Shaping the American Interior

Bringing together 12 original essays, *Shaping the American Interior* maps out, for the first time, the development and definition of the field of interiors in the United States in the period from 1870 until 1960. Its interdisciplinary approach encompasses a broad range of people, contexts, and practices, revealing the design of the interior as a collaborative modern enterprise comprising art, design, manufacture, commerce, and identity construction. Rooted in the expansion of mass production and consumption in the last years of the nineteenth century, new and diverse structures came to define the field and provide formal and informal contexts for design work. Intertwined with, but distinct from, architecture and merchandising, interiors encompassed a diffuse range of individuals, institutions, and organizations engaged in the definition of identity, the development of expertise, and the promotion of consumption. This volume investigates the fluid pre-history of the American profession of interior design, charting attempts to commoditize taste, shape modern conceptions of gender and professionalism, define expertise and authority through principles and standards, marry art with industry and commerce, and shape mass culture in the United States.

Paula Lupkin is a historian of design, architecture, and cities. Her interdisciplinary work focuses on the spatial production of modernity under capitalism, investigating its impact on the designed world and the built environment. Her research and publications, including her first book, *Manhood Factories: YMCA Architecture and the Making of Modern Urban Culture* (University of Minnesota Press, 2010), address the ways that architecture, interiors, cities, and landscapes shaped and were shaped by new ways of living, working, designing, and consuming. Her work has been supported by the Charles Warren Center at Harvard, the Graham Foundation for Advanced Study in the Fine Arts, and the Clements Center for Southwestern Studies at Southern Methodist University.

Penny Sparke is Professor of Design History at Kingston University, London. She studied French Literature at the University of Sussex from 1967 to 1971 and was awarded her PhD in Design History from Brighton Polytechnic in 1975. She taught Design History at Brighton Polytechnic (1975–1982) and the Royal College of Art (1982–1999). She has given keynote addresses, curated exhibitions, and broadcast and published widely. Her publications include *Italian Design from 1860 to the Present* (1989); *The Plastics Age* (1990); *As Long as It's Pink: The Sexual Politics of Taste* (1995); *An Introduction to Design and Culture, 1900 to the Present* (3rd edition, 2004); *Elsie de Wolfe: The Birth of Modern Interior Decoration* (2005); and *The Modern Interior* (2008).

Edited by Paula Lupkin and Penny Sparke

Shaping the American Interior

Structures, Contexts and Practices

LONDON AND NEW YORK

First published 2018
by Routledge
2 Park Square, Milton Park, Abingdon, Oxon OX14 4RN

and by Routledge
711 Third Avenue, New York, NY 10017

Routledge is an imprint of the Taylor & Francis Group, an informa business

© 2018 selection and editorial matter, Paula Lupkin and
Penny Sparke; individual chapters, the contributors

The right of Paula Lupkin and Penny Sparke to be identified as the authors of the editorial material, and of the authors for their individual chapters, has been asserted in accordance with sections 77 and 78 of the Copyright, Designs and Patents Act 1988.

All rights reserved. No part of this book may be reprinted or reproduced or utilised in any form or by any electronic, mechanical, or other means, now known or hereafter invented, including photocopying and recording, or in any information storage or retrieval system, without permission in writing from the publishers.

Trademark notice: Product or corporate names may be trademarks or registered trademarks, and are used only for identification and explanation without intent to infringe.

British Library Cataloguing-in-Publication Data
A catalogue record for this book is available from the British Library

Library of Congress Cataloging-in-Publication Data
A catalog record for this book has been requested

ISBN: 978-1-138-69769-0 (hbk)
ISBN: 978-1-138-69770-6 (pbk)
ISBN: 978-1-315-52073-5 (ebk)

Typeset in Frutiger
by Apex CoVantage, LLC

 Printed in the United Kingdom
by Henry Ling Limited

Contents

Introduction   1
PAULA LUPKIN AND PENNY SPARKE

1   Designing professionals: architects, decorators, clients,
and the interior design process in the nineteenth century   5
ERICA DONNIS AND SUSAN PORTER

2   Dealing in interiors: how Duveen Brothers and Maison Carlhian
shaped an eighteenth-century French salon in 1920s New York   29
ANNE-MARIE SCHAAF AND TERESA MORALES

3   Elsie de Wolfe: a professional interior decorator   47
PENNY SPARKE

4   Designing the gender contest: (re)Locating the gay decorator
in the history of interior design   59
JOHN POTVIN

5   For men by men: furnishing the YMCA   69
PAULA LUPKIN

6   The Art-in-Trades Club: selling style   89
PATRICIA EDMONSON

7   Demonstrating the profession: interior decorating instruction
on early television   107
DANIELLE CHARLAP

8   Coeds and t-squares: interior design education and home economics   125
PATRICK LEE LUCAS

Contents ■

9 "Principles, not effects": Edgar Kaufmann, Jr., MoMA
and the legitimization of interior design 143
LUCINDA KAUKAS HAVENHAND

10 "Apology areas": interior decorating and the marketplace in the 1950s 157
KRISTINA WILSON

11 Imaging interior design: beneath, beside, and within architecture 169
PENELOPE DEAN

12 Modernism's glass ceiling: women in commercial design after WWII 179
MARK HINCHMAN

13 The future of cross-disciplinary practice 195
JOEL SANDERS

Index 205

Introduction

Paula Lupkin and Penny Sparke

The history of interior design practice in the United States is still in its infancy, a neglected stepchild amongst related disciplines like architecture and industrial design. Scholarship in the area has long been dominated by biographies of iconic figures like Elsie de Wolfe and Candace Wheeler.[1] Books and essays trace the trajectories of their careers, their writings, and their relationships with clients. At the same time that these luminaries were forging their identities as individuals, however, the larger profession of interior design began to emerge. Rooted in the expansion of mass production and consumption in the last years of the nineteenth century, new and diverse organizational, educational, and professional structures came to define the field of interiors in the first half of the twentieth century. Based on a successful session at the 2014 Annual Conference of the Society of Architectural Historians, this volume maps out the development and definition of the field of interiors in the United States in the period from 1870 until 1960. Its interdisciplinary approach encompasses a broad range of people, contexts, and practices, revealing the design of the interior as a collaborative modern enterprise comprising art, design, manufacture, commerce, and identity construction. Rooted in the expansion of mass production and consumption in the last years of the nineteenth century, and beginning in the early twentieth century, new and diverse organizational, educational, and professional structures came to define the field and provide formal and informal contexts for design work.

From the late nineteenth century up to the late 1950s "interiors" had operated as an interdisciplinary constellation of discourses and practices devoted to the shaping of public and private interior spaces. Intertwined with, but distinct from, architecture and merchandising, interiors encompassed a broad and diffuse range of individuals, institutions, and organizations engaged in the definition of identity, the development of expertise, and the promotion of consumption. This volume investigates the fluid pre-history of the American profession of interior design, charting attempts to commoditize taste, shape modern conceptions of gender and professionalism, define expertise and authority through principles and standards, marry art with industry and commerce, and shape mass culture in the United States from 1880 to 1960.

Its essays uncover various constellations of individuals, organizations, and institutions; a dramatis personae that includes educators like Frank Alvah Parsons, designers/entrepreneurs like Louis Comfort Tiffany and Gustav Stickley, antiques dealers like Joseph Duveen, merchants and manufacturers like William Sloan Coffin, journalists, interior decorators like Elsie de Wolfe, home economists, and wealthy clients like Frederick Billings. It locates the field of interiors in architecture firms, furniture showrooms, in the pages of professional and popular journals, museum galleries, and television studios. The contributors to the volume reflect the breadth of interior design history as an emerging field, bringing as they do so perspectives from design history, architecture, historic preservation, art history, and other areas. They use a wide variety of sources – letters and organizational archival records, diaries, professional journals to discuss a range of themes: biography and oeuvre, but also stories of entrepreneurship, bureaucracy, and collaboration.

Beginning in the Gilded Age, this chronologically organized volume first considers élite patrons and clients seeking individualized services. Two essays highlight the search for identity, and authority, in a process that involved collaboration and competition between actors that produced the interior. Susan Donnis and Erica Porter offer, through a detailed archival case study of one nineteenth-century client, the Billings family, a fascinating, fine-grained story of élite home decoration as a complex, multifaceted world with different kinds of expertise competing for the control and management of projects. It complicates the narrative of expertise and professionalization in interior design, suggesting the confusion and complexity of the process of interior decoration: a constant push and pull of collaboration, coordination, and competition between architects, artists, landscapers, furnishings manufacturers, and the clients themselves. Teresa Morales and Anne-marie Schaaf focus on a single interior, the drawing room of socialite Mrs. Rice, who sought élite identity through the design of interiors with European art and antiques. Their concentration on the close working partnership of antiques, dealer Joseph Duveen and French craftsmen Maison Carlhian also sheds light on the business side of interiors work, emphasizing the need for efficiency, and the means of communication, advertisement, and client relations. Morales and Schaaf highlight the canny branding and marketing strategies, including the furnished showrooms used by antique dealers to exhibit and sell taste as well as products. Essays by Penny Sparke and John Potvin offer stories that further the "problem" of gender, as represented by the gay male decorator and the dilettante lady decorator. Potvin reveals, through detailed theoretically informed analysis of popular and professional literature, the association of decoration with the effeminate that begins in the Jazz Age. Sparke, by contrast, uncovers Elsie de Wolfe as a successful businesswoman who models her practice on the more developed creative industries of advertising, theatre, and fashion. By the 1920s, other players entered the market, selling taste and style to a booming middle market, both at home and in the public sphere. As the new European "modernistic" style began to penetrate the American living room and lobby, the competition to provide expertise and services grew, as did a growing tension over gender, skill, and taste that was born in the nineteenth century and developed more intensively as the so-called lady decorators entered the field in the early twentieth. As essays on the YMCA Furnishings Service by Paula Lupkin, and the Art in Trades Club, by Patricia Edmonson, suggest, architects, furniture manufacturers, and other male tastemakers, including Frank Parsons and William Sloane Coffin, sought to marry taste and commerce together in a rational, efficient framework influenced by the masculine fields of business and architecture. Danielle Charlap's essay adds a new dimension to the discussion showing that television proved an ideal medium for disseminating the ideas of the professional interior decorator. Her case-study focuses on the programmes devised by Paul MacAlister from 1941 onwards which depended upon his Plan-a-Room kit as a means of communicating his approach and showing a female amateur audience the rights and wrongs of

Introduction ∎

interior decorating. Using extensive archival material, Charlap reveals an important development in the "instructional" role that interior decorators assumed as part of their claim for expertise and professionalism. Patrick Lee Lucas continues to address gender tensions in the changing educational structures offered at land grant universities for the study of interiors throughout the mid-twentieth century. Highlighting the "constellation" of disciplines and practices that have contributed to the professionalization and codification of interiors, he traces the changing placement, nomenclature, and mission of the academic study of interiors from home economics to design schools, examining the students, the curricula, and the expectations for the application of design expertise to homemaking or career development. In the postwar years, Lucinda Havenhand's essay focuses on Edgar Kaufmann's merchandising background and its application to the curatorial and educational work undertaken by MoMA to promote modern design. It brings together several themes that appear earlier in the chronology. Kaufmann's background in department stores links him with William Sloane Coffin. Both businessmen sought to promote interior design as a rational, principled, modern profession. Kristina Wilson's essay, which focuses on AAA and Herman Miller, is an investigation of the overlap between commerce and interior decoration. From the late nineteenth century through to the postwar period the author addresses the use of interior design to sell products and art, from the most élite, like Duveen, to the middle classes in the 1920s Art in Trades Club discussed by Edmonson, to the AAA's DIY emphasis post war. Archival research reveals an important development in the "instructional" role that interior decorators assumed as part of their claim for expertise and professionalism. An emphasis on billing, and the squabble/power play over income and sales highlighted in Penelope Dean's essay "Imaging Interior Design: beneath, beside and within architecture" is an interesting and relevant contribution to the volume. It makes a nice counterpoint to other contributions about professionalization in the postwar period, which focus more on education and other issues. Dean's essay picks up, once again, the strong allegiance between interior design and architecture and focuses on the ways in which postwar journals depicted the changing relationship between the two professional fields, with a growing emphasis on the equivalencies between them. The main difference lies, claims Dean, on the difference between a "spatial" (architecture) approach and a "sum of the parts" (interior design) one. Delving into oral histories from the Art Institute of Chicago, Hinchman continues the investigation of professionalization in the postwar period with a piece that links the contemporaneous rise of curtain wall skyscrapers, contract interior design, and the career challenges faced by individual female interior designers in the modernist world of macho architects. This essay addresses the development of the profession as well as gender roles and identity in a way that is echoed in other contributors' essays. The closing essay is written by one of the most important early and critical voices on the tensions and relationship between architecture and interior design, Joel Sanders.[2] His exploration of the contemporary boundaries, structures, business practices in design education and practice today demonstrates clearly and concretely the outcomes of nineteenth- and twentieth-century attempts to assert disciplinary expertise, control, and order over the process. In this manifesto he calls for a more fluid view of the design of the environment, with fewer disciplinary distinctions between architecture, landscape, and interiors, especially during this juncture in history. It provides an excellent coda to the volume; both its goals and its findings. It recognizes the complexity of the past, the inherent interdisciplinarity of interiors, and looks forward to meet the challenges of contemporary and future with a call for collaboration.

To date, national stories of interior design have been few and far between.[3] Recent scholarship has tended towards wider-focus studies, intended to support pedagogy.[4] Although this volume sets out to chart the situation in the United States, it shows it to be the home of the modern practice of interior decoration and design and a good example, therefore of the complex forces that underpinned their development. Arguably the American model was subsequently transferred across the Atlantic, albeit with inevitable national nuances.

NOTES

1   Penny Sparke, *Elsie de Wolfe: The Birth of Modern Interior Decoration* (New York: Acanthus Press, 2005); Bridget May, "Nancy McClelland (1877–1959) Professionalizing Interior Design in the Early 20th Century," *Journal of Design History* 21, no. 1 (March 2008), 59–74; Amelia Peck and Carol Irish, *Candace Wheeler: The Art and Enterprise of American Design 1875–1900* (New York: Metropolitan Museum of Art, 2001).

2   Joel Sanders, "Curtain Wars: Architects, Decorators, and the Domestic Interior," *Harvard Design Magazine* 16 (Winter/Spring 2002): 14–20.

3   Some recent examples of a national perspective on the study of interiors include Kristina Wilson, *Livable Modernism: Interior Decorating and Design During the Great Depression* (Yale University Press, 2004); Anca Lasc and Mark Taylor, eds., *Designing the French Interior: The Modern Home and Mass Media* (London: Bloomsbury, 2016).

4   For example, the American scholar John Pile's *History of Interior Design* (New York: Wiley) was first published in 2000. In the UK Simon Calloway's *Twentieth-Century Decoration: The Domestic Interior Since 1900 to the Present Day* (London: Weidenfeld and Nicholson) appeared in 1988. Anne Massey's *Interior Design of the 20th Century* (London: Thames and Hudson) was first published in 1990; and the work of the Modern Interiors Research Centre (MIRC), based at Kingston University, London, has been taking place since 2005. Scholars from the UK, the United States, and Australasia have placed emphasis on the global picture, with foci on the Victorian domestic interior; the modernist interior; and the emergence of the interior decorator/designer as a specialist practitioner. (http://fada.kingston.ac.uk/research/modern-interiors-research-centre/).

Chapter 1: Designing professionals

Architects, decorators, clients, and the interior design process in the nineteenth century

Erica Donnis and Susan Porter

The decoration and furnishing of domestic spaces was a complex and dynamic process in the individualistic, entrepreneurial, and competitive culture of nineteenth-century America. As the century progressed, middle and upper class consumers enjoyed unprecedented access to a burgeoning array of consumer goods, including home furnishings, in a wide range of styles suitable for a variety of tastes and budgets. For many Americans, the appearance, design, and character of domestic architecture and interiors came to signify powerful religious and moral values as well as expressions of individuality and, for some, status.[1] As families attempted to navigate not only issues of personal taste and preference but also cultural tensions between economy and consumption, tradition and innovation, and restraint and extravagance, the goal of creating beautiful, tasteful, and comfortable homes became increasingly complex.[2]

Many entrepreneurial architects, artists, furniture manufacturers, decorative painters, upholsterers, and other craftsmen perceived in these social tensions an opportunity to position themselves as experts, professionals, and arbiters of taste. They offered to help clients create their ideal homes by providing design concepts, proposing furnishings, and managing projects. Calling themselves interior decorators, they established firms, often with showrooms retailing furniture, carpets, curtain and upholstery fabrics, and other furnishings, and employed junior designers and craftsmen to fabricate and install their merchandise. While decorators competed with each other to win contracts and clients, they also frequently collaborated, and they sometimes developed enduring working relationships.[3]

In the formative years of the interior design profession, as this case study demonstrates, clients, architects, and decorators engaged in negotiations about taste, style, and suitability that highlighted the complexity of the design process and the potential for disputes over matters that were both culturally influenced and extremely personal. Those who positioned themselves as design professionals were eager to promote themselves as experts, but clients knew their own preferences best, and they held the power of the purse. This often led to conflict, but design professionals who learned to listen to their clients and collaborate with each other were often rewarded with loyalty and ongoing work.

Between 1869 and 1890, Frederick and Julia Billings of Woodstock, Vermont and New York City employed a bevy of architects and decorators for multiple building, renovation, and redecoration projects, as well as other periodic updates and purchases. Born in Vermont, Frederick Billings

(1823–1890) was a lawyer who made his first fortune in San Francisco during the Gold Rush as an attorney and real estate investor and his second as a railroad entrepreneur. In 1862, he married Julia Parmly (1835–1914) of New York City, the daughter of a prosperous dentist and real estate investor. A self-made man who came from old New England stock, Billings was fascinated with new technologies and progress, but he also had a nostalgic vision of the past and a deep attachment to traditional New England values. He was a devoted family man, but he was also keenly aware of his social, political, and economic status in the larger world, and he was actively involved in civic, institutional, and religious affairs throughout his life.

Frederick loved art, history, nature, and the built environment, understood structural and technical data, and was familiar with current architecture and interior design literature. He believed that aesthetics were important; as he wrote Julia in 1865, "There is a way of making a room & a house win anybody's endorsement by its adjustment of color, its comfortable furniture – and its putting anybody at ease. It is art more than money that comes in play." Billings' concept of "art" was both literal and figurative; he had begun to collect artwork in the early 1860s, and he sought the same high level of quality, workmanship, balance, and beauty he admired in paintings for his surroundings. Frederick's focus on "ease" was equally significant. He valued physical comfort, and he also understood that pleasing aesthetics – simple room arrangements, comfortable furniture, careful "adjustment of color" – could provide well-being and relaxation for both mind and body in a way that ornate, extravagant surroundings designed only for show could not. Frederick wanted the best for himself and his family, and he was willing to pay for it, patronizing high-end stores, and investing in new domestic technologies. But he was also strategic about spending and determined to obtain good value for his money.[4]

An energetic, driven man with strong ideas and high expectations for himself and others, Billings respected expertise, and he generally hired architects and decorators with growing reputations. But he saw them as advisors and facilitators rather than final authorities, and he treated them like other employees. He knew his own taste and developed an unwavering confidence in his sense of design through his home renovation and redecoration projects as well as the many other civic, institutional, and religious building projects in Woodstock, New York, and elsewhere that he oversaw and bankrolled.

Julia Billings had a very different personality than her husband, but she also had strong feelings about her domestic environment. She had managed her father's home for five years after the death of her mother, and later became increasingly adept at handling her own domestic affairs as her household grew to include seven children and several servants. Julia was a devout Christian, and she believed deeply in the moral value of the home. Like many other brides of her era, she was strongly influenced by the Beecher sisters' books on domestic economy, which promoted frugality, disavowed fashion as wasteful and extravagant, and exhorted their readers to maintain "Economical, Healthful, Beautiful, and Christian Homes." Such homes would be designed with up-to-date household technologies that fostered good health and efficiency, and filled with practical, tasteful, well-made furnishings, including older items with useful and sentimental value that could be refurbished with new paint or coverings.[5]

In some ways Julia and Frederick's attitudes toward their home conformed to the gender stereotypes of the period, wherein the woman served as the moral advisor to her more competitive, entrepreneurial husband, but left the decision making to him. Julia certainly had more modest taste and was more cost-conscious than Frederick, who admired and collected expensive artwork and other costly furnishings. Both had sentimental attachments to many of their older possessions, and they did not believe in discarding things of beauty, quality, usefulness, and/or sentimental value just because they were no longer in style. Nonetheless, Frederick was tempted by new technologies and fresh looks despite his wish to appear modest, and he relished new projects. Julia, on the other hand, was generally more reluctant to embark upon major household renovations than her husband; more attached to things as they were, she was concerned about unnecessary expenditures and always worried about the disruption that such work would cause.

Julia was generally calm and reasonable, but Frederick tended to be volatile. While he considered himself the final arbiter, he always sought Julia's counsel and was often swayed by her opinions because he was eager to please her and valued her approval. As a result, she always played a key role in shaping the building, renovation, and redecoration projects that the couple undertook. In the end, she invariably became deeply involved, offering both practical and aesthetic suggestions, monitoring progress when Frederick was away, advising him about purchases, and assembling rooms as projects concluded.[6]

In matters of taste, Frederick and Julia concurred, at least in theory, about the kind of home they wished to create. Both consistently expressed disdain for "fashion" in favor of "simple, harmonizing and homelike" designs that blended old and new, and both always stated that they wished to be "as economical as propriety would permit." Even though their wealth increased significantly over the course of their married life, they continued to renovate and rebuild rather than build from scratch, to repair, reupholster, and reuse furnishings, and to mingle new purchases with old favorites. Both spoke condescendingly about *nouveau riche* magnates like Frederick's railroad rival Henry Villard, who they felt had more money than taste; when Villard built a townhouse in the style of an Italian Renaissance palazzo in 1883, Frederick dismissed the "palace" as "very costly but unsuited to a home in this country." They often thought new design proposals too ornate or extravagant and asked for simpler plans, but they were both quick to make purchases that they felt would make their houses more comfortable, convenient, and pleasant.[7]

Frederick and Julia had lived in San Francisco for the first two years of their marriage, but they then settled in Woodstock, Vermont, where Frederick had grown up. He had always admired the Marsh farm, a large property with a substantial Federal-style brick house, for its beautiful setting overlooking Woodstock village and its association with the locally prominent Marsh family. In 1865, he wrote Julia that "I should like to have a house big enough to have our friends come & visit us when they pleased, giving them a warm welcome without any parade or aping of fashionable life. What do you think of the Marsh place?" At that point, Julia was concerned that the house, constructed in about 1805 and little altered thereafter, "would require so many improvements within & without I fear it would be a burden to you." Four years later, however, when the property became available, just before Julia gave birth to their fourth child, Frederick eagerly purchased it.[8]

He and Julia immediately began to plan the "improvements" that would transform the Marsh farm into their vision of an appropriate "country seat" with an expanded, modernized house, several new outbuildings, and reforested grounds, gardens, and greenhouses. Frederick quickly brought in designers to reconfigure the grounds and the house: Robert Morris Copeland (1830–1874), a successful Boston landscape gardener and the author of *Country Life: A Handbook of Agriculture, Horticulture and Landscape Gardening* (1859), and William Ralph Emerson (1833–1917), a young Boston architect. Emerson, the son of a Maine doctor, had trained with the Boston architect-builder Jonathan Preston. Between 1864 and 1874, he and his partner, Carl Fehmer (1838–1903), designed several townhouses in Boston's Back Bay, two city grammar schools, and the Milton Sanford House in Newport, Rhode Island, among other buildings, but Fehmer had no direct involvement with the Billings' project.[9]

The projected work on the Marsh house was extensive; when demolition began in June 1869 the local newspaper reported that, "Little else than the bare walls remain of the old Charles Marsh mansion. Mr. Billings has a large force of men transforming the place into something to his taste."[10] Those walls would provide a deliberate physical link to the house's history, but Emerson's plan would make the dwelling a modern three-story residence with a Second Empire and Stick-Style exterior and a Renaissance-Revival-style interior. The design added dormers and a Mansard roof to the main block and a new wing containing a library, master bedroom, and nursery. The dining room and the rooms directly above it, as well as the rear service ell, were enlarged, and gas lighting and hot and cold water plumbing were installed on all floors. Although no plans or agreements for this project survive, it is clear that Emerson was also contracted to design the interior trim, paneling, and several built-in features, and to oversee the selection of mantels, wallpaper, and paint treatments.[11]

Figure 1.1

The Billings residence in Woodstock, Vermont, soon after completion of the William Ralph Emerson rebuild, stereograph, summer 1870. Box P9, Billings Family Archives, The Woodstock Foundation, Inc., Woodstock, Vermont.

Frederick was enthusiastic about the project and initially happy with Emerson, and Julia quickly became involved as well. The exterior construction progressed, with Emerson making several changes that the Billings proposed, through the summer and fall of 1869. By the time the work moved inside for the winter, however, Frederick and Julia were concerned about the pace of the project and their architect's taste. While Julia admired the library finishes, they were both upset that Emerson had not delivered the plan for the sideboard. They found the mantels he had chosen for several bedrooms "insufferable" and decided to replace them with "plain ones of better marble." Later, Frederick would also reject another shipment of mantels he deemed "hideous."[12]

Emerson also failed to complete his designs for the wall finishes, and, by February 1870, Frederick complained that "He ought to have taken charge of painting etc. – but I cannot stand his neglect & inefficiency." Concerned that Emerson would not be able to achieve the "simpler, harmonizing, and homelike" look the couple envisioned, and convinced that they would need some additional help with the decorating, he turned to his landscape gardener, Robert Morris Copeland. Copeland's expertise was not interior decorating, but he promptly submitted plans for wallpaper and decorative paint treatments. Julia was horrified:

> [H]e proposed doing a great deal too much . . . his ideas of coloring were theatrical & not tasteful . . . the following suggestions for the parlor: Crimson & gold paper Rose & Salmon ceiling, cornice lined, center & corners allegorically treated – "purple largely introduced & warm wood tints!! – for my sitting room he advises a *green* & gold paper with *blue* & gold ceiling." Now dear, can a man of good taste desire such combinations?[13]

Frederick agreed that Copeland's plans were more "extravagant" than the "simple modest and economical" interiors they envisioned, but he also worried that "I do not know what to do about painting & papering – I know nothing about such things – and I have no time to study them up . . . some system should be adopted for the whole . . . we must be careful not to make a piece-meal business of it devoid of harmony." He pushed Julia to continue to work with Copeland, but she continued to resist.[14]

Frederick and Julia knew what they liked and what they cared about, and they preferred to control the decision-making process. But, at this point, they needed help translating their vision of good taste and harmony into reality. They also needed someone to do the legwork, as Frederick was preoccupied with his railroad work and Julia was busy caring for their four very young children. Ultimately Frederick hired an interiors specialist, William J. McPherson (1821–1900), an aspiring Boston decorative painter, to "attend to the details." Born in Scotland, McPherson had trained there with David Ramsay Hay, a well-known decorative painter and color theorist. After immigrating to Boston in 1837, McPherson established a successful business as a "House Painter . . . Glazier . . . and Fresco Painter in Enamel, Oil, and Distemper Colors." By March 1870, when he met the Billings, McPherson was developing a national reputation as an interior decorator; in 1872 he advertised his specialties as "all aspects of interior decoration," including "the selection and adaptation of Carpets, Draperies, Furniture and the arrangement of all things appertaining to the proper and tasteful harmonizing and perfection of any work that may be intrusted [sic] to his care."[15]

In 1870–1871, McPherson designed and painted decorative wall and ceiling treatments for the Billings' principal rooms and selected wallpaper for several family bedrooms.[16] McPherson also helped the Billings choose the additional furnishings they needed for their new, and much larger, home, sometimes accompanying them as they shopped for furniture, carpets, and other items in the Boston area.

By the mid-nineteenth century, Boston had become an important center of "modern" furniture manufacturing, whereby companies produced high-quality furniture and interior architectural elements roughed out on steam-powered equipment and then finished by hand. The entrepreneurial owners of these manufactories had showrooms with large furniture inventories in many fashionable styles, took custom orders, and retailed imported curtain and upholstery fabrics. It was difficult for such firms to stay afloat in the fluctuating economy, and they frequently went bankrupt or lost a partner. As a result, businesses reconstituted themselves frequently with new partners under new names.[17]

One such furniture manufactory that catered to high-end private and commercial customers was Doe & Charmois, whose owners advertised themselves as "Designers & Manufacturers of all Kinds of First Class Furniture of Every Description. Mantels, Mirrors, Etc Draperies, Curtains & Shades." The manufactory itself had been in operation for decades; Doe & Charmois, established in 1869,

Figure 1.2
The Billings parlor in Woodstock, depicting William McPherson's decorative painting and furniture purchased from Doe & Charmois, c. 1879. Box P29b, Billings Family Archives.

was the third firm to operate it. The Billings probably ordered much of their new furniture, including two large groups of Renaissance-Revival-style furniture for the dining room and parlor, from Doe & Charmois with the guidance of McPherson and Victor Charmois (1826–1883). Charmois, a seasoned designer of furniture and architectural elements from France, had worked for the company for several years before becoming Joseph Merrill Doe's partner.[18] McPherson and Charmois also worked together to help the family arrange furniture, hang pictures, and place carpets after the furnishings were delivered.[19]

When the Billings' project was completed in the spring of 1871, they were enchanted with every aspect of their new home, and their attachment to it continued to deepen in the ensuing years. The house was the locus of the Billings' religious and social life as well as their daily activities: they gathered together there for prayers every morning, held Bible lessons and Sunday evening hymn sings, and hosted extended family and friends for reading groups, card games, and holiday celebrations. The seven children played tag in the halls, ran races on the veranda, and were schooled at home by Julia and the family's live-in governess.[20]

All this activity, of course, took a toll on the house. The Billings were frequently busy with maintenance, repairs, and updates, and new items were often purchased to meet the changing needs of the children as they grew older. In addition, a number of structural deficiencies in Emerson's architectural designs caused settling that severely damaged plaster walls and ceilings, wallpaper, and floors in certain areas and required regular mitigation. Sometimes the Billings managed this work themselves; in 1879, for example, they had the sagging floor and subfloor in the dining room replaced and chose new carpeting and furniture for the reception room. At other times, they called upon McPherson, who, for instance, helped the Billings select new wallpapers and oversaw the design and application of coordinating "frescoes" in several rooms in 1880.[21]

Frederick had planned to have McPherson paint the rest of the rooms in 1881, but his attention was diverted when the couple purchased a townhouse in New York City, where Frederick spent much of his time doing business. The Billings had always hoped to buy a winter residence there, where they could be together more, their children could attend day schools rather than boarding schools as they grew older, and the entire family could take advantage of the city's social and cultural opportunities. By 1881, having consolidated his fortune as president of the Northern Pacific Railroad and left that position much enriched, Billings could well afford the extra cost of maintaining an urban establishment, and when a large, sunny four-story furnished townhouse in a convenient location on the corner of Madison Avenue and 40th Street became available, he and Julia purchased it.[22]

The Billings hoped to avoid extensive renovation and redecoration work on the townhouse, and they planned to reuse many of the existing furnishings. However, they soon discovered that the building, its systems, and its contents were in "dreadful" shape, and would need "overhauling." By this time, they felt more self-confident about interior decoration, but they still needed a professional to manage the multiple subcontractors required. Frederick passed over McPherson in favor of "Mr. Douglas," a more "moderate-priced" New York decorator recommended by his brother. Douglas was hired to work on the billiard room and servants' rooms; if he proved satisfactory, he would continue with the principal rooms. But the experiment did not go well. Frederick felt that the work progressed too slowly and that Douglas' design for the painted billiard room ceiling was "too elaborate." He discharged Douglas and, with relief, called in McPherson to manage the remainder of the project, as he "knows our tastes – and he will respect my wishes – and not go beyond the limits we may agree on."[23]

The Billings hired another firm they knew well, Doe, Hunnewell & Company, successor to Doe & Charmois, to work with McPherson on the furniture they wanted to reuse and to supply new furniture, woodwork, and draperies. The Billings dealt directly with Elias R. Hunnewell (1840–1895), the company's owner. A Maine native, Hunnewell had trained as an upholsterer and spent his early career working as a salesman. In 1871, Hunnewell purchased the company as a sole proprietorship, renamed it Doe & Hunnewell (Doe, Hunnewell & Co. after 1880), and gradually expanded the well-known high-end furniture manufactory into a full-service interior decorating company that offered design consultations and an expanded inventory of furnishings. By 1877 the firm provided "Interior Woodwork, Bank Counters, Screens, Desks &c. also First Class Furniture, Draperies, Mirrors, Shades &c. Upholstery Goods. Wholesale & Retail."[24]

Hunnewell had worked with McPherson before, and they collaborated over the next eight months to redecorate most of the Billings' townhouse. The project proceeded very slowly; when family members arrived for their first New York winter, the principal rooms were not ready, and the workmen were present for three more months. Frederick and Julia abhorred some of McPherson's designs, ordered him to rectify several errors, and returned many of the items he selected. By the end of the project, Frederick was thoroughly disgusted with McPherson's "blunders" and excuses, fuming that "McP is foxy & outrageous – wish I had employed someone else." When the decorator's bill arrived, Frederick felt "swindled" and was indignant "about the injustice of paying a percentage on his mistakes." The Billings would not hire McPherson again, but they did remain good customers of Doe, Hunnewell & Co.[25]

Frederick was never satisfied with McPherson's work on the townhouse, and he later decided to redo some of the rooms where he hosted his business associates and friends, hiring a prominent New York decorator, Auguste Pottier (1823–1896), for this work. Frederick liked to examine the goods in various showrooms when he was considering new purchases, and he had been "delighted" with Pottier's work on one such visit in 1882. President of the Pottier & Stymus Manufacturing Company, one of the leading furniture manufacturer/decorators in the United States, Pottier trained as a wood carver in his native France and immigrated to New York City in 1847; in 1859, he established Pottier & Stymus with upholsterer William Pierre Stymus Sr. In 1885 Frederick hired Pottier to completely redecorate his New York library, office, and guest room. Julia thought the work unnecessary, but Frederick overruled her and was pleased with the results. Even so, the work took a long time, and he did not employ the firm again.[26]

In 1882, Frederick also began to consider renovations to the Woodstock house. In addition to the redecorating he had been planning since 1880, he wanted to address the building's ongoing structural problems, raise the roof on the main block, and enlarge the service ell. Frederick asked Henry Hudson Holly (1834–1892), an architect whom he had previously hired for a Woodstock Congregational Church project, to measure the house. The son of a New York merchant, Holly had apprenticed with the British émigré architect Gervase Wheeler before opening his own firm in 1857. By the early 1880s, Holly had become one of the foremost proponents of the Queen Anne style, and he had published several architectural style books that also discussed structural matters, household systems, and interior design.[27]

Between 1882 and 1885, Billings and Holly considered several plans for the Woodstock house. Frederick judged Holly's initial plans "rather too elaborate" and requested the architect "to make a plan simply for L [ell] part of house. He wants to do too much." Later, he asked Holly to draw up new plans for "general improvements," and at least two "sketches" were completed by 1883. But Frederick was ambivalent about Holly's designs and the scope of the project, and the project lay dormant for two years.[28]

In 1885, Frederick decided to move forward again with structural mitigations and other major work that would refashion the house in the Queen Anne style: raising the roof to create a full-height third floor and attic on the main block of the building, rebuilding the service wing as a three-story structure, resurfacing the entire exterior in brick, moving a chimney to widen the dining room, and expanding the library by combining it with an adjoining room. Since the project would affect almost all of the interior spaces, requiring new woodwork, plasterwork, wall finishes, and/or flooring, Frederick also asked Holly to design new architectural features for the interiors.[29]

However, Julia and Laura Wheeler, the Billings' long-time governess who had become a close family friend, were furious, and they both voiced uncharacteristically strong objections. Frederick recorded that Laura "attacked the proposed changes in the house – & Julia . . . went at me in such a way, that being tired I got all out of temper." The women saw no need to change spaces they liked, and they knew that much of the disruption that the work would entail would devolve on them. In response, a possibly abashed Frederick instructed Holly to scale back the project by eliminating the

Figure 1.3
The Billings residence in Woodstock, after the Henry Hudson Holly renovations, c. late 1880s. Box P22c, Billings Family Archives.

proposed modifications to the library and the rooms above the dining room. Even so, he proceeded with the bulk of the work, hoping that Julia would come around, and was quick to inform her when her architect nephew Ehrick Kensett Rossiter approved Holly's plans.[30]

The 1885–1886 project demonstrated Frederick Billings' mature approach to home improvement work. Frederick took a hands-on approach from the outset (in part because he was, by this time, less engaged in business affairs), carefully reviewing and proposing alterations to the plans submitted by Holly, directly supervising the work, and deciding on and implementing changes on site. The scheme was complex and, as with earlier projects, he was at first willing to trust the expert he had hired. As a result, he allowed Holly to contract with decorators, subcontractors, and suppliers he knew from the New York area. However, as in earlier projects, Frederick quickly became disillusioned, and he insisted on bringing in and convening vendors from both New England and New York, including some he had used and trusted for many years.[31]

From the outset, Frederick found numerous practical and aesthetic deficiencies with the details of Holly's plans and, when he disagreed with his architect, he repeatedly stopped work. As he noted in November, "The balcony & perspective on East front too heavy – spoils Ehricks room – & takes away cheerfulness of 2d story hall-belts of brick so low as to interfere with blinds." This led to considerable drama. At first, he demanded that Holly revise and resubmit his designs, and then he began to devise and implement his own solutions and changes, trusting his own redesigns more than those of his architect. When he learned that architectural finishes supplied by Holly's New Jersey subcontractor were seriously delayed, he became furious about Holly's poor project management as well: "So many mistakes made by him I was severe with him. He confessed to many . . . Wish I cd get rid of him."[32]

Holly promised to do better, but, by the time construction shifted indoors, Frederick professed himself "afraid of his [Holly's] judgment." When the architect's plans for the interiors arrived, Frederick reacted strongly, rejecting them as "too elaborate & will destroy the simplicity & beauty of house." This response reflected a larger pattern of ambivalence towards major modifications to his family's beloved home; while he desired "improvements," he worried that the end result would appear too showy and extravagant. He considered hiring another architect, but then merely requested "more simple drawings." Eventually he approved the original design, won over by its aesthetic appeal and modern look.[33]

At the same time, he determined to improve the work process by assuming full control over the subcontracting. He fired Holly's problematic New Jersey supplier and commissioned Doe, Hunnewell & Co., the furniture company he had used for the New York townhouse (which had also supplied many items to the Woodstock house over the years), to contract with a nearby lumber mill to fabricate and install the interior finishes specified in Holly's plans at a better price. Billings also engaged Doe, Hunnewell & Co. to repair, refresh, and reupholster the furniture they were reusing, and to supply many additional new pieces of Aesthetic-style furniture.[34]

Elias Hunnewell, with whom the Billings had worked in New York City, was present for the initial consultations, but most of Doe, Hunnewell & Co.'s work on the 1885–1886 Woodstock renovation was supervised by Joseph T. Hazelton (1831–1916), an experienced employee who offered further advice, managed production and site installation, and helped to assemble rooms. Hazelton and his father, Jonathan Eastman Hazelton, had had a long history with this furniture manufactory. The elder Hazelton, a furniture maker and "renovator," had been a partner in the business from 1849 to 1858, when it was called Doe & Hazelton, and Joseph Hazelton joined his father as a partner from 1859 to 1869, along with John A. Ellis, in its next iteration as John A. Ellis & Co. Joseph Hazelton had returned to the firm as Hunnewell's employee in 1872.

In January 1886, Frederick also hired a second professional decorating firm to help design and provide furnishings, fittings, and other items for the first-floor public rooms that were intended to impress visitors and showcase his art and other collections. The Tiffany Glass Company of New York City, which had been formed the previous month by innovative artist and decorator Louis Comfort Tiffany (1848–1933), would later advertise "facilities for designing and executing interior decorative works in a variety of media and techniques, including painting and fresco, papering, fabrics, relief ornament, leather, metal, interior woodwork, stained and leaded glass, glass tiles, and mosaic facings and floorings." Tiffany's career as an interior decorator had taken off after he designed rooms at New York City's Union League Club and the Seventh Regiment Armory in 1881 and redecorated several state rooms in the Aesthetic style at the White House in 1882. Just as Tiffany's fashionable redecoration of the East Room replaced the neo-Grec decorations William McPherson had completed in the White House in 1874, Tiffany's work would replace McPherson's 1869 work in the Billings' home.[35] The Billings worked with one of Tiffany's lead designers, architect John L. Du Fais (1855–1935). A New Yorker, Du Fais had studied architecture at the Massachusetts Institute of Technology, and he had previously worked for John La Farge and McKim, Mead & White.

As usual, Frederick judged Du Fais' first proposal "too ornate & expensive," but he promptly accepted a revised plan. Over the next eight months, Du Fais coordinated the redesign of the house's principal living spaces in the Aesthetic style, helping the Billings select wallpaper and paint treatments, floor coverings, lighting fixtures, fireplace tiles, and carpeting, and design at least one of the three stained-glass windows the Billings ordered from Tiffany. Some of the new furnishings were produced by the Tiffany Glass Company; others were purchased through Tiffany from other manufacturers and retailers.[36]

Despite her initial opposition to the project, Julia took an active role in the decision-making process for the interiors. She was present when Holly described his preliminary plans for the finishes in October 1885, and she probably attended at least some of the design meetings that winter. By February 1886 she was pleasantly surprised: "We find the house nearly ready for wallpaper . . . The changes are all great improvements and the third story is especially improved."[37]

As the interior work continued, Frederick brought Du Fais, Holly, Hunnewell, and Hazelton together on multiple occasions to advise and collaborate on the interiors. In late January, they "spent almost an entire day" together with the New Hampshire lumber supplier in Woodstock; they "settled a good many things," determining the wood types for the parlor finishes and the flooring material in several rooms. In February, Billings, Du Fais, and Holly met in New York to discuss "[wall] papers & decorations;" Hunnewell joined them the following day to confer on furniture. Two weeks later, concerned about the design of the woodwork in the main hall, Frederick halted the installation and convened Holly, Hunnewell, and Hazelton to revise the plans. At this meeting, they also selected the interior color schemes and revised the design for the built-in sideboard in the dining room. In April, Hunnewell, Holly, and an "iron man" recommended by Hunnewell met to settle on a way to safely support the ceiling in the enlarged library that Holly had envisioned in his initial plans, and

Frederick approved the work. Later, Julia, Frederick, and Du Fais selected floor coverings and globes for the lighting fixtures, and Julia persuaded Frederick to install a stained-glass window in the parlor. Julia met with Hazelton and Du Fais to discuss the style of the draperies, and they all arranged the rooms together as the project concluded.[38]

The work required careful coordination, mostly orchestrated by Frederick. Doe, Hunnewell & Co. built the frames for the stained-glass windows produced by the Tiffany Glass Company, Du Fais sent carpet samples to Hazelton to coordinate with the drapery and upholstery fabrics, and the design for the draperies fabricated by Hunnewell was a group effort.[39] By June, Frederick noted that, "The house is far from done but is fine already – and I was much impressed with its dignified beauty," and Julia was "much delighted especially with the Halls." When the project was completed in August 1886, and Doe, Hunnewell & Co.'s invoice for the bulk of the work arrived, Frederick remarked, without rancor, "Rec'd Doe H. & Co. bill about [$] 37.000–5.000 more than I expected . . . They charge very high – but do their work well."[40]

The Billings also clearly appreciated Joseph Hazelton's contributions. That fall, they hired him to update the bathrooms at their Woodstock house, adding wainscoting produced by Doe, Hunnewell, and Co., as well as new fixtures. In 1887, when Hazelton left Doe, Hunnewell & Co. to form a new company, Hazelton & Goddard (later Hazelton Goddard & Kitfield), they promptly transferred their business there until at least 1904, purchasing new furniture from him on occasion and engaging him

Figure 1.4
The Billings parlor in Woodstock, as redesigned in 1886. Box P29b, Billings Family Archives.

Designing professionals ■

Figure 1.5
The Billings library in Woodstock, depicting the mantel and bookcases designed by William Ralph Emerson in 1870 and the wall finishes and furniture installed in 1886.
Photography by Gilbert Ask, 1947. Box P35, Billings Family Archives.

annually to prepare the Woodstock house for the summer and do work on other buildings they owned in Woodstock. Hazelton's firm, which specialized in "Artistic Furniture, Upholstery and Draperies," operated until at least 1900, and Hazelton continued as sole proprietor for some years thereafter.[41]

After Frederick's death in 1890, Julia and her daughters also continued to employ Hazelton and Lewis Comfort Tiffany's successive firms for renovation projects in Woodstock that ranged from decorative carvings for the dining room mantel to the installation and refurbishing of several bathrooms. The Tiffany Glass & Decorating Company designed at least one of the bathrooms and supplied the tile and some of the fixtures, but the work for all of them was completed by Hazelton's subcontractor, Boston plumber Isaac N. Tucker. Tiffany's firms were also hired for other updates in New York and other Woodstock buildings during this period.[42]

Frederick and Julia Billings deeply valued aesthetically pleasing, comfortable domestic environments and kept their homes well maintained and up to date. Over a 40-year period, they had myriad experiences with architects, furniture manufacturers, and others with a variety of backgrounds and training. There was some hierarchy among the decorators that the Billings hired, and Frederick treated those who, like McPherson and Du Fais, had professional training, with more respect than other employees unless they proved themselves unworthy or incompetent. But the Billings always remained loyal to those whose work they appreciated, whether they were well-known decorators or talented plumbers.

The Billings had a clear vision of the kind of home they wanted from the beginning, and, over time, they learned how to achieve it. Frederick, and to some extent Julia, were exacting clients who demanded excellence, and they gained self-confidence with every project they undertook. Determined that their image of "dignified beauty," rather than the one proposed by the architect and/or decorator, should prevail, Frederick (and occasionally Julia) felt entitled to criticize their decorators, reject their advice, and overrule them. Frederick eventually even served as his own project manager, taking control of projects by convening and consulting several "experts" about design decisions, playing them off against each other, weighing their ideas and suggestions, and orchestrating collaborations and alliances among them. This approach helped him make decisions in a way that, at least in part, mitigated the friction of one-on-one confrontations, and may also have resulted in better designs.

The architects, decorators, and craftsmen of all kinds who sought to impress clients like the Billings with their superior sensibilities and expertise quickly learned that both taste and design are in the eye of the beholder, and that their success depended on negotiation, tact, and submission to the client who paid the bills and would occupy the property. Eager for work, recognition, and status, they promoted themselves as experts in interior decoration. Those who were arrogant, incompetent, inefficient, and uncompromising were likely to have a rough time of it, but designers and decorators who were willing to accommodate the clients' demands were rewarded with enduring loyalty. In addition, those who developed ongoing relationships with clients and their families also developed strong associations with each other that led to further work.[43]

In the early years of the interior design profession, most designers and decorators had begun their careers as specialized craftsmen of particular skill and strong ambition who broadened their scope in response to a growing population of consumers who needed help in creating modern, stylish homes that expressed their personal taste and values. For a decorative painter it was a small step from wall and ceiling designs to wallpaper, carpets, woodwork, and lighting fixtures, and it was an equally minor leap for a furniture manufacturer to woodwork, upholstery, carpets, and draperies. But it would take longer for families like the Billings, who were used to appreciating craftsmen for high-quality workmanship while treating them as employees, to esteem and venerate interior decorators as artists, experts, and tastemakers.

NOTES

1 This article is based on research published in Susan Porter, PhD, Susan Walton, PhD, and Erica Donnis, MA, *Historic Furnishings Report, Marsh-Billings-Rockefeller National Historical Park*, Vols. 1–4 (Charlestown, MA: Northeast Museum Services Center, National Park Service, 2013–2014). We thank Susan Walton for her many contributions, the National Park Service for its support, and Marianne Zephir of the Marsh-Billings-Rockefeller National Historical Park and Woodstock Foundation for her assistance. Edgar de N. Mayhew and Minor Myers, Jr., *A Documentary History of American Interiors From the Colonial Era to 1915* (New York: Charles Scribner's Sons, 1980), 193–310. Harvey Green, "The Ironies of Style: Complexities and Contradictions in American Decorative Arts, 1850–1900," in *Victorian Furniture: Essays*

Designing professionals ■

From a Victorian Society Autumn Symposium, ed. Kenneth L. Ames (Philadelphia, PA: Victorian Society in America, 1983), 19–34. David P. Handlin, *The American Home, Architecture and Society, 1815–1915* (Boston: Little, Brown and Company, 1979), 4–19. Clifford Edward Clark Jr., *The American Family Home, 1800–1960* (Chapel Hill: University of North Carolina Press, 1986), 3–4, 15–16, 25, 29.

2 Martha Crabill McClaugherty, "Household Art: Creating the Artistic Home, 1868–1893," *Winterthur Portfolio* 18, no. 1 (Spring 1983): 9.

3 Dell Upton, "Pattern Books and Professionalism: Aspects of the Transformation of Domestic Architecture in America, 1800–1860," *Winterthur Portfolio* 19, no. 2/3 (Summer/Autumn 1984): 129–139. Dianne H. Pilgrim, "Decorative Art: The Domestic Environment," in *The American Renaissance, 1876–1917* (New York: Brooklyn Museum, 1979), 114, 116. McClaugherty, "Household Art," 1–26. Janna Jones, "The Distance From Home: The Domestication of Desire in Interior Design Manuals," *Journal of Social History* 31, no. 2 (Winter 1997): 307–326.

4 The Billings' collection contains several books on design, including Charles Eastlake, *Hints on Household Taste in Furniture, Upholstery, and Other Details* (London: Longmans, Green and Co., 1868) and Clarence Cook, *The House Beautiful: Essays on Beds and Tables, Stools and Candlesticks* (New York: Charles Scribner's Sons, 1881). Frederick Billings (hereafter FB) to Julia Parmly Billings (hereafter JPB), 26 November 1865, Box A5a, Billings Family Archives (hereafter BFA), The Woodstock Foundation, Inc., [2004.003], Woodstock, VT. Robin Winks, *Frederick Billings, a Life* (Berkeley: University of California Press, 1998), 147.

5 Catharine E. Beecher, *A Treatise on Domestic Economy, for the Use of Young Ladies at Home, and at School* (Boston: Marsh, Capen, Lyon, and Webb, 1841). JPB Diary, 24 January 1870, BFA. Catharine E. Beecher and Harriet Beecher Stowe, *The American Woman's Home: Or, Principles of Domestic Science; Being a Guide to the Formation and Maintenance of Economical, Healthful, Beautiful, and Christian Homes* (New York: J. B. Ford And Company, 1869; reprint: Arno Press, Inc., 1971), i–ii, 89. Jr. Clark, Jr. *The American Family Home*, 59. Katherine C. Grier, *Culture & Comfort: Parlor Making and Middle-Class Identity, 1850–1930* (Washington, DC: Smithsonian Institution Press, 1988), 6–9.

6 "For Frederick and her relatives Julia often was an arbiter of taste, appearing to defer to her husband yet usually getting her way;" Winks, *Frederick Billings, a Life*, 147.

7 Villard's house, at 451 Madison Avenue in New York City, was designed by McKim, Mead, and White. FB Diary, 3 December 1883, BFA. "Let us have the whole simpler harmonizing and homelike;" FB to JPB, 22 February 1870, Box A5c, BFA. "Took Julia Mary Ward & Laura over [Henry] Villard's new palace, very costly but unsuited to a home in this country;" FB Diary, 3 December 1883, BFA.

8 At that time the Billings were living in a family home in Woodstock with FB's widowed sister. The Marsh house, a large two and one half story dwelling with a gable roof, a cellar, an attic, and two chimneys on the north and south end walls respectively, was constructed between 1805 and 1807 by a local architect-builder, Nathaniel Smith, for lawyer and gentleman farmer Charles Marsh Sr.; Barbara Yocum, *The Mansion: Preliminary Historic Structure Report, Marsh-Billings-Rockefeller National Historical Park* (Lowell, MA: Building Conservation Branch, Northeast Cultural Resource Center, National Park Service, 2001), 9, 21. FB to JPB, 17 October 1865, Box A5a, BFA. JPB to FB, 17 November 1865, Box A4b, BFA. "I believe if I could have one more streak of luck I would buy the Marsh place – and gradually fix it up – and have it for a country seat;" FB to JPB, 30 September 1868, Box 5a, BFA. Warrantee Deed, Charles Marsh Jr. to FB, 17 March 1869, Box A24, BFA.

9 "F. & I looked over the plans for the Marsh house;" JPB Diary, 17 April 1869, BFA. "Frederick & I decided upon some changes at the house;" JPB Diary, 7 March 1870, BFA. Daniel Joseph Nadenicek, William H. Tischler, and Lance M. Neckar, "Copeland, Robert Morris," in *Pioneers of American Landscape Design*, ed. Charles A. Birnbaum and Robin Karson (New York: McGraw-Hill, 2000), 68–70. *Boston City Directories*. Bainbridge Bunting, *Houses of Boston's Back Bay, An Architectural History, 1840–1917* (Cambridge: Harvard University Press, 1967). Cynthia Zaitzevsky and Myron Miller, *The Architecture of William Ralph Emerson, 1833–1917* (Cambridge: Harvard University, 1969), 2–3. Roger G. Reed and Richard Cheek, *A Delight to All Who Know It, The Maine Summer Architecture of William R. Emerson* (Augusta: Maine

19 □

Historic Preservation Commission, 1990), 11–12. Samuel Atkins Eliot, *Biographical History of Massachusetts; Biographies and Autobiographies of the Leading Men in the State, Volume VI* (Boston: Massachusetts Biographical Society, 1916).

10 *Vermont Standard*, 3 June 1869.

11 No architectural drawings, business correspondence, or invoices for the 1869–1871 project have been found and few of the finishes from this rebuild survive. The appearance of the house is documented by several photographs in the BFA. Yocum, "The Mansion," 22–23. Virginia and Lee McAlester, *A Field Guide to American Houses* (New York: Alfred A. Knopf, 1984), 211, 241, 255.

12 "Mr. Emerson and I had a talk over the library and we agreed upon all the main features – leaving the North wall as it is. I like him exceedingly;" FB to JPB, 2 April 1869, Box A5c, BFA. "The house goes on very slowly – and the big chimney in dining room I must take down – It projects so far as to spoil the dining room & billiard room awkward;" FB to JPB, nd [summer 1869], Box A5b, BFA. "Lizzie [Allen] & I . . . saw the alteration of the parlor walls. It is a great improvement;" JPB to FB, 15 December 1869, Box A4b, BFA. "Remembering your request about the 3rd story mantles. . . . the effect they produced upon me must have been quite as unfavorable as you described in your own case. . . . I told Mr. Barker to have them exchanged for some plain ones of better marble;" JPB to FB, 15 February 1870, Box A4b, BFA. "Lizzie went up to see the mantles yesterday & says they looked even worse than she expected and she fully agrees with you in thinking them insufferable;" JPB to FB, 15 February 1870, Box A4, BFA. "The walnut wood in the library is very handsome;" JPB to FB, 17 February 1870, Box A4, BFA. "I am glad you ordered down those hideous mantels – How could Emerson have sent such things – Let us have those pretty tasteful ones – They don't cost much;" FB to JPB, [1870], Box A5c, BFA.

13 JPB to FB, 24 February 1870, Box A4b, BFA. FB to JPB, 22 February 1870, Box A5c, BFA. "I have seen Mr. Copeland . . . and I think that under you he should take charge of painting and papering. It is a considerable job – I want you to make such suggestions and give such directions as may occur to you – Let us have the whole simpler harmonizing and homelike;" FB to JPB, 22 February 1870, Box A5c, BFA. "I feel . . . that instead of attempting to do it all ourselves – in the family – we should have somebody in – and attend to the details. Now Emerson I can't trust;" FB to JPB, 25 February 1870, Box A5c, BFA. "The plan of silver safe in side-board is as decided upon long ago – but Emerson never has drawn the plan of the side-board – although he promised it long ago – He has annoyed me by much of his conduct – He ought to have taken charge of painting etc – but I cannot stand his neglect & inefficiency;" FB to JPB, 23 February 1870, Box A5c, BFA.

14 FB to JPB, 22 February 1870, Box A5c, BFA. "I am very much impressed with what you say . . . about Copeland – I feel this however that the painting and papering ought to be going on very soon. . . . Copeland seems to me to be the only available outside aid . . . I told him that you didn't like his suggestions – thought them too extravagant – and he must talk the matter over with you – that you were to be chief – and I impressed him with my desire to be simple modest and economical"; FB to JPB, 25 [February 1870], Box A5c, BFA. FB to JPB, 26 February 1870, Box A5c, BFA.

15 FB to JPB, 25 [February 1870], Box A5c, BFA. William McPherson, advertisement in *Boston City Directory*, 1872, 1272. "Copeland & MacPherson [sic] dined, tea'd & passed the evening;" JPB Diary, 4 March 1870, BFA. The Billings may have learned about McPherson through Emerson. Emerson was working on the Sanford house at the same time; it has decorative paint treatments that resemble other McPherson commissions of the same period; Historic American Buildings Survey, Creator, Architects Fehmer And Emerson, Builders A. A. Low And Co, and Milton H Sanford, *Sanford-Covell House, 72 Washington Street, Newport, Newport County, RI*, documentation compiled after 1933, Pdf, retrieved from the Library of Congress, www.loc.gov/item/ri0012. McPherson completed myriad East Coast decorative painting projects, and in the early 1870s he designed and executed decorative work for the White House's East Room and other federal projects, including the Office of the Secretary of the Navy in the East Wing of the White House (1873). Alfred Mullett, Supervising Architect of the US Treasury Department, declared McPherson "the most accomplished architectural decorator in the United States;" Antoinette J. Lee, *Architects to the*

Designing professionals ■

Nation, The Rise and Decline of the Supervising Architect's Office (New York: Oxford University Press, 2000), Ch. 4, 82.

16 View of the Parlor, Box P29b, BFA. "Find a letter from McPherson saying he wished to have carpets selected & furniture come before sending up painters;" FB to JPB, 13 March 1870, Box A5c, BFA. "Buying carpets in Boston. Mr. McPherson dined with us & in the afternoon we went to look at pictures & furniture;" JPB Diary, 24 March 1870, BFA. "The painters were in Parmly's room yesterday – I think there is little else to do except the parlors;" JPB to FB, 19 April 1870, Box A4, BFA. "We saw 2 papers hung in F.'s room;" JPB Diary, 13 June 1870, BFA.

17 Doe & Charmois, advertisement in *Cambridge City Directory*, 1871. Doe & Hunnewell, advertisement in *Boston Morning Sun*, 21–22 April 1877. Doe, Hunnewell, & Co., advertisement in *Boston City Directory*, 1885. Doe, Hunnewell, & Co., "Design for Library in Empire Style;" "Design for Dining-Room in Renaissance;" "Design for Elizabethan Hall;" "Design for Parlor, Louis XVI Style," in Boston Society of Architects and Boston Architectural Club, *Catalogue of the Architectural Exhibition Held in the New Public Library Building, October 28 to November 4, Inclusive* . . . (Boston: [s.n.], 1891). Edward S. Cooke Jr., "The Boston Furniture Industry in 1880," *Old-Time New England* 80 (1980): 83, 87–88. Ann Gilkerson, "Furniture Manufacturing in East Cambridge, 1851–1916, John A. Ellis Co.," unpublished paper, Cambridge Historical Commission, 13 September 1982.

18 The Billings may have known of the company prior to 1870, as they knew others who had patronized it, and also made a purchase themselves in early 1869: "The new furniture from Boston arrived;" JPB Diary, 19 January 1869, BFA. Gilkerson, "Furniture Manufacturing in East Cambridge." John A. Ellis & Co. to Trenor Park, 2 October 1865, 19 & 29 January 1866, John A. Ellis & Co. to Mrs. Trenor Park, 1 December 1865, and Invoices, John A. Ellis & Co. to Trenor Park, 20 January 1866 and 2 January 1867, all in Box 40A, Park-McCullough Papers, University of Vermont Special Collections. Founded by Jonathan Eastman Hazelton (1803–1888), who was in the furniture business in Cambridge by 1845, and Joseph Merrill Doe, Doe & Hazelton was in business from 1849 to 1858. In 1859, Hazelton, his son Joseph T. Hazelton, and John A. Ellis, another Cambridge cabinetmaker, established John A. Ellis & Co. Ellis' partnership with the Hazeltons was dissolved in January 1862, and Doe became Ellis' partner; they operated the firm together until Ellis' death in March 1869; *Boston City Directory*, 1845–1875; *Cambridge City Directory*, 1851–1869; United States Census, 1850, 1860, National Archives and Records Administration, accessed at www.ancestry.com; *Cambridge Chronicle*, 2 May 1868, 27 March 1869.

19 "We all went to the Hill at 5, to sit in council over the new dining table. . . . Kirwan thinks it can be altered sufficiently to improve its appearance & make it a pleasanter table & he sends word to Doe & Charmois . . . that we think of having that done;" JPB to FB, 6 July 1870, Box A4, BFA. "Mr. McPherson came and he and F. discussed the housefurnishing [sic];" JPB Diary, 22 June 1870, BFA. "Mr. McPherson came to help F. about the house;" JPB Diary, 16 July 1870, BFA. "I have written McPherson to know if can meet me at Woodstock Saturday – if not, if he could send up Charmois;" FB to JPB, 27 March 1871, Box A5c. "Hung some engravings w. McP. help;" JPB Diary, 1 April 1871, BFA. "Mr. McPherson & Charmois were busy discussing changes etc. almost every moment of their stay;" JPB to FB, 12 April 1871, Box A4b. "I thought Doe & Charmois were to have the parlor *fitted* by this time – but you say nothing of them;" FB to JPB, 23 April 1871, Box A5c, BFA.

20 For example, "We were all in the parlor to sing hymns in eve.g;" JPB Diary, 12 March 1876, BFA. "I sat w. E. & Parm. while the Arth. Les. proceeded. They made designs w. blocks on the piazza. . . . Parmly studied his arth. w. Miss W. & then recited to me. We had a pleasant Bible reading in Laura's room;" JPB Diary, 11 July 1876, BFA. "Tis getting to be nine o'clock and I must gather my chickens; they are just now playing tag in the hall, and twould do your hearts good to hear the merry voices;" Laura Wheeler (governess) to JPB and FB, 8[?] March 1877, Box A9, BFA.

21 FB's brother Frank Billings, and his sister Lizzie Allen also helped with various projects. In the 1870s and early 1880s, FB also hired McPherson to work on several civic projects in Woodstock; Henry Swan Dana, *History of Woodstock, Vermont* (Boston: Houghton, Mifflin and Company, 1889, reprint: Countryman

Press, 1980), 439; JPB Diary, 15 June 1876 and 20 August 1876, BFA; JPB, "Autobiographical Notes thru 1908," c. 1904–1909, Box A12, BFA, 27; Laura Wheeler to JPB, 19 September and 2 October 1880, BFA; Receipt, Emerson to FB, 24 December 1882, copy, MABI 13045, Marsh-Billings-Rockefeller National Historical Park, Woodstock, Vermont. "Our painter, Bailey, might have been at a loss for work this rainy day but for restoring the dining room paper & patching here & there in the nurseries;" JPB to FB, 10 June 1872, Box A4b, BFA. "Mr. McPherson called and accompanied us to Edward Hixon at 180 Washington St. [Boston] and then to Bliss & Perkins. Selected the color for new coverings to parlor furniture where it showed the repairs;" FB Diary, 4 November 1874, BFA. "Bailey – painter . . . said he thought the repairs to dining-room ceiling would take two days;" JPB to FB, 24 July 1876, Box A4b. "We shall have our reception room in order. . . . Mr. Abbott is now helping Amos lay the new carpet over the old one. . . . The carpet suits the paper well & being of a rather dingy shade will accord nicely with our old things;" JPB to FB, 1 November 1879, Box A5, BFA. "The work went on a while by gaslight in the dining room, it was necessary to take down the under flooring – it had settled so much;" JPB to FB, 5 November 1879, Box A5, BFA. "The recep.tn furniture came – Is very approp.;" JPB Diary, 11 December 1879, BFA. "Rec'd samples of wall paper selected by McPherson – agreed to all except Dining Room which is too dark;" FB Diary, 2 April 1880, BFA. "The decorators have just finished your rooms. . . . The frescoes are heavier than before & altogether different but accord beautifully with the paper. . . . The new dining room paper is handsomer than either of the others;" Laura Wheeler to FB and JPB, 5 May 1880, Box A9, BFA. "Mary's room is very pretty with its new paper & fresco;" Laura Wheeler to JPB and FB, 8 May 1880, Box A9, BFA. "We were delighted with the newly papered rooms;" JPB Diary, 14 May 1880, BFA. "Saw the finished rooms & are delighted;" FB Diary, 14 May 1880, BFA.

22 "Told [McPherson] next spring – to paint the rest of my house;" FB Diary, 15 May 1880, BFA. "I believe if I could have one more streak of luck I would buy the Marsh place . . . and at the same time gradually increase the amount of your money until we had enough to buy a house in the city;" FB to JPB, 30 September 1868, Box A5a, BFA. FB to JPB, 10 January 1881, Box A5j, BFA. FB Diary, 12 January 1881, BFA. "Well, the Arnold house is to be yours. . . . Now, no more questions about where we are to live – Woodstock in summer New York in winter – sunny dear houses—& room & to share;" FB to JPB, 16 March 1881, Box A5j, BFA.

23 "Mr. Douglas" may be Alfred Douglass, listed in the 1880 *New York City Directory* with an occupation of "h. furnishing." FB to JPB, 3 April 1881, Box A5j, BFA. "[T]he house is really in a dreadful condition;" FB to JPB, 5 April 1881, Box A5j, BFA. "I telegraphed Frank not to employ Mr. McPherson – The man who had charge of Oliver's house – is good enough for the basement and the 4th story – and a moderate-priced good man. I propose to let him do what is necessary in those two stories – and then we will see;" FB to JPB, 6 April 1881, Box A5j, BFA. "I'm inclined to think it will be a great relief to let McPherson take charge of the three principal stories;" FB to JPB, 9 April 1881, Box A5j, BFA. "[H]ouse – work goes slowly – Too elaborate painting on billiard room ceiling;" FB Diary, 7 May 1881, BFA. "McPherson. . . . is to . . . decide on all that is to be done – He took in the situation completely. . . . Mr. Douglass, Oliver's man, showed his incompetency by the way he has painted the billiard room;" FB to JPB, 14 May 1881, Box A5j, BFA. "Requested [housekeeper] to have Douglas send in his bills & keep away;" FB Diary, 21 July 1881, BFA.

24 *Boston City Directory*, 1863–1871. Massachusetts Vital Records for Boston, MA, 1895, accessed at www. ancestry.com. Doe & Hunnewell, Advertisement, *Boston Morning Sun*, 20–21 April 1877. *Cambridge City Directory*, 1877. Gilkerson, "Furniture Manufacturing in East Cambridge." Christopher Hail, *Cambridge Buildings and Architects* (Cambridge, MA: Christopher Hail, 2001), 634–635.

25 One Hunnewell and McPherson collaboration was Cedar Hill (now known as Clouds Hill) in Rhode Island; Marissa Sarah Hershon, "An Egyptian Revival Reception Room: Cedar Hill, Warwick, Rhode Island, 1872–1877" (Master's thesis, Smithsonian Associates and Corcoran College of Art + Design, 2010), n36. By the 1880s, the light, elegant decorative style of McPherson's earlier work was becoming less fashionable, but he was still in business in 1888; W. J. McPherson, Trade Catalog (Providence: Livermore and Knight, 1888), F-186, Rakow Library, Corning Museum of Glass, Corning, New York. FB Diary, 11 August 1881,

Designing professionals ■

BFA. "To house . . . We decided carving of furniture in Laura's room hideous & ordered it changed;" FB Diary, 28 October 1881, BFA. William McPherson to JPB, [October or November 1881], Box A31b, BFA. "F . . . a good deal tried by MacP.'s many blunders;" JPB Diary, 12 November 1881, BFA. "Found little progress in house . . . and I was a bit cross with McPherson;" FB Diary, 16 November 1881, BFA. "Am growing sick of the yellow furnishings of my & Julia's room. The furniture returned to Boston;" FB Diary, 21 November 1881, BFA. "FB Diary, 5 December 1881, BFA. "The last of McPherson's men left today . . . what a strung out imposition his work has been;" FB Diary, 10 December 1881, BFA. "Overhauled McPherson's account – some of the charges are outrageously high;" FB Diary, 1 February 1882, BFA. "F. wrote McPherson about the injustice of paying a percentage on his mistakes;" JPB Diary, 3 February 1882, BFA. FB Diary, 3 October 1883, BFA.

26 "To Pottier & Stymus – Delighted;" FB Diary, 2 December 1882, BFA. Pottier & Stymus redecorated sections of the White House for President Ulysses Grant and decorated the newly-built homes of Thomas Edison and Leland Stanford. The company was liquidated in 1888; Ruth Lutgens, "The Pottier & Stymus Manufacturing Company's 1876 Centennial Exhibition Furniture" (master's thesis, Sotheby's Institute of Art, 2011), 7–10, 17; Doreen Bulger Burke, ed., *In Pursuit of Beauty: Americans and the Aesthetic Movement* (New York: Metropolitan Museum of Art, 1986), 116; Kristin Herron, "The Modern Gothic Furniture of Pottier & Stymus," *The Magazine Antiques* 155 (May 1999): 762–769. "Pottier of P & Stymus Came to see about mirrors in dining room – Cambric kin[?] in sitting room. Liked him – wish he had fixed my house – wh. I was so swindled in by McPherson;" FB Diary, 3 October 1883, BFA. "Pottier called & we talked over my office & library – He is to get estimates and designs;" FB Diary, 6 May 1885, BFA. "Pottier came over & decided to entirely fix over my office – changing every thing . . . – Julia & Laura object to doing over Library – but will clean ceiling;" FB Diary, 20 May 1885, BFA. FB Diary, 27 May 1885. FB Diary, 25 July 1885, BFA. FB to JPB, 6 September 1886, BFA. FB to JPB, 8 September 1885, Box A5k, BFA. "Pottier & Stymus went out of the house with their paint pots last night – 6 weeks & 3 days beyond the time period in the agreement. The rooms are very nice;" FB to JPB, 17 September 1885, Box A5k, BFA.

27 "Holly architect. . . . took measurements at house;" FB Diary, 3 August 1882, BFA. Henry Hudson Holly, *Holly's Country Seats* (New York: D. Appleton & Co., 1863), *Church Architecture* (Hartford: M.H. Mallory, 1871), and *Modern Dwellings in Town and Country in Town and Country Adapted to American Wants and Climate, With a Treatise on Furniture and Decoration* (New York: Harper & Bros., 1878). Michael A. Tomlan, "The Domestic Architectural Stylebooks of Henry Hudson Holly," in *Country Seats & Modern Dwellings: Two Victorian Domestic Architectural Stylebooks by Henry Hudson Holly*, ed. Henry Hudson Holly (Watkins Glen, NY: Library of Victorian Culture, 1977). George B. Tatum, "Introduction to the Dover Edition," *Holly's Picturesque Country Seats, a Complete Reprint of the 1863 Classic* (New York: Dover Publications, 1993), iii–xiii. Obituary for Henry Hudson Holly, *New York Times*, 7 September 1892, www. nytimes.com.

28 A plan for the first floor of the service ell probably dates from this period; Holly, "Plan of First Story Extension," in Yocum, "The Mansion," Figure 11. FB Diary, 16 August 1882, BFA. FB Diary, 17 August 1882, BFA. FB Diary, 29 January 1883, BFA. FB Diary, 19 February 1883, BFA. FB Diary, 13 March 1883, BFA.

29 "Discussed w. Julia the changing of roof on house and raising servants part according to Holly's plans;" FB Diary, 30 July 1885, BFA. "Holly arrived & spend day in discussing changes – Left minl' changes which not altogether satisfactory – will revise them;" FB Diary, 4 August 1885, BFA. "With Holly & determined good many things about house – his commission agreed on 8% & he pays all expenses;" FB Diary, 5 August 1885, BFA.

30 The library clearly needed structural reinforcement, but FB and JPB may have been concerned that enlarging the span of the room would exacerbate the problem. FB Diary 9 August 1885, BFA. FB Diary, 10 August 1885, BFA. "Holly writes can set back fireplace in dining room without disturbing rooms above – wh. pleases me;" FB Diary, 13 August 1885, BFA. "I have a note here from Ehrick who thinks the proposed changes will be a great addition to our comfort – I know they will be – and when you go up next Spring

and see the house in its new shape and new paint you will be glad;" FB to JPB, 19 August 1885, Box A5k, BFA.

31 He may have taken a supervisory role, at least in part, because the general contractor, Austin Abbott, seemed overwhelmed; "Holly left – and I staid nearly the whole day at the Hill driving the work which is altogether too big for Abbott;" FB Diary, 3 September 1885. FB Diary, 4 September 1885.

32 FB Diary, 11 November 1885, BFA. For example, "Dissatisfied with gable on South side of L – the extra window to light that upper hall is hideous;" FB Diary, 2 October 1885, BFA. "Discussed with Abbott & Austin two gables on L part – & directed where they should go – unless sketches to arrive from Holly show an improvement – Sketches arrived – Holly's plan rejected & instructed mine to be followed;" FB Diary, 5 October 1885, BFA. "F. was happy but for the defects in Holly's plans. . . . F. was annoyed at the looks of the high gables & a great defect in the nursery balcony windows," JPB Diary, 9 October 1885, BFA. "It was a trying day for F. who had many mistakes of Holly to rectify;" JPB Diary, 11 November 1885, BFA. "[Ca]r of finish had not arrived according to promise – Feel indignant with Holly;" FB Diary, 20 November 1885, BFA.

33 FB Diary, 23 November 1885, BFA. FB Diary, 24 November 1885, BFA. "Holly called & I told him, so many mistakes & delays – & his interior plans so much more elaborate than I wished – and then I would get someone else. He was willing – Did not decide save to say he might try his hand at something more simple;" FB Diary, 25 November 1885, BFA. FB Diary, 30 November 1885, BFA. FB Diary, 1 December 1885, BFA. "Holly to make more simple drawings – & get detail estimates of first plans & of these – & then I will determine;" FB Diary, 2 December 1885, BFA. "Holly arrived morning train – spent good deal of time with him at house – rather disposed to yield to his first plans;" FB Diary, 10 December 1885, BFA. "Saw Holly . . . & told him to go ahead substantially with first plans;" FB Diary, 11 December 1885, BFA.

34 "Contracted with Doe Hunnewell & Co. of Boston for hard wood finish f.o.b. [$] 8200 [?] – lower price than Fairchilds – Delighted to be done w. Fairchilds & New Jersey;" FB Diary, 6 January 1886, BFA. "Ordered chamber set from Doe Hunnewell & Co. to Woodstock for butler;" FB Diary, 22 May 1884, BFA. "Wrote Frank [Billings] various suggestions about house to submit to Holly & Hunnewell;" FB Diary, 7 January 1886, BFA. "Kilner [FB's secretary] saw Holly about mantels for Woodstock;" FB Diary, 11 January 1886, BFA. "[M]et Hunnewell from Boston about furniture for Woodstock house – To cost more than I expected – with the repair and covering of old furniture – certainly [$]5.500 – He went to see DuFais and Holly;" FB Diary, 12 February 1886, BFA. "Hunnewell called & we substantially settled the furniture question;" FB Diary, 13 February 1886, BFA. "Hazelton overhauled all furniture;" FB Diary, 22 April 1886, BFA. "Went over many things with Mr. Hazelton – decided substantially on fine furniture &c.;" FB Diary, 11 June 1886, BFA. Yocum, "The Mansion," 30.

35 *Decorator and Furnisher* 10, no. 5 (August 1887), 164. "Louis Comfort Tiffany," in Burke et al., *In Pursuit of Beauty*, 474–475. William Seale, *The President's House, a History*, Volume 1, Second edition (Baltimore: Johns Hopkins University Press, 2008), 517–523.

36 Du Fais had served as the director of architecture for Louis Comfort Tiffany's previous decorating firm, Louis C. Tiffany & Company, before becoming secretary of the Tiffany Glass Company; Alice Cooney Frelinghuysen, *Louis Comfort Tiffany and Laurelton Hall: An Artist's Country Estate* (New Haven: Yale University Press, 2006), 6–7, 11, 20–21, 226. "Louis Comfort Tiffany," in Burke et al., *In Pursuit of Beauty*, 474–475. Roberta A. Meyer and Carolyn K. Kane, "Disassociating the 'Associated Artists': The Early Business Ventures of Louis C. Tiffany, Candace T. Wheeler, and Lockwood de Forest," *Studies in the Decorative Arts* 8, No. 2 (Spring–Summer 2001): 2–36. "John Du Fais Dead," *New York Times,* 15 March 1935, www.nytimes.com. "Looked over with Julia & Laura samples of papers &c. sent by Tiffanys for Woodstock & made memoranda of criticism – too ornate & expensive;" FB Diary, 10 February 1886, BFA. "DuFais came with portfolio of sketches papers & decorations for house – &c we agreed;" FB Diary, 16 February 1886, BFA. FB Diary, 12 April 1886, BFA. "DuFais called . . . with samples of carpets – Most of them satisfactory – also plan for stained glass window in Library – which he sends to Abbott;" FB Diary, 29 April 1886, BFA. "Went with Julia, Mary & Miss W. to Arnold C[onstable] & C. to meet Mr. DuFais & select carpets for

Woodstock;" FB Diary, 1 May 1886, BFA. "DuFais & Hazelton went to Woodstock with me . . . DuFais's work long way behind – He will send up 4 more men;" FB Diary, 29 May 1886, BFA. "To Tiffany Glass Co. with Julia to see about globes for gas fixtures;" FB Diary, 7 June 1886, BFA. "Mr. Hazelton arrived – with a good many things – Telegraphed for DuFais;" FB Diary, 25 June 1886, BFA. "Mr. Dufais was so helpful we got on quite fast in deciding matters for the parlor & dining room;" JPB Diary, 26 June 1886, BFA.

37 "Holly. . . . discussed plans for fireplaces and finish of rooms with the ladies;" FB Diary, 27 October 1885, BFA. JPB to Parmly Billings, 25 February 1886, Box A6a, BFA.

38 "Holly, Hunnewell, DuFais (Tiffany & Co.) arrived morning train – as also Mason of Mead, M[ason] & Co. Spent almost entire day at Hill—& settled a good many things – to change hood over South kitchen door – to change South gable – to put railing on coping of driveway – determined on maple rather than birch for finish parlor – floor Laura's Mary's Julia's & Music Room hardwood &c DuFais to submit plans and estimates;" FB Diary, 28 January 1886, BFA. FB Diary, 11 February 1886, BFA. "[M]et Hunnewell from Boston about furniture for Woodstock house. . . . He went to see DuFais and Holly;" FB Diary, 12 February 1886, BFA. "Holly, Hazelton & Hunnewell designer arrived morning – We made changes in hall finish taking out first beam & spindles – & moving the other one &c – Decided to put dressers in dining room each side of side board;" FB Diary, 2 March 1886, BFA. "Met Holly, Hazelton & Hunnewell men at Hill & we decided on the hall changes from Holly plans – & substantially on colors for interior of house;" FB Diary, 3 March 1886, BFA. FB Diary, 13 April 1886, BFA. "Rec'd from Hunnewell plan of how he would arrange ceiling, throwing So-hall into Library. . . . The proposed beams coming down into room with it so large a room will make ceiling very heavy. Must take time and study matter;" FB Diary, 16 April 1886, BFA. "Telegraphed for Holly & iron man from Boston to be here in morning to decide about girder;" FB Diary, 22 April 1886, BFA. JPB Diary, 1 May 1886, BFA.

39 "Saw DuFais & told him Mrs. B. wanted the parlor stained glass window – Wrote so to D. Hunnewell & Co. – directed frame to be sent to DuFais – for window to be fitted & sent there;" FB Diary, 12 April 1886, BFA. "Stopped at DuFais – who will send specimens of carpets to D.H. & Co. today;" FB Diary, 3 May 1886, BFA. FB Diary, 17 May 1886, BFA.

40 FB Diary, 14 August 1886, BFA. FB Diary, 10 June 1886, BFA. JPB Diary, 10 June 1886, BFA.

41 Hazelton & Goddard, which advertised as specialists in "Artistic Furniture, Upholstery and Draperies," was in business from 1887 to about 1894. From 1894 to late 1899, the company operated as Hazelton, Goddard & Kitfield, purveyors of "Furniture and Fabrics, Woodworkers and Interior Decorators;" Invoices, Hazelton, Goddard & Kitfield, to Trustees Estate of FB, 1 October 1894 and 29 May 1899, copies, MABI 13045; Hazelton to George Aitken, 10 June 1904, Aitken Correspondence from Various, May–August 1904, Billings Farm Records, The Woodstock Foundation, Woodstock, Vermont [hereafter BFR]. By 1905, Hazelton had his own business, Joseph T. Hazelton, Furniture, Upholstery, and Wallpaper, on Massachusetts Avenue in Boston. In 1910, he was still working as a furniture manufacturer; United States Census, 1910, accessed at www.ancestry.com. Every spring Hazelton's employees varnished or polished the furniture and floors, repaired and reupholstered furniture, supplied new slipcovers and curtains, and performed other maintenance at the Woodstock house. Invoices and Receipts, Hazelton & Goddard/Hazelton, Goddard & Kitfield to FB and Invoices to Trustees of Estate of FB, copies, MABI 13045 and Billings Farm Fiscal Records, MABI Curator Files, Marsh-Billings Rockefeller National Historical Park. Mary Holland to George Aitken, 20 May 1904, Aitken Correspondence with Billings Family and Associates, BFR.

42 The decorative carvings were one of the earliest commissions completed by Boston wood carver Johannes Kirchmayer (1860–1930); Douglass Shand-Tucci, *Boston Bohemia, 1881–1900, Ralph Adams Cram: Life and Architecture*, Volume 1 (Amherst: University of Massachusetts Press, 1995), 305; E. Shirley Prouty, *Master Carver Johannes Kirchmayer, 1860–1930: From Germany's Passion Play Village to America's Finest Sanctuaries* (Portsmouth, NH: Peter E. Randall, 2007); *Boston Daily Globe*, 15 January 1911. Among other projects, in 1899, the Tiffany Glass & Decorating Company installed electrical wiring in Woodstock and refreshed the first-floor living spaces in New York; Invoice, Tiffany Glass and Decorating Company to JPB, 1 December 1899, copy, MABI Curator Files. Tucker provided his own subcontractors and supplied fixtures

and accessories; Invoices, Isaac Tucker to Estate of FB, copies, Billings Farm Fiscal Records, MABI Curator Files. JPB Diary, 24 January 1890, BFA. JPB Diary, 21 May 1890, BFA.

43 "It's strange Mr. Emerson should show so little concern but he is sensitive. . . . He, probably, has never overcome his indignation at your plain speaking last summer;" JPB to FB, 27 February 1870, Box A4, BFA. Emerson apologized in the spring of 1870: "I am much pleased with the way Mr. Emerson has written you. He is a very agreeable gentleman and proves himself manly by admitting himself in fault about our work;" JPB to FB, 10 March 1870, Box A4, BFA. "Letter from Holly showing his feeling that I do not put more confidence in him;" FB Diary, 30 November 1885, BFA. "Wrote Holly we better hold together & see if we could not agree about interior finish;" FB Diary, 1 December 1885, BFA.

BIBLIOGRAPHY

Beecher, Catharine E. and Harriet Beecher Stowe. *The American Woman's Home: Or, Principles of Domestic Science; Being a Guide to the Formation and Maintenance of Economical, Healthful, Beautiful, and Christian Homes*. New York: J.B. Ford And Company, 1869, reprint: Arno Press, Inc., 1971.

Beecher, Catharine E. *A Treatise on Domestic Economy, For the Use of Young Ladies at Home, and at School*. Boston: Marsh, Capen, Lyon, and Webb, 1841.

Billings Family Archives. The Woodstock Foundation Inc., Woodstock, Vermont.

Boston City Directory. 1845–1875. Historic New England Library and Archives, Boston, MA.

Boston Morning Sun. 1877. Historic New England Library and Archives, Boston, MA.

Boston Society of Architects and Boston Architectural Club. *Catalogue of the Architectural Exhibition Held in the New Public Library Building, October 28 to November 4, Inclusive, in Conjunction With the Annual Convention of the American Institute of Architects, and Under the Direction of the Boston Society of Architects and the Boston Architectural Club*. Boston: [s.n.], 1891.

Bunting, Bainbridge. *Houses of Boston's Back Bay, an Architectural History, 1840–1917*. Cambridge: Harvard University Press, 1967.

Burke, Doreen Bulger, ed. *In Pursuit of Beauty: Americans and the Aesthetic Movement*. New York: Metropolitan Museum of Art, 1986.

Cambridge Chronicle. 1868–1869. Historic New England Library and Archives, Boston, Massachusetts.

Cambridge City Directory. 1851–1930. Historic New England Library and Archives, Boston, MA.

Clark Jr., Clifford Edward. *The American Family Home, 1800–1960*. Chapel Hill: University of North Carolina Press, 1986.

Collard, Frances. "Historical Revivals, Commercial Enterprise and Public Confusion: Negotiating Taste, 1860–1890." *Journal of Design History* 16, no. 1 (2003): 35–48.

Cook, Clarence. *The House Beautiful: Essays on Beds and Tables, Stools and Candlesticks*. New York: Charles Scribner's Sons, 1881.

Cooke Jr., Edward S. "The Boston Furniture Industry in 1880." *Old-Time New England* 80 (1980): 82–98.

Dana, Henry Swan. *History of Woodstock, Vermont*. Boston: Houghton, Mifflin and Company, 1889, reprint: Countryman Press, 1980.

Eastlake, Charles. *Hints on Household Taste in Furniture, Upholstery, and Other Details*. London: Longmans, Green and Co., 1868.

Eliot, Samuel Atkins. *Biographical History of Massachusetts; Biographies and Autobiographies of the Leading Men in the State, Volume VI*. Boston: Massachusetts Biographical Society, 1916.

Ettema, Michael J. "Technological Innovation and Design Economics in American Furniture Manufacture of the Nineteenth Century." *Winterthur Portfolio* 16, no. 2/3 (Summer/Autumn 1981): 197–223.

Frelinghuysen, Alice Cooney. *Louis Comfort Tiffany and Laurelton Hall: An Artist's Country Estate*. New Haven: Yale University Press, 2006.

Gilkerson, Ann. "Furniture Manufacturing in East Cambridge, 1851–1916, John A. Ellis Co." Unpublished paper, 13 September 1982. Cambridge Historical Commission.

Green, Harvey. "The Ironies of Style: Complexities and Contradictions in American Decorative Arts, 1850–1900," in *Victorian Furniture: Essays From a Victorian Society Autumn Symposium*, ed. Kenneth L. Ames. Philadelphia, PA: Victorian Society in America, 1983, 19–34.

Grier, Katherine C. *Culture & Comfort: Parlor Making and Middle-Class Identity, 1850–1930*. Washington, DC: Smithsonian Institution Press, 1988.

Hail, Christopher. *Cambridge Buildings and Architects*. Cambridge, MA: Christopher Hail, 2001.

Handlin, David P. *The American Home, Architecture and Society, 1815–1915*. Boston: Little, Brown and Company, 1979.

Herron, Kristin. "The Modern Gothic Furniture of Pottier & Stymus." *The Magazine Antiques* 155 (May 1999): 762–769.

Hershon, Marissa Sarah. "An Egyptian Revival Reception Room: Cedar Hill, Warwick, Rhode Island, 1872–1877." Master's thesis, 2010. Smithsonian Associates and Corcoran College of Art + Design.

Historic American Buildings Survey, Creator, Architects Fehmer And Emerson, Builders A. A. Low And Co, and Milton H. Sanford. "Sanford-Covell House, 72 Washington Street, Newport, Newport County, RI." Documentation Compiled After, 1933. Pdf. Retrieved from the Library of Congress. Accessed at www.loc.gov/item/ri0012.

Holly, Henry Hudson. *Church Architecture*. Hartford: M.H. Mallory, 1871.

———. *Holly's Country Seats*. New York: D. Appleton & Co., 1863.

———. *Modern Dwellings in Town and Country in Town and Country Adapted to American Wants and Climate, With a Treatise on Furniture and Decoration*. New York: Harper & Bros., 1878.

Houghton, Janet. "FINISH, FURNISHINGS and WORKS of ART in the DINING ROOM: A Brief Description of the Notable Items in the Room." February 2005. MABI Curator's Electronic Records, Marsh-Billings-Rockefeller National Historical Park.

Hounshell, David A. *From the American System to Mass Production, 1800–1932: The Development of Manufacturing Technology in the United States*. Baltimore: Johns Hopkins University Press, 1984.

Howe, Katherine S., Alice Cooney Frelinghuysen, Catherine Hoover Voorsanger et al. *Herter Brothers: Furniture and Interiors for a Gilded Age*. New York: Harry N. Abrams and The Museum of Fine Arts, Houston, 1994.

Jones, Janna. "The Distance From Home: The Domestication of Desire in Interior Design Manuals." *Journal of Social History* 31, no. 2 (Winter 1997): 307–326.

Lee, Antoinette J. *Architects to the Nation, The Rise and Decline of the Supervising Architect's Office*. New York: Oxford University Press, 2000.

Lutgens, Ruth. "The Pottier & Stymus Manufacturing Company's 1876 Centennial Exhibition Furniture." Master's thesis, 2011. Sotheby's Institute of Art.

MABI Collections. Marsh-Billings-Rockefeller National Historical Park, Woodstock, Vermont.

Massachusetts Vital Records for Boston and Cambridge, MA, 1850–1895. Accessed at www.ancestry.com.

Mayhew, Edgar deN. and Minor Myers, Jr. *A Documentary History of American Interiors From the Colonial Era to 1915*. New York: Charles Scribner's Sons, 1980.

McAlester, Virginia and Lee. *A Field Guide to American Houses*. New York: Alfred A. Knopf, 1984.

McClaugherty, Martha Crabill. "Household Art: Creating the Artistic Home, 1868–1893." *Winterthur Portfolio* 18, no. 1 (Spring 1983): 1–26.

McPherson, William J. Trade Catalog. Providence: Livermore and Knight, 1888. F-186, Rakow Library, Corning Museum of Glass, Corning, New York.

Meyer, Roberta A. and Carolyn K. Kane. "Disassociating the 'Associated Artists': The Early Business Ventures of Louis C. Tiffany, Candace T. Wheeler, and Lockwood de Forest." *Studies in the Decorative Arts* 8, no. 2 (Spring-Summer 2001): 2–36.

Nadenicek, Daniel Joseph, William H. Tischler, and Lance M. Neckar. "Copeland, Robert Morris," in *Pioneers of American Landscape Design*, ed. Charles A. Birnbaum and Robin Karson. New York: McGraw-Hill, 2000.

New York City Directory. 1880. Accessed at www.ancestry.com.

New York Times. 1892, 1935. Accessed at www.nytimes.com.

Park-McCullough Papers, University of Vermont Special Collections, Burlington, Vermont.

Pilgrim, Dianne H. "Decorative Art: The Domestic Environment," in *The American Renaissance, 1876–1917*. New York: Brooklyn Museum, 1979.

Porter, Susan, Susan Walton, and Erica Donnis. *Historic Furnishings Report, Marsh-Billings-Rockefeller National Historical Park*, Vols. 1–4. Charlestown, MA: Northeast Museum Services Center, National Park Service, 2013–2014.

Prouty, E. Shirley. *Master Carver Johannes Kirchmayer, 1860–1930: From Germany's Passion Play Village to America's Finest Sanctuaries*. Portsmouth, NH: Peter E. Randall, 2007.

Quimby, Ian M. G. and Polly Anne Earl. *Technological Innovation and the Decorative Arts*. Charlottesville: University of Virginia for Henry Francis du Pont Winterthur Museum, 1974.

Reed, Roger G. and Richard Cheek. *A Delight to All Who Know It, The Maine Summer Architecture of William R. Emerson*. Augusta: Maine Historic Preservation Commission, 1990.

Seale, William. *The President's House, a History, Vol. 1, second edition*. Baltimore: Johns Hopkins University Press, 2008.

Shand-Tucci, Douglass. *Boston Bohemia, 1881–1900, Ralph Adams Cram: Life and Architecture, Vol. 1*. Amherst: University of Massachusetts Press, 1995.

Stern, Robert A. M., Gregory Gilmartin, and John Massengale. *New York 1900: Metropolitan Architecture and Urbanism, 1890–1915*. New York: Rizzoli, 1995.

Strazdes, Linda. "The Millionaire's Palace: Leland Stanford's Commission for Pottier & Stymus in New York City." *Winterthur Portfolio* 36, no. 4 (Winter 2001): 213–243.

Tatum, George B. "Introduction to the Dover Edition," in *Holly's Picturesque Country Seats, a Complete Reprint of the 1863 Classic*. New York: Dover Publications, 1993.

Tiffany Glass Company. Advertisement. *Decorator and Furnisher* 10, no. 5 (August 1887): 164.

Tomlan, Michael A. "The Domestic Architectural Stylebooks of Henry Hudson Holly," in *Country Seats & Modern Dwellings: Two Victorian Domestic Architectural Stylebooks by Henry Hudson Holly*, ed. Henry Hudson Holly. Watkins Glen, NY: Library of Victorian Culture, 1977.

United States Census. Schedule 1 (Population). 1850, 1860, 1870, 1880, 1890, 1900. National Archives and Records Administration. Accessed at www.ancestry.com.

United States Passport Applications. 1891, 1910. National Archives and Records Administration. Accessed at www.ancestry.com.

Upton, Dell. "Pattern Books and Professionalism: Aspects of the Transformation of Domestic Architecture in America, 1800–1860." *Winterthur Portfolio* 19, no. 2/3 (Summer/Autumn 1984): 107–150.

Varner, Elizabeth Chantale. "Bolstering A National Identity: President Andrew Johnson's Pottier & Stymus Furniture in the United States Treasury Department." Master's thesis, Smithsonian Associates and Corcoran School of Art + Design, 2008.

Vermont Standard. 1857–1869. Woodstock Historical Society, Woodstock, Vermont.

Winks, Robin W. *Frederick Billings, a Life*. Berkeley: University of California Press, 1998.

Withey, Henry F. and Elsie Rathburn Withey. *Biographical Dictionary of American Artists (Deceased)*. Los Angeles: New Age Publishing Company, 1956.

Wright, Gwendolyn. *Moralism and the Model Home: Domestic Architecture and Cultural Conflict in Chicago, 1873–1913*. Chicago: University of Chicago Press, 1980.

Yocum, Barbara. *The Mansion: Preliminary Historic Structure Report, Marsh-Billings-Rockefeller National Historical Park*. Lowell, MA: Building Conservation Branch, Northeast Cultural Resource Center, National Park Service, 2001.

Zaitzevsky, Cynthia and Myron Miller. *The Architecture of William Ralph Emerson, 1833–1917*. Cambridge: Harvard University Press, 1969.

Chapter 2: Dealing in interiors

How Duveen Brothers and Maison Carlhian shaped an eighteenth-century French salon in 1920s New York

Anne-Marie Schaaf and Teresa Morales

Surrounded from childhood by magnificent works of art of many different periods, Mrs. A. Hamilton Rice[1] devoted herself single-mindedly to one, the French dix-huitième. Her houses in New York, Newport and Paris were alike filled with its products. Her choicest treasures, however, were assembled and combined with unerring taste in her great New York drawing room, with its rich Louis XVI[2] panelling.

Fiske Kimball, "The Rice Bequest"[3]

Mrs. Rice's New York drawing room/salon[4] showcased the best of her superb collection of eighteenth-century French decorative arts. (See Figure 2.1: View of Room at Philadelphia Museum of Art.) With the assistance of an interior designer, a fine arts dealer, an architect, and an abundance of money and taste, she created a complete historicist interior. An imported antique floor, custom-made antique-style wall paneling, and semi-antique chandeliers provided a Louis XVI/neo-classical setting for antique porcelains, tapestries, sculpture, and a large assemblage of antique, semi-antique, and reproduction furniture. Such a display of pre-Revolutionary French decorative arts evoked the wealth and taste of a much-mythologized bygone era and confirmed Mrs. Rice's social and financial status as a cosmopolitan collector and traveler, elegant hostess, and wealthy heiress. Now in the Philadelphia Museum of Art, the ensemble remains a legacy to both Louis XVI France and Gilded Age America, presenting a luxurious, tranquil oasis juxtaposed against the political turmoil and intense commercial activity of both eras.[5]

In addition to Mrs. Rice, two firms involved in selling antiques and shaping interiors – Duveen Brothers and Maison Carlhian – worked on the design and furnishings for this luxurious townhouse salon. Separately and together, Duveen and Carlhian attended to their client, tracked details, procured antiques, created made-to-order draperies and furniture, and coordinated transportation and installation. They also shared many other clients, partnered in a mutually beneficial arrangement, and worked on new construction, remodeling, and furnishing projects for the lavish residences of American millionaire industrialists. Both firms kept extensive records but left little in the way of theory or intentions related to their interior designs – no manifestos, no articles, and no books.

Taking a material culture approach, this essay draws on the extensive documentary evidence left behind by Duveen and Carlhian. We focus on both process and product of their sometimes uneasy collaboration, describing the dealers' practices and their interactions with Mrs. Rice. While looking

Figure 2.1

Drawing Room from a Town House: 901 Fifth Avenue, New York City, 1923. Painted and gilded oak. Philadelphia Museum of Art, Bequest of Eleanore Elkins Rice, 1939–41–62.

closely at each interior design element, we trace the room's evolution and examine the intent and effect of the design and furnishings provided by each firm.

DUVEEN AND CARLHIAN

In response to the strong American demand for paneling and furnishings in the 1890s, Duveen Brothers contracted with the Paris firm of Carlhian and Beaumetz in order to get first call on their artisans. With this agreement, Duveen committed to bringing Carlhian at least $500,000 of business each year.[6] In October 1919, after working together for 30 years, the two firms signed a secret business agreement that spelled out the terms of their partnership for the next three years. Duveen recommended Carlhian for interior decoration commissions, advanced them money each month, made out the invoices for Carlhian's work, and added a fixed percentage as commission. Carlhian paid a kickback, and Duveen agreed that this would be the firm's only commission. Duveen promised to do his utmost to promote French styles and the Carlhian firm and to commission only Carlhian to manufacture French interior decorations and furniture in both New York and Paris. Without Duveen brokering, Carlhian could buy and sell "old paneled rooms, overmantels, chimneypieces, frames, and other decorative objects" of any grade independently but had to include Duveen's brokering if furniture items were valuable enough to offer competition in Duveen's realm.[7] To facilitate communication, the two firms shared a private telephone line between their Paris offices.

Due to the secrecy of the arrangement and the greater prominence of Duveen Brothers, many interiors that Carlhian actually designed and executed were attributed to Duveen. On the other hand, Duveen's strong voice did guide both the content and execution of these commissions, even when Carlhian designed them. While Carlhian certainly welcomed the business and the stability of a long-term commitment, at least one employee – Ernest L. Brothers, head of the New York office and vice president of the firm – chafed at Duveen's interference. The records of both firms reveal their constant monitoring of each other's activities and of their clients.[8] On the Rice townhouse project, Duveen checked in with architect Horace Trumbauer to be sure that Carlhian got "the entire contract,"[9] went to Paris to see the wall panels in person,[10] and continued to meddle with furnishing details, constantly stimulating new purchases.

DUVEEN BROTHERS

Beginning with tapestries, Asian porcelain, and silver, the English firm of antique dealers known as Duveen Brothers steadily grew in importance in the late nineteenth century, adding a New York office in 1886, a Paris office in 1897, and a new emphasis on paintings around 1907. During this time the status of antique dealers improved greatly, going from mere used-goods dealers to the social equals of their (also newly rich) clients; Joseph Duveen (1869–1939) was both the most prominent example and a prime motivator of this change in status. In the service of selling artworks – paintings, sculptures, tapestries, porcelains, and furniture – the firm also researched, catalogued, exhibited, and published artworks and collections.

From the beginning, Duveen Brothers used schemes for interior decoration as an effective means to both market and sell large quantities of high-priced works of art to extremely wealthy clients. After selling many individual objects to J. P. Morgan, the firm furnished entire houses for him in London. By making and presenting an extremely expensive plaster *maquette* (model) of his new Fifth Avenue mansion, Duveen convinced Senator William Andrews Clark to furnish it to Duveen's taste and from Duveen's stock. After purchasing the entire collections of the Kahn brothers in 1907, Duveen left the spectacular paintings and decorative arts *in situ*, using the furnished Paris residences as both galleries from which to sell individual pieces and examples of the epitome of French interior decoration. In similar fashion, he took great care establishing his New York gallery, creating a series of elegant jewel-box settings containing select, carefully staged artworks. Room names evoked the luxury of eighteenth-century France and set the tone for the interiors he inspired in his clients' homes: Rose Sèvres Room, Royal Blue Sèvres Room, Queen Marie Antoinette Room, Gabriel Room, and Rose Tapestry Room. When completed, clients' homes – newly furnished with treasures he provided, in arrangements that echoed those in his showrooms – also became gallery outposts: Duveen wrote of Henry Huntington's San Marino home that it "will be one of the greatest advertisements my Firm can have."[11] Duveen even invited such clients as Andrew Mellon, William Randolph Hearst, and the John D. Rockefellers to visit Huntington, and their favorable reactions led to more business for the firm.

Joseph Duveen, who took over the New York office in 1907 and led the entire firm soon after, preferred to advise clients on the selection of decorators, rather than taking full control of such complex commissions. Guiding both clients and decorators, alternately commiserating with clients about frustrations and scolding decorators about lapsed timetables, he avoided tarnishing his own reputation with responsibility for the inevitable delays and cost increases.[12]

Duveen's business process included careful tracking of both works of art and clients, in hopes of matching them up. The firm kept detailed notes of clients' whereabouts, vacation and travel patterns, viewing and shopping habits, purchases, and other preferences. Duveen did endless favors to ingratiate himself and the firm with his most important clients, sometimes arranging travel plans – which also facilitated his spying.[13] As a full-service personal concierge, he stored clients' cigars, repaired their broken vases, insured their collections, offered vans for collections transport, and provided amenities such as lilies, orchids, and fresh fruit baskets in Paris and London hotel rooms, all in the service of keeping his name ever in his clients' sight.

As a part of their business process, Duveen Brothers kept extensive correspondence with clients, collectors' files, and reference photographs of artworks. Bound albums of photographs recorded the most important works of art in stock, clients' collections, and related works of art. In addition to vast photographic reference files, the firm kept a library of published books, exhibition and sales catalogs, and periodicals. To track marketing, they kept callers' books with notes on client visits and lists of objects viewed by clients. To promote sales, they prepared descriptive sales brochures, much like today's auction catalogues. To monitor potential sources for new stock, the firm employed scouts who visited European estates, recording lists and descriptions of potential acquisitions.

MAISON CARLHIAN

In 1867 the Carlhian family of Paris founded an exporting firm that evolved into a respected decorating and furnishings business with a Paris headquarters and a New York branch office.[14] From 1918 on, André Carlhian (1883–1967) directed the firm and did most of the designing. Ernest L. Brothers (1891–1974), from an English family of antique dealers and decorators, joined around 1919, heading up the New York office. The firm employed around 30 craftspeople and office staff in various departments: a business office, a drawing office, a photography department, and workshops for woodworking, cabinetmaking, painting, and scenic wallpaper. Additional skilled workers executed gilding, upholstery, window treatments, and plasterwork. With deep knowledge of period styles and extensive stocks of paneling, furniture, wallpaper, and textiles, the firm had both the capacity to design and create reproductions and the connections to obtain antique furnishings, especially paneling. Often collaborating with noted architects, they specialized in creating eighteenth-century French interiors, skillfully blending antiques and modern reproductions. They attended to every detail, even tinting electrified chandelier bulbs yellow to simulate the warmth of candlelight.[15]

Carlhian's principal stock was antique paneling, ranging in style from Gothic through Empire. Stored in their crowded Paris warehouse, the collection was by turns stacked on the floor, propped against the walls, and installed upright in a maze of makeshift rooms. (See Figure 2.2: Carlhian warehouse.) Over time, nearly 300 sets of paneling passed through the firm, often removed directly from old buildings. Carlhian workers restored, adapted, and/or extended them for installation in clients' interiors.

Dealing in interiors ■

Figure 2.2
Stock of *boiserie* on display, [undated]. Getty Research Institute, Los Angeles (930092). © J. Paul Getty Trust

Most often beginning with the paneling, Carlhian designed complete interiors and provided accompanying furnishings – again original antiques, period-style reproductions, or some combination – with integrated custom upholstery, drapery, and elaborate trimmings. The firm also sold *à la carte* antiques and reproductions, from architectural fragments and scenic wallpaper to furniture in many forms. When necessary, they commissioned other firms to reproduce items while Carlhian retained the models' physical and intellectual property.[16]

Carlhian's business practice included much more careful financial record keeping than Duveen Brothers. The firm kept stock books of antique and modern furniture and objects and soft goods (textiles for upholstery and window treatments), registering items that the firm acquired, sold, or placed on consignment with other dealers. They listed proposed projects in order books, describing the work and services in detail, and tabulated actual goods sold and work performed in complementary debit books. To document specific commissions, the firm preserved bundles of fabric samples identified by client, date, location, and fabric information, so that orders could be completed or renewed at a later date. They also kept extensive visual documentation of rooms, architectural elements, furniture, drapery, and furnishings plans, along with a library of printed reference works used as sources of antique models. They retained certain antique paneling, chairs, and wallpaper as models for reproductions, ranking the paneling by quality grades and pricing them accordingly.[17]

To direct their complex commissions, Carlhian used many tools for project management, long before the term was common. They followed approval processes and documented progress and products at every stage with numbering systems, stock books, and photography logs. Staff carefully tracked the business side of transactions and created reams of lists of tasks done and yet to be done, objects to import, objects to find, and objects ready to send. They enumerated difficulties to resolve by cabling or discussion with the client, whether in New York or Paris. They created typed matrices of work completion dates; room-by-room lists of lighting, paint, window glass, locks and hinges, parquet flooring, carpet, upholstery, and drapery fabric needs; and wall paneling plans with specific sizes needed, shipping information, and dates for cutting, carving, gilding, and painting. Other lists tracked items farther up the supply chain, as they were received in Paris from various French suppliers and were then assigned to ship names and dates of sailing to New York. All the elements for decorating an entire residence came together in this complex web of organization.

To begin a commission, a designer, usually André Carlhian, selected a paneling source and drew elevations, detail views, and a floor plan. To develop a furnishings plan, they might begin with photographs of furniture pinned to a sketch of a room, progress to a rough floor plan drawing with furniture shapes surrounded by photographs of antiques or reproductions, and conclude with beautifully painted watercolor vignettes of object groupings, including alternatives for upholstery and textiles for window hangings and white "ghost" versions of items not yet obtained. The firm more often was known for making *maquettes*, scale models of rooms in pencil, ink, and watercolor on paper, cardboard, or wood. (See Figure 2.3: *Maquette* in sections and Figure 2.4: Canvas *maquette* for wall panel.) To give clients a sense of proportion and perspective, Carlhian staff also set up and photographed the models with lights and scale figures.

THE CLIENT

Born the daughter of a greengrocer in 1861, Eleanore Elkins – the future Mrs. Alexander Hamilton Rice – grew up in a successful Philadelphia merchant family that grew steadily more prosperous through investments in oil, gas, and urban transit systems. In 1883 she married George D. Widener, son of her father's business partner, gaining still more wealth. Entering into America's Gilded Age aristocracy, they raised three children in the Widener family home in the Philadelphia suburb of Elkins Park. In 1912 Eleanore and George traveled to Europe with their oldest son Harry, who eagerly purchased rare books for his growing collection. They boarded the *Titanic* to return to America, but only Eleanore survived.

Prior to the tragic voyage, Eleanore and George had been planning a summer home in Newport, Rhode Island, with Horace Trumbauer as architect and Carlhian as one of the decorators.[18] Eleanore resumed the project, and Miramar, her 30,000-square foot French neoclassical mansion, opened in August 1915 with a lavish 500-guest, three-orchestra gala. Later in 1915 Eleanore married again, to

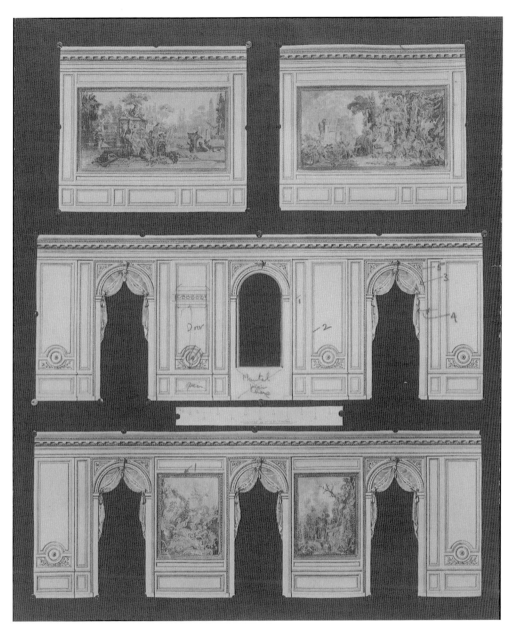

Figure 2.3
Room elevations for *maquette*, 1923. Paper. Getty Research Institute, Los Angeles (930092). © J. Paul Getty Trust

Figure 2.4

Canvas *maquette* for wall panel *(Maquette grandeur d'un coin circulaire du grand salon de Mrs. Hamilton Rice, New York)*, c. 1923. Getty Research Institute, Los Angeles (930092). © J. Paul Getty Trust

Dr. Alexander Hamilton Rice, an explorer from an old Boston family, adding Amazon expeditions to her regular travel for European shopping and touring.

In 1921, at the age of 60, Eleanore began working with Trumbauer again, initiating plans for a townhouse for herself and her husband at 78th Street and Fifth Avenue in New York City. She again commissioned Carlhian (alone this time) to design and decorate the interiors. With Duveen's encouragement, she accelerated her purchases from both dealers. Her letters describe her motivation – a desire to enjoy the home while she still could[19] – but this was supplemented by outside pressure. As usual, Duveen had ulterior motives: he took the creation of any new client residence as an opportunity to sell more high-priced items, and he wanted to use the finished interiors as additional gallery spaces to demonstrate his exquisite taste and goods. As with the aging J.P. Morgan, Benjamin Altman, Henry E. Huntington, and Eleanore's father-in-law P.A.B. Widener, Duveen recognized the limited time remaining with a valuable client and self-interestedly urged specific purchases.

DESIGNING THE SALON

The townhouse exterior and plan employed elements of a Parisian *hôtel particulier* from the era of Louis XVI, though early twentieth-century New York demanded fewer, larger rooms used as both public and private spaces rather than the smaller, specific-use rooms found in French townhouses. The eighteenth-century French model included public rooms for reception, large gatherings, and concerts on the entrance floor of the home's principal block. Salons hosted literary, intellectual, musical, and social gatherings and also gave their name to such gatherings. Mrs. Rice used her salon both for social gatherings – as a drawing room, in British parlance – and as her favorite space for private leisure.

The room's external architecture – windows, doors, and ceiling height – came from Trumbauer's Louis XVI design for the home. Though located on the second floor, Mrs. Rice's salon opened onto a garden terrace to the east, echoing the garden front of the most admired eighteenth-century salons, which allowed the entertainment to continue outside. Carlhian reshaped the interior, designing and supplying flat and curved wall panels, built-in frames for the tapestries and glass cases for the porcelain, and ornamentation for door, window, and fireplace openings. Strong symmetry and balance in all dimensions emphasized the room's sober, delicate Louis XVI style. Two mirrored doors and an over-mantel mirror on the east wall, with porcelain-filled vitrines between, reflected the three full-length windows and two tapestries on the west wall. The shorter north and south walls each featured a central tapestry flanked by decorated wall panels. All doors and windows had the same treatment, with pilasters, arches, and full-length drapes pulled back at both sides.

With the exception of a Gothic library room for Dr. Rice, the architecture and interiors of the New York townhouse were uniformly eighteenth-century French, as at Miramar, reflecting Mrs. Rice's preferred taste and Duveen and Carlhian's most expensive furnishings.[20] Carlhian designed the salon as an elegant setting for Mrs. Rice's distinguished collection of French decorative arts, featuring her Beauvais tapestries and her outstanding collection of Sèvres porcelain and her expanding collection of French furniture.[21] As in the Miramar salon, the room included two smaller showcases for porcelain.[22]

In contrast, the interior design of a similar class of eighteenth-century French room would have derived entirely from the architecture, rather than from a pre-existing collection of decorative arts. Such a salon would have included suites of seat furniture, both those placed against the walls and those in the center of the room, along with console and card tables, mirrors, draperies and *portières*, often tapestries, and a chandelier or wall lights. There would be no desks, no carpets, no sculptures, and no plants or flowers.

SALON FURNISHINGS

Carlhian built the room around the four large tapestries, which dominate the walls.[23] Each tapestry, from the *Story of Psyche* after designs by François Boucher, includes a woven border resembling a gilded wood frame and is further enclosed in a gilded wood frame of wall paneling. The framing emphasizes both the tapestries' value – they came from the French royal tapestry manufactory – and their parallel with paintings as wall decoration. The two largest tapestries, hung on the shorter end walls, differ in width, but Carlhian made their frames and the surrounding panels the same size, thus maintaining the room's symmetry and postponing decisions about tapestry placement until the final installation.[24] Though large expanses are rather faded, the areas of strong pinkish-red and blue, complemented by the gilt frames in both the tapestry and the wall itself, set the tone for the room's color scheme. These colors – and more pictorial tapestry – also appear as furniture covering, as seen in a fire screen, two sofas, and ten of the room's chairs.

Carlhian's paneling design was fairly simple, following the understated Louis XVI style, but with a bold cornice that shaped an appealing oval line linking the walls and ceiling and empha- sized the curved corner panels. With most of the panels serving as frames for the tapestries, windows, doors, and vitrines, the curved corner panels offered the room's one unbroken area of paneling and were thus the only panels with additional decoration. Carlhian derived their gilded circular decorative element (a central rosette encircled by a floral garland and various moldings above a leafy spray) from an impeccable Louis XVI source – Jacques-Ange Gabriel.[25] The muted panel color – a matte, slightly mottled and green-toned ivory that effectively sets off the warm gilding – both implied age and communicated luxurious yet restrained taste. It also kept the panels in the background, admirably setting off the tapestries while not upstaging the room's treasured collections.

Taking advantage of the room's height, Carlhian designed the full-length drapes with a blue brocade border to echo some of the upholstery color and to draw the eye upward to the level of the tapestries, effectively integrating the cornice and the lofty ceiling with the rest of the room. His initial drapery design, seen on the *maquette*, involved much shorter drapes, which appeared insubstantial in the context of the room's grand scale. The final installation included shirred sheers installed behind the decorative drapes, in front of both windows and doorways.

Following eighteenth-century precedents, Trumbauer and Carlhian helped fill the generous space with plenty of natural light from the three tall windows that faced Fifth Avenue and Central Park. But twentieth-century norms also required strong, festive evening illumination in the form of five rock crystal chandeliers, all electrified and hanging very near the ceiling to avoid obstructing the tapestries. Electric lights in the vitrines, gilt bronze wall lights and mounts on the case furniture, and gilded wall panels and wooden seat furniture offered further brilliance. Reflections multiplied in the glass vitrine shelves, the over-mantel mirror, and the mirrored doors on the east (fireplace) side of the room.

Carlhian laid an antique European parquet floor and initially provided several small carpets that harmonized with the color scheme and period. But in 1924, Duveen sold Mrs. Rice a large, luxurious, brightly colored, Baroque Savonnerie carpet that competes with the prevailing color scheme and violates the period unity. The carpet's beauty, rarity, and provenance – made for Louis XIV's Grand Galerie du Louvre and previously owned by J.P. Morgan – and Duveen's eagerness to sell such an expensive treasure explain its inclusion, despite its seventeenth-century origin and overpowering effect.

Carlhian arranged the salon's plentiful furniture primarily for show. Chairs and sofas could be drawn up at desks or tables, but no lamps, books, or writing materials indicated frequent letter writing or reading. In the main, the surfaces displayed vases, sculpture, or flowers; desk fronts remained closed and locked; and cupboards served as beautiful objects masking the heat registers rather than as functioning storage furniture.[26] The sheer number of pieces precluded an arrangement with a single focus. At least 20 chairs,[27] four sofas, six small writing desks, four flat writing tables (two large and two small), four cabinets or chests of drawers, two small tiered tables with candlesticks, one plant stand, one folding screen, and one fire screen filled up the room.[28] Excepting the two larger writing tables and the two small tiered tables, the desks, tables, and some chairs were set against the walls in nearly strictly symmetrical positions. Chairs were consistently matched in pairs, usually with members of a suite grouped together or at least symmetrically, and evenly distributed throughout the room.[29] Upholstery ranged from eighteenth-century tapestry[30] to contemporary silk brocades and velvet; the predominant blues and pinks echoed the tapestries and porcelain, while the yellow added another note.

Once the walls, floors, lighting, draperies, tapestries, and furniture were in place, Duveen took the opportunity to provide (through sale or trade) additional expensive *objets d'art*. A white marble bust of a woman sat on the mantelpiece, and at least one bronze sculpture sat on a large desk, adding the "darker notes" that Duveen had also recommended for Huntington's colorful tapestry-filled library room.[31] Two small white marble neoclassical sculptures, three more exuberant Rococo terracotta sculptures by Clodion, and two Chinese porcelain vases with French gilded bronze mounts adorned additional surfaces. While most of the Sèvres porcelain – nearly all vases – was displayed in the vitrines, a few paired pieces sat on chests or cabinets against the walls. Ferns in an eighteenth-century plant stand[32] and flowers in vases or pots on the tiered tables and large desks and in a tall stand added living color to the room, complementing the floral motifs woven on the tapestry chairs and painted on the porcelain.

Two painted portraits of the room by prominent society artists immortalized it. (See Figure 2.5: William Ranken painting.) While in New York in 1925–1926 for an exhibition of his paintings in Duveen's New York gallery, Sir John Lavery, an Irish-born portraitist, painted the Rices' salon and their Gothic library.[33] In each painting, the small figures of the couple blend in with the crowded furnishings, dwarfed by the high ceilings and with their features as indistinct as those of the mantel bust and the bronze tabletop sculpture. Lavery's salon painting captured most of the room, emphasizing its lighting and color harmonies.

Anne-Marie Schaaf and Teresa Morales ■

Figure 2.5

William Ranken, *The Salon, 901 Fifth Avenue*, 1927. Oil on board. Philadelphia Museum of Art, Gift of Edith R. Dixon, 2009–9–1.

On a mid-1920s trip to America, Scottish-born William Bruce Ellis Ranken, a socially well-connected oil painter and watercolorist, also recorded Mrs. Rice's celebrated New York salon—about eight years after painting at least one view of the treasures at the Widener family home. He painted less of the room than Lavery but portrayed individual pieces of furniture, chandeliers, and textiles with more loving detail. Ranken's distinct outlines and lower viewpoint—and the prominent Savonnerie carpet—make the room look even more crowded.[34]

Friends, connoisseurs, and many visitors – from art dealers such as Mr. Samuels of French & Co. to society women such as Mrs. J.B. Duke – praised the room for the beauty and quality of its collections, promoting both Duveen's and Carlhian's achievements within a circle of potential clients. But only one professional observer wrote a lengthy critique, tactfully expressing both admiration and puzzlement about various aspects of the room. In a long internal memo to André Carlhian, written in January 1925, Ernest L. Brothers of Carlhian's New York office assessed the paneling, upholstery, drapery, carpet, and specific suites of furniture in the context of the dominant tapestries and porcelain, concentrating on the elements supplied by Carlhian.[35] Admiring the tapestries on the walls and on the seat furniture, he measured other pieces against them and considered the cumulative effect.

Brothers appreciated the salon's paneling and drapery but faulted much of the seat furniture for its lack of delicacy and subtlety. He did not think the furniture was the type "that Americans would desire to use in their Salon or Drawing Room and [it] is not up to the scale of the tapestries, decoration, and works of art belonging to this client." He told Carlhian he was "at a loss to understand what effect you wished to achieve [with the furniture] in this room" and criticized the proportions of the larger, "comfortable" (Louis XV) chairs, preferring the smaller (Louis XVI) chairs.[36] He thought the yellow and blue silk brocades more appropriate "for a pretty lady's boudoir," some of the antique brocades "a little shabby for the tapestry furniture," and the expanses of blue satin ground too prominent on the larger chairs. These vivid, shiny, large-figured satins may have attracted more than their share of attention amidst the subtler charms of the somewhat faded tapestries, the less conspicuous marquetry furniture, and the modestly sized – though brightly colored and gilded – pieces of Sèvres porcelain in the vitrines and on some of the pieces of furniture.[37]

Brothers seems to have disdained Carlhian's concessions to the client's convenience and comfort. Like other decorators, Carlhian had to supply chairs of lesser quality in order to meet his client's need for more seat furniture – all armchairs. Even with ten tapestry chairs and two tapestry sofas, Mrs. Rice commissioned Carlhian to furnish an additional large sofa covered in yellow brocade and more chairs covered either in blue brocade or blue velvet. Brothers did not speculate, but Mrs. Rice may have required these pieces because of her entertaining needs – to allow her older guests to sit rather than stand – or because she retained an affection for the crowded Victorian rooms of her youth.[38]

STYLE AND MEANING

From the 1880s to the 1920s, wealthy Gilded Age Americans still embarked on European Grand Tours, furthering both their cultural education and their social position. Through tourism and shopping, these *nouveaux riches* acquired the knowledge, manners, and often the goods of hereditary European nobility. On returning, newly made millionaires could prominently display their valuable antiques, cloaking themselves in the prestigious mantle of connoisseurship. They might disdain the *ancien régime* link to monarchy and politics, but they welcomed the link between economics and culture.

Expanding upon Victorian revival styles, many late nineteenth- and early twentieth-century decorators[39] shared Carlhian and Duveen's taste for eighteenth-century French architecture and interiors and created more or less historicist spaces for their American clients, often the newly rich industrialists and financiers.[40] The "Louis style" that Jules Allard created for Alva Vanderbilt at her Newport mansion combined eighteenth-century French pieces with modern (late nineteenth-century) reproductions and Victorian fringed seat furniture. White, Allom & Co. blended eighteenth-century French pieces with contemporary (early twentieth-century) pieces, especially comfortable seating furniture, following the fashion of the Rothschilds' domestic interiors and the art dealers' galleries.[41] Carlhian's design for the Rice townhouse mixed Louis XV and Louis XVI styles with the twentieth-century conveniences of electrified light fixtures, an elevator, and modern heating and plumbing. Rather than aiming to recreate a specific historical moment, all of these designers and clients created a glittering atmosphere to showcase their precious antiques – but the implicit association with aristocracy was not unwelcome.

The 1920s saw many of Mrs. Rice's peers convey their private American collections of French or other decorative arts, often in period room settings, to the public. Henry Clay Frick died in 1919, willing his New York home as a public museum[42]; Henry Huntington transferred his San Marino, California, estate and collections to the public in 1922[43]; the Pierpont Morgan Library opened in New York in 1924[44]; and Isabella Stewart Gardner died in 1924, endowing her Boston museum.[45] These gifts to the public cemented their namesake millionaires' reputations for wealth and power, expressed through taste, transforming their monetary success into lasting cultural monuments.

American collectors looked to eighteenth-century French interiors as the most secure of all status symbols, prizing them as emblems of the ultimate in luxury with a pre-French Revolution lack of self-consciousness and guilt.[46] Since French royalty and aristocracy were Europe's trendsetters, the refined aesthetic and acknowledged elegance of these styles asserted social and financial status in their own time. In later eras, Marie-Antoinette's reputation for taste and refinement fueled particular interest in the Louis XVI style. Her story's romantic associations, which mingle extreme privilege, whimsy, misunderstanding, and tragedy, compound the appeal even now.

Connection with the original royal and aristocratic patrons provided another attraction for American collectors of French decorative arts. Philadelphia Museum of Art Director Fiske Kimball made the connection clear: "No field of art has attracted more distinguished and discriminating collectors than French decorative art of the eighteenth century, itself created for patrons as insatiable as Marie Antoinette, as enlightened as the duc d'Aumont."[47] Furthermore, new owners gained reputations as discerning connoisseurs not only through associations with the original owners but through affinity with more recent owners, especially British nobility. As one recent scholar has noted, "Provenances from such esteemed sources passed on an almost tangible patina to the next generation of collectors."[48]

In the nineteenth century, many factors sustained interest in eighteenth-century France at various social and economic levels in multiple countries. George IV, the Rothschilds, the Victoria and Albert Museum, and the Wallace Collection provided celebrated examples of British collecting at the top of the market. At a range of economic levels, displays at universal expositions, "French Style" porcelain more or less influenced by Sévres, and department store reproduction furniture in "Louis" styles offered elements of this look for middle-class interiors. In the decades around 1900, prominent American millionaire patrons such as Alva Vanderbilt and Arabella Huntington commissioned French interior decorators to create wholly European period-style interiors in their multiple homes. Most of these clients – and the dealers who sold to them – were unconcerned with historical accuracy and authentic recreations; they merely wanted a magnificent, lavish ambiance for their collections and their social activities.[49]

LEGACY

Mrs. Rice, however, got it all: a glittering display of genuine eighteenth-century French objects in a suitable setting; plenty of seats for entertaining; associations with royalty, aristocracy, and

Dealing in interiors ■

prominent citizens of two centuries and three countries; secure status; and public recognition as a tastemaker. Ever abreast of the gossip – and eager to promote his own influence – Duveen cabled a report from Paris: someone "told us that Mrs Rice's house was a tremendous success and was the talk of New York with the result that the taste for XVIIIth Century was being revived in New York."[50] He had already noted her reaction in a characteristically flattering cable to his Paris office: "Mrs. Rice delighted. House marvellous and most beautiful in town."[51]

Since her death in 1937, Mrs. Rice's legacy has lived on through a bequest to the Philadelphia Museum of Art, where it has remained an example of elegance and taste. Her gift of a consciously created room, abundantly filled with desirable, museum-quality objects and supported by the copious documentation available in the Carlhian and Duveen archives, remains a benchmark for museum period rooms. Now publicly accessible, the salon offers both specific aesthetic specimens from eighteenth-century France and a social and cultural setting from early twentieth-century America. Mrs. Rice's achievement reflects her fortune, taste, and opportunity; the sometimes uneasy collaboration of Carlhian and Duveen; and both firms' grasp of aesthetics, project management, and client cultivation. Duveen shaped his clients' visions and encouraged their collections; Carlhian shaped their spaces; and their shared legacy has in turn inspired viewers for nearly a century.

NOTES

1 Eleanore Elkins (1861–1939) spent 29 years married to George D. Widener and three years as his widow before she married Dr. Alexander Hamilton Rice (1875–1956).
2 King Louis XVI of France reigned from 1774 to 1792.
3 *Philadelphia Museum Bulletin* 35, no. 183 (November 1939): 2.
4 Kimball used the British term *drawing room*. This paper will use the French term *salon,* to emphasize the room's French origin.
5 Maison Carlhian, *Drawing Room From a Town House: 901 Fifth Avenue, New York City*, 1923. (1939–41–62). Philadelphia Museum of Art.
6 Edward Fowles, *Memories of Duveen Brothers* (London: Times Books, 1976), 7.
7 Carlhian-Duveen Agreement, 15 October 1919, Box 411, Carlhian Records (930092), Getty Research Institute (hereafter cited as CR).
8 "I am very much obliged to you for your letter of June 12th and for the information you gave me about our lady friend in Paris." Joseph Duveen to André Carlhian, 17 June 1925, Box 518, f. 6, CR.
9 Horace Trumbauer to Joseph Duveen, 25 August 1922, Box 381 (reel 236), Duveen Brothers Records (960015). Getty Research Institute. (hereafter cited as DBR).
10 Duveen Brothers, London to New York, cable, 27 June 1922. Box 500, f.4 (reel 355), DBR.
11 Joseph Duveen to Mrs. C.P. Huntington, 11 August 1908. Arabella Duval Huntington Papers, reels 4279–80, Archives of American Art, quoted in Shelley M. Bennett, "Henry and Arabella Huntington: The Staging of Eighteenth-Century French Art by Twentieth-Century Americans," in *French Art of the Eighteenth Century*, ed. Shelley M. Bennett and Carolyn Sargentson (New Haven: Yale University Press, 2008), 18–19.
12 Nicholas Penny and Karen Serres, "Duveen and the Decorators," *Burlington Magazine* 149 (June 2007): 403–404.
13 Duveen liberally tipped hotel and ship staff to keep him informed about persons of interest to his business, and he expected the London and Paris staff to know clients' whereabouts when they were in town.
14 The Paris headquarters, known as Carlhian & Beaumetz and later Carlhian & Cie, was active from 1867 to 1975. Under André's management, begun in 1918 after his service in World War I, the firm was known as

Maison Carlhian. The New York office, known as Carlhian of Paris, was active from 1907 to 1953, except for closure during World War II. The Buenos Aires office was active from 1908 to 1923.

15 Recipe for tinting light bulbs, n.d., Box 750, f. 3, CR.

16 Subcontractors had to affirm that the models given them to copy remained Carlhian's property and that the right to copy them also came only from Carlhian. They also had to promise to protect the models against damage and never to photograph, reproduce, or keep the models for any purpose except Carlhian's. See examples of these promises in letters from various subcontractors in Box 520, f. 16, CR.

17 *Tableaux des boiseries en stock*, 1927–1960, Box 827*, CR.

18 Trumbauer and Carlhian had already worked on homes for the Elkins and Widener families.

19 Duveen Brothers, Paris to New York, 6 June 1924, and cable, Paris to New York, June 26, 1924, Box 501, folders 1–2 (reel 356), DBR.

20 Duveen's most expensive objects were Old Master paintings. He only succeeded in selling two to Mrs. Rice: a Holbein and a Memling, which both hung in the Gothic library.

21 Some of these treasures had previously been displayed in Miramar's larger Grand Salon. Many pieces continued to adorn both salons, as Duveen's staff regularly moved them from Newport to New York, following Mrs. Rice's seasonal routines.

22 There were about 30 pieces of porcelain in the two vitrines, with pink or "rose du Barry" pieces to the left of the fireplace and turquoise blue pieces to the right.

23 Mrs. Rice bought the tapestries around 1914 and hung them at Miramar.

24 Though Carlhian and Duveen had both recommended cutting a tapestry rather than changing the panel, Mrs. Rice evidently refused to do so; they compromised by folding over an edge.

25 The circular decorative element matches a detail in the paneling of Madame du Barry's dining room at Louveciennes, designed by Jacques-Ange Gabriel (1698–1782), architect to Kings Louis XV and XVI, royal mistresses Madame de Pompadour and Madame du Barry (whose name is the source of the "rose du Barry" color found in the room's tapestries, porcelains, and upholstery), and Queen Marie-Antoinette. The paneling's other notable decorative feature – the central volute and gilt scrolls in the spandrels above the arched windows and doors – is not found in Gabriel's work. See photographs of the room and the detail: CN 7847 and 7848, Box 69, CR.

26 This was an intentional issue mentioned in Ernest L. Brothers' critique of the room.

27 There may have been as many as 26; some members of a set of eight originally at Miramar may have stayed there, or they may have been stored in the chair storage room in the New York townhouse.

28 These 43 pieces – particularly the chairs – may not have all been in the room at all times, but the evidence of photographs and paintings attests to only minor changes over time. The New York house had a designated Chair Storage Room, which may have stored pieces at times, or some pieces may have traveled to Miramar.

29 Duveen and other dealers often made up and sold matched pairs or sets of furniture, capitalizing on the desire for symmetry and unity to multiply their profits.

30 The Gobelins tapestry upholstery for the chairs and sofas featured designs by Boucher and Jean-Baptiste Oudry. The tapestry on the fire screen is probably from Beauvais.

31 Joseph Duveen to Henry E. Huntington, 11 April 1916, Box 135, no. 10633, fols. 2–3, Henry E. Huntington Archives, Huntington Library, Art Collections and Botanical Gardens, quoted in Shelley M. Bennett, *The Art of Wealth: The Huntingtons in the Gilded Age* (San Marino, CA: Huntington Library, Art Collections, and Botanical Gardens, 2013), 219. Successfully using this argument, Duveen managed to sell Huntington 22 of the many bronzes from the J.P. Morgan collection, from which he also sold to Mrs. Rice.

32 The Museum still keeps a fern in this plant stand. For decades after Mrs. Rice's death, her son George D. Widener, Jr., a Museum trustee, underwrote the cost of maintaining the plants in his mother's recreated room in the Museum.

33 Sir John Lavery, *The Salon, 901 Fifth Avenue* (2009–206–2), Philadelphia Museum of Art, and Sir John Lavery, *The Gothic Room, 901 Fifth Avenue* (2009–206–1), Philadelphia Museum of Art.

34 William Ranken, *The Salon, 901 Fifth Avenue* (2009–9–1), Philadelphia Museum of Art. In addition to painting interiors, Ranken was friendly with interior designers such as Elsie de Wolfe and Basil Ionides. See Basil Ionides, *Colour and Interior Decoration,* illustrated by Ranken and published by Country Life in 1926.

35 Ernest L. Brothers, "Mrs. A. Hamilton Rice. Criticisms Salon," 21 January 1925 (photocopy), Curator's File, Drawing Room 1939–41–61, Philadelphia Museum of Art.

36 The simplest distinction between these styles is that Louis XV chairs have curved legs and Louis XVI chairs have straight legs.

37 Brothers', "Criticisms Salon." Some of his complaints may have stemmed from a suppressed frustration with Duveen's interference. Mrs. Rice's many late purchases from Duveen may have altered Carlhian's plans.

38 Following more modern taste, the Museum has chosen to display only 12 chairs and three sofas in the room.

39 White, Allom & Co.; Jules Allard and Sons; Maison Jansen; Alavoine & Co; Elsie de Wolfe.

40 J. P. Morgan, Henry Clay Frick, Arabella and Henry Huntington, Horace Dodge, William Andrews Clark, Julius Bache, P.A.B. Widener, William L. Elkins, E.T. Stotesbury.

41 Shelley M. Bennett, "Henry and Arabella," 1–27.

42 The Frick Collection opened in 1935, four years after his widow died.

43 The Huntington Library, Art Collections, and Botanical Gardens opened in 1928, after Huntington's death in 1927.

44 J.P. Morgan's son made it a public institution, following his father's will. It is now known as the Morgan Library & Museum.

45 She had already opened it to the public as Fenway Court in 1903. After her death, the collection was frozen and took the name of its founder as the Isabella Stewart Gardner Museum.

46 Penny Sparke, "Taste and the Interior Designer," in *After Taste: Expanded Practice in Interior Design*, ed. Kent Kleinman (New York: Princeton Architectural Press, 2011), 18.

47 "The Rice Bequest," 2. The duc d'Aumont (1709–1782) was a prominent patron and collector of French decorative arts. Louis XVI and Marie-Antoinette, among others, purchased items from the collection after d'Aumont's death.

48 Charissa Bremer-David, "Why Boucher? The Enduring Appeal of Boucher Tapestries," in *French Art*, 288.

49 Shelley M. Bennett, "Henry and Arabella Huntington," 9–16.

50 Duveen Brothers, Paris to New York, cable, 23 March 1925, Box 501, f. 1–2 (reel 356), DBR.

51 Joseph Duveen, London to Paris, cable, 26 January 1925, Box 501, f. 1–2 (reel 356), DBR.

BIBLIOGRAPHY

Bennett, Shelley M. *The Art of Wealth: The Huntingtons in the Gilded Age*. San Marino, CA: Huntington Library, Art Collections, and Botanical Gardens, 2013.

Bennett, Shelley M. and Carolyn Sargentson, eds. *French Art of the Eighteenth Century at The Huntington*. San Marino, CA: Huntington Library, Art Collections, and Botanical Gardens; New Haven: Yale University Press, 2008.

Bouvet, Vincent. "La continuité du grand goût: La maison Carlhian ou le Louis XVI-moderne." *Monuments Historiques* 195 (March 1995): 38–44.

Carlhian (Firm). Records, 1867–1988. 930092. Getty Research Institute. Accessed at http://hdl.handle.net/10020/cifa930092.

Duveen, James Henry. *The Rise of the House of Duveen*. New York: Knopf, 1957.

Duveen Brothers. Records, 1876–1981. 960015. Getty Research Institute. Accessed at http://hdl.handle.net/10020/cifa960015.

Duveen Brothers. Stock documentation from the dealer's library. 1829–1965. 2007.D.1. Getty Research Institute. Accessed at http://hdl.handle.net/10020/cifa2007d1.

Fowles, Edward. *Memories of Duveen Brothers*. London: Times Books, 1976.

Harris, John. *Moving Rooms: The Trade in Architectural Salvages*. New Haven: Yale University Press, 2007.

Kimball, Fiske. "The Rice Bequest." *Philadelphia Museum Bulletin* 35, no. 183 (November 1939): 2–15.

Penny, Nicholas, and Karen Serres. "Duveen and the Decorators." *Burlington Magazine* 149 (June 2007): 400–406.

Pons, Bruno. *French Period Rooms, 1650–1800: Rebuilt in England, France, and the Americas*. Dijon: Editions Faton, 1995.

Simpson, Colin. *Artful Partners: Bernard Berenson and Joseph Duveen*. New York: Macmillan, 1986.

Sparke, Penny, "Taste and the Interior Designer," in *After Taste: Expanded Practice in Interior Design*, ed. Kent Kleinman. New York: Princeton Architectural Press, 2011.

Chapter 3: Elsie de Wolfe

A professional interior decorator

Penny Sparke

The (mostly) recent work undertaken to date on early twentieth-century female interior decorators – Eleanor McMillen, Nancy Lancaster, Sister Parish, Elsie de Wolfe, Dorothy Draper, Nancy McClelland, Syrie Maugham, Rose Cumming and others – has emphasized their exceptional biographies.[1] Indeed, the very size and glossy nature of many of the publications highlight the individual, celebrity nature of the decorators in question. It was through their determination, strength of character and often flamboyant personalities, these publications suggest, that they transformed what had hitherto been seen as an unpaid amateur feminine activity – the decoration of the home – into a modern career for women.

The fact that so many of the lady decorators focused on the home is made much of in several of the studies. In the foreword to the book about their mother and grandmother by Sister Parish, Apple Bartlett and Susan Crater, for example, Albert Hadley stressed that,

> The beauty and harmony of her surroundings were expressed with conviction and clarity in the environments she helped to create for others. At the core were all the elements of refined taste, but taste flavored by a sometimes wicked wit and a degree of jovial irreverence that possibly explains the magic of her creative genius – her genius for the art of living, the art of home.[2]

Only May's article on McClelland points out that that particular decorator contributed to the profession of interior decoration in a more institutional manner by becoming the first women to be the national president of the American Institute of Interior Decorators. Mostly, the other publications are more interested in the lives, the styles, and the individuality of their colorful subjects.

This focus on individual feminine achievement has been at the expense, perhaps, of an account of a history of interior decoration/design that might have placed more emphasis on the development of professionalization through the roles of generic structures, such as educational and professional organizations and institutions. In other contexts, these are often cited as the catalysts of profession formation, especially in the neighboring fields of architecture and graphic design. In her study, *Origins of Graphic Design in America*, for example, Ellen Mazur Thomson stated that the professional status of graphic designers was achieved through "education, self-imposed standards and [the formation of] professional gate-keeping organizations."[3] Although individual designers are also dealt with in Thomson's study, the role of institutions in defining and overseeing standards is seen as core.

The so-called amateur backgrounds of many of the lady decorators; their (for the most part) seeming lack of interest in the development of formal interior design education; and their (again, for the most part) apparent lack of attention to shared professional standards and regulations, has tended to create a binary divide in scholarship in the field of interior decoration/design history. That divide separates the activities of the decorators from the story of the evolution of the profession of interior design as it developed through the twentieth century. It is a divide that has gender difference at its core and it partly derives from the fact that, in the years after 1945, a number of neo-modernist, male interior designers and apologists accused de Wolfe and her entourage of holding back the interior design profession because of their commitment to historical styles. Robsjohn-Gibbings, for example, wrote in his book, *Goodbye Mr Chippendale*, "Decoratively speaking, American women live in the shadow of Elsie de Wolfe and if it was the Chicago World's Fair that held American architecture back fifty years, it was she who did the same thing for American furniture design."[4] His vitriolic attack on de Wolfe derived from his essentially modernist positioning, that is he abhorred historicism and was anxious about the role that taste played in the decoration of the domestic sphere. Taking their lead from architects Robsjohn-Gibbings, and others, they preferred the taste-free (or so they believed) world of the public sphere.

That masculine point of view was already manifesting itself earlier on in the century, however. Frank Alvah Parsons, a male apologist for interior decoration, was a contemporary of de Wolfe's. He was undoubtedly aware of her work and not impressed by the way that female decorator's projects were closely linked to the social aspirations of many of her clients. In 1915 Parsons, who created one of the first educational programs in interior design in the United States, published his book, *Interior Decoration: Its Principles and Practice*. In it he wrote, in stark opposition to de Wolfe's idea that the home is a feminine sphere, that, "The house is but the externalized man: himself expressed in colour, form, line and texture."[5] He went on to argue against the use of "feeling" in making aesthetic decisions, and of historical styles, at least as he saw them being used. "The periods, too" he wrote, "have been treated as strange and incomprehensible, too deep and mysterious for anything but unquestionable admiration and slavish copy."[6]

In this chapter I would like to suggest that, where the formation of the profession is concerned, the divide between individualistic feminine interior decoration and collective masculine interior design is a false construct, and that, in spite of their historicist preferences where the styles of the interiors they created were concerned, de Wolfe, along with several of her contemporaries and followers, was as fully engaged in forming and defining a new profession as was Parsons by setting up his educational program. Although the lady decorators may not have been responsible for putting in place the educational and regulatory institutions that set and oversaw the standards expected of the profession, they intuitively, I believe, established many of the commercially-oriented practices and strategies that underpinned interior decoration and design through the twentieth century, and which continue to do so to this day.

De Wolfe's assumption was that decorators acquired knowledge about their clients and the market through working with them and that the best way of learning how to promote their activities to others in a world in which the media through which that information was disseminated was constantly changing, was to engage in practice. Also, given the important client orientation of, and the role of taste in the practice of interior decoration, a number of broadly-based skills and bodies of knowledge could only be acquired in the working environment, especially those relating to the concepts of life-style and fashion, and to the practices of marketing and advertising linked to changing definitions of the concept of the brand.

One of the reasons why we link de Wolfe with amateur, rather than professional, interior decoration is that she came to our notice through the publication of her 1913 book, *The House in Good Taste*.[7] In as much as it targeted amateur practitioners that tome (falsely) presented its author as a quasi-amateur herself. Just as Hadley claims for Sister Parish later, having unquestioningly bought the self-presentation that that decorator offered to the world, de Wolfe presented herself as a private individual with innate taste who could offer it to others, especially in the all-important (where social status was concerned) arena of the home. This was little more than a subtle marketing ploy, however, which positioned her as someone who could offer people the taste that they did not necessarily have themselves.

Many of her clients were second-generation *nouveaux riches* – the William H. Crockers, for example, for whom she designed the interior of their home, *New Place*, in Burlingame, California, made their money through banking and the railroad, while J. Ogden Armour, for whose family she worked on the interiors of *Mellody Hall* in Lake Forest, Illinois, was in the meatpacking business.[8] Both families wanted to be able to present themselves as tasteful and the elegant eighteenth-century interiors that de Wolfe provided them with what was needed to do that.

Throughout *The House in Good Taste* de Wolfe emphasized the schemes she had developed for her own homes, from the one on East 17th Street in New York, to her residence on East 55th Street in the same city, to her French home in Versailles. The decorator turned her own life and life-style into a commodity that was highly attractive to the clientèle with whom she sought to work. It was a marketing strategy that remained in place through the twentieth century where selling goods for the home was concerned, brought to the fore in the 1960s by the British retailer Terence Conran, through his Habitat store. *The House in Good Taste* was published at the point at which de Wolfe's career had really taken off and the book sold in very large numbers. It undoubtedly served to bring her the notice of large numbers of people and assist her in her career. The fact that she went to the lengths of employing a ghost-writer for it – Ruby Ross Goodnow (later the decorator Ruby Ross Wood) – suggests its importance for her as a commercial strategy.

In spite of her lack of a formal education and non-adherence to a professional body, in this essay I want to suggest that de Wolfe contributed to and reinforced a number of commercial strategies that have helped shape the working practices of the modern interior design profession. She was not necessarily the first, or indeed unique, in developing them but she was notable for being quick to borrow models established in adjacent areas and adapting them for her own purposes.

Before she even became a decorator, de Wolfe's first career as a paid actress on the Broadway stage at the turn of the nineteenth and twentieth centuries, for instance, provided her with a set of skills that were directly transferable to the newly-emerging activity of interior decoration. Above all it taught her how to promote herself through the media. Several articles about the actress in her own home appeared in New York magazines, such as *Town Topics*, in the 1890s. The writer, Margherita Arlina Hamm, also commented in her book, *Eminent Actors in the Their Homes*, about de Wolfe's East 17th Street home, that "No neighbourhood is more appropriate as the home of a famous actress."[9] She continued to use the printed mass media as a form of self-promotion. She first published *The House in Good Taste*, as instalments in *The Delineator* and the *Ladies Home Journal*, popular women's magazines, aware that this was a hugely effective form of advertising the work of her new office. Her marketing strategy was thought through from the outset. As well as involving herself with the media she sent out a card with an image of a wolf on it, a distinctive visual branding exercise that she used for many years.

De Wolfe was also clearly aware of the importance of networking. The first paid projects she was involved with were commissions from people she knew from her theater days. She quickly expanded that circle when she took on the project of working with Stanford White on the interiors of Colony Club in New York, an all-woman's club the membership of which came from across the United States. So well publicized was her work on the club's interiors that many of its members (including Ethel Crocker and Lolita Ogden Armour) commissioned work from her. De Wolfe had met White through Sunday afternoon open house sessions that she and her partner, Elizabeth Marbury, held regularly at their home on East 17th Street, a networking event that proved extremely professionally beneficial for the aspiring interior decorator.

Another of de Wolfe's professional/personal contacts was Condé Nast who owned *Vogue* magazine, which was published at first in the United States, but soon afterwards in Paris and London. De Wolfe was a regular in its pages over several decades. Not only did the magazine report on her decorating achievements it also noted her dress and her entertaining – in fact, her whole life-style. Their marketing strategies were finely attuned as Nast claimed that he wanted *Vogue* to appeal to people "whose criterion was taste rather than mass popularity."[10] In 1924 the decorator refurbished Nast's apartment on Park Avenue.[11]

De Wolfe's commercial strategies – networking, marketing and branding among them – were undoubtedly developed intuitively as she had a strongly entrepreneurial side to her character and she clearly followed her nose rather than a textbook. When *The House in Good Taste* finally appeared it contained, as its frontispiece, an image of de Wolfe leaning against the mantelpiece of her own home in East 17th Street. The fact that the decorator's hand-written name was added confirmed her self-identification as an early "signature designer," a phenomenon that came to the fore in the United States in the 1930s and, again, in Europe in the 1980s. Although that marketing strategy had been used earlier by the pioneering couturier, Charles Frederick Worth, who had added his name to his garments, de Wolfe was the first to employ it as a decorator.[12]

Indeed, de Wolfe owed a great deal to the growing couture industry that was establishing itself in Paris just before the rise of the interior decorator. She had had direct contact with it when she was working on the stage. In the era before catwalk shows, it was actresses on the stage who had worn couture gowns and de Wolfe, with her slim figure had been an ideal clothes horse. She had worn gowns designed by Worth, Jacques Doucet and Jeanne Paquin among others.[13] In performing that role she would have undoubtedly become aware of the sophisticated promotion and marketing strategies utilized by the new, highly aggressive fashion industry and would have unconsciously absorbed them. When the need came for her to promote her own business she most probably drew on that knowledge. It also reinforced her understanding of interior decoration as a lifestyle business.

The branding of oneself as a means of selling a creative individual's identity and celebrity as a guarantee of taste (seen in this context as a commodity in the commercial marketplace) became a key element within the marketing strategies employed by designers working across a range of

Elsie de Wolfe ■

specialisms through the twentieth century. Fashion designers, such as Worth, borrowed the idea of the creative individual from nineteenth-century Romantic art. In the process they characterized their own work as an art form, which gave it added value. The practice remained part of the world of haute couture through the twentieth century, and until very recently, with couturiers such as Coco Chanel, Yves Saint-Laurent, Christian Dior and latterly Giorgio Armani, among many others, depending on the same strategy.[14] From fashion it moved into interior decoration and on into the worlds of graphic design, industrial design, and architecture. By the 1930s the product designer, Raymond Loewy, had become a creative celebrity par excellence, featured, among other places, on the front cover of *Time* magazine. Half a century later the French industrial designer, Philippe Starck was to promote himself as a celebrity in a similar way, even to the extent of appearing on a television series.

By the 1930s the decorator had extended the reach of the "Elsie de Wolfe" brand, offering herself as a model of good taste and of a modern lifestyle by, like Loewy, endorsing a wide range of products, from cigarettes to carpets. While Loewy designed the all-white Lucky Strike cigarette pack, de Wolfe's advertisement for the brand, clearly aimed at women, played on the slimness of her own body. The advertisement showed her – described as a noted interior decorator – clothed in an elegant couture gown and pearls, and the text read, "I recommend a *Lucky* in place of a sweet. Toasting has taken out every bit of harshness in the *Lucky Strike* tobacco. All that remains is the splendid *Lucky* flavour – an excellent substitute when your appetite craves a sweet but your figure must be considered." (Figure 3.1) In an advertisement for Gulistan carpets, de Wolfe (now Lady Mendl), was described as an "internationally famous actress, hostess and decorator."[15] The female audience was told that it also could become successful hostesses. "What pleasures will be yours when your guests see *your* room" the text explained.

As the twentieth century progressed de Wolfe's decorating operation grew in size. In 1910 a newspaper article explained that, "she now keeps fourteen [staff] busy all the time and she has so many demands on her time that she finds it absolutely impossible to accept more than half the contracts that are offered to her."[16] By 1914, it was claimed, she had expanded her business significantly and was earning more than any of the lawyers in New York.[17]

From working from her own home in East 17th Street, in 1906 de Wolfe moved to her first office at 4 West 40th Street, where she supplied both interiors and *objets d'art*. Nine years later, at the height of her success, she moved again, this time to 2 West 47th Street, where she installed, on one floor, what she described as a mixture of salons, offices and studios, carefully decorated for visits from clients. A second floor was dedicated to workshops, staffed by a team of craftspeople who were employed to fabricate reproduction furniture items and the props needed for her interiors. They also made the curtains and other soft furnishings for her ongoing projects.

The idea of bringing production and sales into a single location was also taken from the couturiers. They in turn had taken it from early factories engaged in the manufacture of consumer goods, such as sewing machines, which, back in the mid-nineteenth-century, had opened showrooms adjacent to their manufacturing plants, thereby bringing selling into the environment of production. Even before that, the model had been used in the mass production furniture industry, which had implemented it from the early nineteenth century. The main reason was efficiency; but it also meant that it was easier to have control over everything that went on. In her showroom de Wolfe could show her clients the kind of items they could include in their interiors.

Penny Sparke

Figure 3.1
Advertisement for Lucky Strike cigarettes with an endorsement from Elsie de Wolfe (From the collection of Stanford Research Into the Impact of Tobacco Advertising [tobacco.stanford.edu]).

The decorator described her West 47th Street premises as the "Elsie de Wolfe Studio" in order to downplay the commercialism of her activity and to emphasise her links with artistic practice and the consequent tastefulness of her offer to clients. Couturiers were doing the same. Indeed, it is a model of practice that has continued up to the present in the creative industries, interior decoration and design included. In 1921, after she had made Paris her personal base, de Wolfe took on a whole floor of the new six-story Cammeyer Building at 677 Fifth Avenue where her premises expanded yet again due to the quantity of commissions coming her way. She explained that the showroom there looked more like a private house than a shop, which suggested that she believed that the best way to sell interior decoration was to immerse people in simulated spaces that made them feel at home. The idea of placing the goods she had for sale in cases and on pedestals in emulation of a museum setting was not, for de Wolfe, the right approach.

Elsie de Wolfe ■

While de Wolfe borrowed several of her marketing strategies from fashion design she also took ideas from the early advertising industry, in particular that of the creative office. In the second half of the nineteenth century the advertising industry had developed in the United States as a means of ensuring that the goods produced by manufacturing industry reached consumers. Although manufacturers could sell customers their first sewing machine or automobile by bringing them to the factory, it was harder to make a repeat sale that way. Advertising agencies filled the gap, stimulating consumer desire. J. Walter Thompson was an example of a large advertising agency that was established in New York back in 1864 (originally with the name of Carlton and Smith). By 1902 it was working with Unilever to sell that company's goods through magazine and newspaper advertisements. Thompson pioneered the employment of "creatives," in his case of artists and writers, who worked alongside all the other employees needed to make the agency function.

It was a model that appealed to de Wolfe in as much as she needed to combine creativity with a range of other activities, through from promotion to finance to project management. She was operating at a significant scale and therefore needed to model her practice on companies of a similar size. Although the language used to describe what we now call the "creative and cultural industries" did not fully emerge until the 1990s, the model was established nearly a century earlier. As Justin O'Connor (2011) has written of the creative and cultural industries, "individual artistic practice had to be set within a wide range of professional, managerial and commercial services."[18] The same could be said of de Wolfe's operation a hundred years before that.

Although she sold herself as a lone creative individual, or artist, de Wolfe needed the support of many employees, both creative and otherwise, in order to be able to deliver her decorating service. Regrettably the de Wolfe office's business records have been destroyed, and very little is actually known about her day-to-day business practices. However, we learn from the individual projects that she undertook that Paul Chalfin, later the decorator of Viscaya, James Deering's mansion in Miami,[19] worked as an assistant to de Wolfe in 1910; that a Miss Butler was her assistant when she worked on Henry Clay Frick's house in New York[20]; that an Elena Bachman and an H. Joan Hofford were assistants to the decorator when she worked on a project for Nell Pruyn Cunningham in the 1920s[21]; and that a Josephine Kneissel was her finance manager in 1915. This information, albeit fragmented, suggests that she was hugely dependent upon a large number of direct employees, both administrative and creative, to ensure the smooth running of her operation. In addition, we know that she also worked with subcontractors on a project-by-project basis. Among them was the artist Everett Shinn, later to become a member of the Ashcan school of painting, who she employed to create eighteenth-century decorations for the Colony Club.[22] de Wolfe worked with Shinn again on a painting for a dressing table that was used in the Jay P. Graves' residence in Spokane[23] and yet again in the Frick residence.[24] This kind of work clearly provided an income over many years for Shinn while he was developing his own artistic career.

Following on the heels of the already well-established profession of architecture, and in response to the twin needs of mass production and mass consumption, the new creative industries – advertising, fashion design, graphic design, interior decoration, and industrial design – were all expanding in the United States in the early years of the twentieth century and developing into modern creative professions and commercial operations. There were significant interdependencies, overlaps and borrowing between them in the early days. When, for example, in the late 1920s, the industrial designer, Walter Dorwin Teague, set up his large independent office in New York, he modelled his operation on that of the advertising agency in which he had undertaken his own apprenticeship.

Teague, a trained illustrator at New York's Art Students' League, had worked for the advertising firm of Calkins and Holden, providing decorative borders for the documents they created for clients.[25]

Unlike the advertisers and the industrial designers, however, de Wolfe was not selling her creative skills to manufacturing industry but rather, in a direct sales context, to architects to whom she supplied antiques and *objets d'art*, and with (mostly female) clients who commissioned her to decorate their entire interiors. Where the former was concerned the decorator collaborated with numerous architects over her long career. They included Stanford White, with whom she worked on the Colony Club[26]; Ogden Codman, whom she collaborated with on the design of a show house on East 71st Street in New York[27]; Arthur Heun, the architect with whom she worked on Mellody Farm[28]; Bigelow and Wadsworth, with whom she collaborated on Nell Pruyn Cunningham's residence in Glen Falls, New York[29]; Little and Browne, the architects who designed Suffolk House for the Warren Lanes in St. James, New York[30]; and Carrère and Hastings, who built the Frick residence on East 70th Street in New York.[31] Each collaboration had a character of its own in as much as sometimes she worked closely with architects, as she did with Stanford White before his untimely death, and sometimes she simply supplied them with furnishings. Whatever the nature of the collaboration it was a very important aspect of de Wolfe's business when she was working on new buildings. Indeed, it remains a key part of most interior decorators'/designers' practices in the early twenty-first century.

Above all, though, de Wolfe developed direct relationships with the clients who commissioned decorative schemes from her. Where that (most important) part of her business practice was concerned she borrowed selling strategies from late nineteenth-century couturiers, among them Worth, John Redfern, Jeanne Paquin, Jacques Doucet and others – who sold dresses to women in studios that resembled domestic interiors. Indeed, their operations became known as "fashion houses." Clearly, it was felt that women were more likely to make a purchase if they felt at home while they were trying on dresses and looking in mirrors to see whether different models suited them or otherwise. The relaxed atmosphere undoubtedly had an impact on sales.

De Wolfe borrowed another of her commercial strategies from the World's Fairs where the idea of the use of complete model domestic interiors for commercial purpose had originated in the last decades of the nineteenth century. By 1900 it had become an important way of exhibiting furniture, as exemplified by the rooms created by Eugène Gaillard, George de Feure and others that were displayed at the Paris Exposition Universelle of that year.[32] German and Austrian designers also created rooms at the same event. de Wolfe clearly understood the impact of the model room and, when she created her showroom at West 47th Street, she included one in it. While the other rooms in that venue were rather messy amalgams of furniture pieces displayed as in a warehouse, the little model room that she created brought together a regency striped chair, a boxy sofa, a patterned Louis XVI chair and Chinese wallpaper into a setting that looked as if someone could move into it immediately. Five years earlier, in 1910, the decorator had created a complete show-house at 131 East 71st Street in New York with the architect-decorator, Ogden Codman, that was full of model rooms.[33] Not only did she furnish the entire house right down to the ceramic ornaments on the mantelpieces and pictures on the walls, and open it to the public, she generated even more publicity from it by holding a reception there on the opening night, which was reported widely in the press.[34]

The dependence on the simulated domestic interior as a sales setting not only distinguished de Wolfe's studio from the more production-oriented showrooms of the factories but also from those of the art and antique dealers who were expanding at that time with the fashion for historical interiors, especially in the French styles. De Wolfe worked closely with art dealers and with the antiques trade. From the early days of her decorating career she travelled frequently to France, buying antiques and importing them back for her clients. Sometimes she shopped with them, as was the case with Henry Clay Frick in 1914 with whom she travelled to London and Paris, visiting, among others, the retail outlets of Lenygon and Morant, Frank Partridge and Charles of London in the former, and those of Arnold Seligman, Doucet, Mathelin and Jansen in the latter.

The art and antique dealers were also in the business of creating interiors for clients in the early twentieth century. However, they put less emphasis, than did de Wolfe, on the use of private domestic settings. The 720 5th Avenue showrooms of the Duveen Brothers, prominent New York-based dealers in antiques from the 1860s onwards, for example, contained stands, pedestals, vitrines and showcases. This suggests that they exhibited furnishings and decorative artefacts as if they were being displayed in a public museum, thereby aiming to enhance their value in the eyes of the visitors who came to purchase them.

Large-scale upholstering companies also provided clients with complete interiors in the early years of the twentieth century. Indeed, before the emergence of the lady decorators, firms such as those of Herter Brothers, and of George Platt and A. C. Palmer, among several others, had provided complete decorating services.[35] The Herter brothers had been originally committed to the vertical combination of manufacturing and marketing in one building model described above, and, from 1855 onwards, had housed their manufacturing and marketing in a single building. They separated them over time, however, eventually taking on an enormous building on Ladies Mile in New York. The first-floor showroom in that building was described as a "museum containing over 400,000 articles."[36] The spirit of mass production remained pervasive, however, and the model of the public sphere of the museum, rather than that of the private home, prevailed.

The other venue in which customers could purchase an interior decorating service in early twentieth-century United States was the department store, the most important new form of retail outlet to be developed in the second half of the nineteenth century. There were strong connections between the fashion trade, world exhibitions, and department stores. The department store window was, for example, one of the main ways in which the general public encountered fashionable dress, while at the Paris 1900 exhibition the department store, Bon Marché, displayed its fashion wares on live models. By the end of the nineteenth century a commercial nexus had emerged that served to bring fashion items and consumer goods more broadly to the attention of the general public.

De Wolfe was very conscious of the opportunities that that nexus provided her with and she cleverly inserted interior decoration into the mix. Her clientèle remained one that was socially above that which frequented department stores, however. When those stores began to offer decorating services it helped her indirectly, though, as it defined her clients more clearly as not being department store customers. At the same time de Wolfe was always on the lookout for new clients who were rising (as she had done herself) through the social classes so her marketing was as wide ranging as it could be, especially in the latter decades of her career. The fact that the clientèle for department store interiors were from a social class below the one that sought interiors from de Wolfe, though, explained her closer allegiance to the couturiers who sought to provide a more élite, customized product.

In spite of de Wolfe's absence from that level of the market, borrowing from the French model that had been developed through the second half of the nineteenth century and into the twentieth century in stores such as Le Bon Marché and Le Printemps, American department stores began to offer interior decorating services in the early twentieth century – Wanamakers in New York in particular – under the directorship of Nancy McClelland from 1912. McClelland, as Bridget May has shown us, unlike de Wolfe, was a life-long advocate of education and professional standards, including licensing, for decorators. In 1914 she was joined by Ruby Ross Goodnow (later Ruby Ross Wood) who, as has already been mentioned, ghost-wrote de Wolfe's *The House in Good Taste*.

Although de Wolfe herself worked independently, focusing on the commercial aspects of the developing practice of interior decoration, but presenting herself to her potential clientèle as a quasi-amateur, professional interior decorating groups were forming around her, aided and abetted by the lady decorator movement that she had helped to form. The Decorators' Club, for example, was founded in 1914 in New York by a group of women who set out to promote high standards for interior design education and establish rules for professional practice. In that year 38 members met at the home of decorator Gertrude Gheen Robinson who, like de Wolfe, had begun her professional career as an actress and who delivered her operation in a very similar way. The Club was the precursor of the American Institute of Interior Decorators, formed in 1931, which, when merged in 1974 with the National Society of Interior Designers (formed earlier in 1957), became the American Society of Interior Designers.

This suggests that, rather than there being a divide between them, there was direct continuity between the so-called amateur ladies and the fully formed interior design profession of the second half of the twentieth century. I would like to suggest, although she was personally disinclined to become part of professional groups, that de Wolfe's early understanding of that profession as a modern commercial activity, combined with her ability to learn from practices that were developing in parallel to her own, played a significant part in defining the *modus operandum* of the interior design profession when it finally emerged in the years after World War II. Her understanding of promotion, marketing, branding, and the use of social networks were developed to a high level and she established those practices as being part of the professional practice of interior decoration and subsequently of interior design. Above all, she understood how, in order to be able to acquire clients, a creative service industry that focused on the decoration of the home had to embrace feminine culture and all that that brought with it. At the same time, however, it had to be run as a hard-headed modern business utilizing all the commercial strategies available to a modern businesswoman.

NOTES

1 See E. Brown, *Sixty Years of Interior Design: The World of McMillen* (New York: Viking Press, 1982); R. Becker, *Nancy Lancaster: Her Life, Her World, Her Art* (New York: Knopf, 1996); A. P. Bartlett and S. B. Crater, *Sister: The Life of Legendary American Interior Decorator, Mrs. Henry Parish II* (New York: St. Martin's Press); P. Sparke, *Elsie de Wolfe: The Birth of Modern Interior Decoration* (New York: Acanthus, 2005); C. Varney, *In the Pink: Dorothy Draper: America's Most Fabulous Decorator* (New York: Pointed Leaf Press, 2006); B. May, "Nancy Vincent McClelland (1877–1950): Professionalizing Interior Decoration in the Early Twentieth Century," *Journal of Design History* 21, no. 1 (2008); P. Metcalf, *Syrie Maugham: Staging the Glamorous Interior* (New York: Acanthus, 2010); and J. H. Simpson, *Rose Cumming: With an Introduction by Albert Hadley* (New York: Rizzoli International Publishers, 2012).
2 Bartlett and Crater 2000, xvii.
3 E. M. Thomson, *The Origins of Graphic Design in America, 1870–1920* (New Haven: Yale University Press, 1997), 27.

Elsie de Wolfe ■

4 T. H. Robsjohn-Gibbings quoted in Sparke 2005, 23.
5 F. A. Parsons, *Interior Decoration: Its Principles and Practice* (New York: Doubleday, Page & Company, 1915), vii.
6 Parsons 1915, viii.
7 E. de Wolfe, *The House in Good Taste* (New York: Century Publications, 1913).
8 Sparke 2005, 47–57 and 67–79.
9 M. A. Hamm, *Eminent Actors in Their Homes: Personal Descriptions and Interviews* (New York: James Pott & Company, 1902), 56.
10 E. W. Chase and I. Chase, *Always in Vogue* (London: Gollantz, 1954), 55.
11 Sparke 2005, 229–237.
12 See Diana de Marly, 'Worth: Father of Haute Couture' (London: Elm Tree Books, 1980)
13 Sparke 2005, 126.
14 See J. Potvin, *Giorgio Armani: Empire of the Senses* (London and New York: Ashgate, 2013).
15 Elsie de Wolfe advertisement for Lucky Strike cigarettes in *Ladies' Home Journal*, May 1934, 17.
16 Robinson-Locke Collection of Theatre Scrapbooks (1914) series 3, vol. 373, (New York Public Library), 18.
17 Ibid.
18 J. O'Connor, "The Cultural and Creative Industries: A Critical History," *Ekonomiaz* 73, no. 3 (2011): 4, available in translation online at: www.academia.edu/4147550/The_Cultural_and_Creative_Industries_A_Critical_History, 3. (accessed 4 April 2016).
19 Sparke 2005, 322.
20 Sparke 2005, 167–179.
21 Sparke 2005, 239–245.
22 Sparke 2005, 43.
23 Sparke 20005, 119.
24 Sparke 2005, 176.
25 P. Sparke, "From a Lipstick to a Steamship: The Growth of the American Industrial Design Profession," in *Design History: Fad or Function* (London: Design Council, (1978), 21.
26 Sparke 2005, 37–47.
27 Sparke 2005, 79–91.
28 Sparke 2005, 67–77.
29 Sparke 2005, 239–243.
30 Sparke 2005, 326.
31 Sparke 2005, 167–177.
32 P. Sparke, *The Modern Interior* (London: Reaktion Books, 2008), 66.
33 Sparke 2005, 79–91.
34 Sparke 2005, 89.
35 L. Frankel, ed., *Herter Brothers: Furniture and Interiors for a Gilded Age* (New York: Harry N. Abrams in association with The Museum of Fine Arts, Houston, 1994), 57.
36 Frankel, 1994, 83.

Chapter 4: Designing the gender contest

(Re)Locating the gay decorator in the history of interior design

John Potvin

> *But it's not just the ratty part of town. The upper class in San Francisco is that way. The Bohemian Grove, which I attend from time to time – it is the most faggy goddamned thing you could ever imagine, with that San Francisco crowd. I can't shake hands with anybody from San Francisco. Decorators. They got to do something. But we don't have to glorify it.*
>
> (Richard Nixon)[1]

In his now infamous conversation with John D. Ehrlichman and H. R. Haldeman in 1971, then US President Richard Nixon infamously characterized male interior decorators as the glorification, or perhaps more aptly the professionalization, of an aberrant sexuality.[2] By entering into the profession, these "faggy" men put a public, visible face to their sexuality, an identity best left in the closet rather than in the interiors of respectable Americans. In the shadow of the Stonewall Riots of 1969 and a general move toward sexual emancipation, Nixon's shaming words provocatively point to an all-too-common cultural trope in the United States that conflates the profession of interior design with homosexuality. Nearly 40 years earlier the so-called dean of interior decorators, Billy Baldwin, drew attention to the near invisibility of male decorators in the 1930s by noting how few men were involved in the profession: "You notice that during this period not many men are mentioned. For the good reason that not many men were decorators."[3] Sandwiched between Baldwin's and Nixon's highly divergent points of reference was the creation in 1957 of the National Society of Interior Designers which, once and for all, set out to lend legitimacy and credibility to the profession and bring educators, designers, and the industry closer together. The desire to organize and standardize professional practice, however, can be traced back to the 1910s and the years immediately following World War I. In combination, these brief snap shots unwittingly conjure a composite impression of the role and position of the male decorator within the twentieth-century American cultural landscape. At first glance, the impression one gets of the initially absentee figure is, by the post-war period, purportedly transformed into a sexual aberrant, or in other words a *faggy* (read flamboyant and effeminate) professional decorator. This chapter argues that a concern for both gender and sexuality was concomitantly and irrevocably folded into and embedded in this desire to professionalize and standardize.

Today the effeminate gay decorator has become all but a truism within popular culture, its historical roots, biases and assumptions rarely questioned, challenged or examined. Stuart Hall defines identities as "the names we give to the different ways we are positioned by, and position ourselves in, the narratives of the past."[4] Identities are therefore mutable, shifting and contingent and yet they can also be tenacious and steadfast cutting across time and space, particularly as they develop into cultural clichés and stereotypes. These stereotypes, naturalized over time, "threaten not only our knowledge of the past, but our ability to imagine, reshape, and make claims for identifications in the present and future as well." These threats "have been particularly virulent in recent years, abetting the forces that would render us sexually anxious, isolated in dynamics of shame and guilt."[5] Sexuality, effeminacy, and interior design are three terms inextricably braided together within the cultural imagination. Yet, as contemporary architect and essayist Joel Sanders has asserted: "If the history of the professional decorator has been neglected, the subject of homosexuality and interior decoration has been largely ignored."[6] Not all aspects of stereotypes, however, are negative. As a result, my aim here is not to proceed by removing any associations of camp or effeminacy largely attached to the stereotype of the (gay) male decorator, but rather to challenge the negative connotations and the shame that necessarily still comes with this triangulation.

Despite the limitations of space and scope, my ambition for this essay is driven by larger and on-going historiographical concerns made clear here through a close examination of a particular historical conjuncture. Seeking to challenge the current historiography of interior design, rather than reaffirm what is quickly becoming a canonical reading of the field's history, I posit that two intersecting axes have defined the very foundation and creation of interior design not only as a viable career, but a symptom of modernism and modernity alike.[7] The first axis marks out the tensions between professionalism and amateurism while the second outlines the culturally contingent and socially burdened gender/sexuality continuum. These two axes intersect at the point where industrial production, consumer culture, women's growing emancipation and the creation of sexual typologies converge and collide. It is this dynamic and volatile nexus, where the second axis has largely been ignored in the history of interior design, defined equally by industrial, lifestyle modernism, and registers of gender and sexuality that mark, I posit, a pivotal, and yet neglected, point of shame ingrained in the very fabric of the profession's history. My contention is that it is precisely this embedded and unexamined shame that distinguishes the profession from all others. As a means to offer evidence of this collision and rupture, I explore a small slice of the history of the development of the profession, the years concomitant with World War I and its immediate aftermath, a period I assert was a, if not the, defining moment that would forever determine the social perceptions, codes, ethics, and standards of the profession of interior decoration and design in the United States.

THE GENDER "DRIFT"

As part of my discussion, the short history I examine and offer up as the embryonic period that led to twentieth-century American perceptions held by people like President Nixon hinged on a gendered contest, which can be traced back the last quarter of the nineteenth century, when upholsterers and architects were largely responsible for the design and decoration of the domestic interior. Both professions were seen to be dictating from a distance rather than decorating from within and as a result were detached from the supposed feminizing influence of the home and its

Designing the gender contest ■

mundane domestic realities. Prior to the emergence of interior decorators, it was taken as given that upholsters and architects were men whose masculinity (and sexuality by extension) was rarely, if ever, called into question.

Candace Wheeler was the first women to publicly acknowledge and assert that interior decoration was an ideal and logical profession for women, for, according to her, the domestic realm was already largely understood to be the purview of women, themselves relegated to its confines. However, for Wheeler it was less social realities than a seemingly inherent aptitude that gave women their clear advantage. According to her, "[t]he apparently instinctive knowledge which women have of textiles, and which men have not, the intimate knowledge of the conveniences of domestic life – conveniences which may also be used as factors in a scheme of beauty – are great advantages to women who make this choice of a profession."[8] Throughout the 1910s and 1920s, however, men and women competed to define what constituted good design and who was best suited to decorate the modern American home.[9]

The long-held ideal divide of the separate spheres determined by sexual difference assumed to guarantee a privileged position for women given that they were relegated to the realm of the domestic. By the early twentieth century women were seen as the driving force behind the professionalization of interior decorating, becoming its custodians, exemplars, and in some instances its celebrity personalities. As Stephen Vider has recently argued,

> according to the U.S. census, even as the total numbers of decorators (grouped with drapers and window dressers) increased from 1900 to 1940, men consistently outnumbered women. Rather women redefined the field in the popular press and cinema as a field best left to women – a field not of contractors but aesthetic experts, with an intuitive sense for beauty and taste. By the 1920s and 30s, many of the nation's best known and most successful decorators were women.[10]

Indeed, notoriety and perception have played a significant role in the development of the profession and its social, cultural and even political standing in American society. Figures like Elsie de Wolfe, among others, were seen as the consummate paragons of both successful professionalism and arbiters of public taste.

de Wolfe made clear that the interior was not a man's space, but the dominion of women when she famously proclaimed that

> [w]e take it for granted that every woman is interested in houses – that she either has a home in course of construction, or dreams of having one, or has had a house long enough wrong to wish it right. And we take it for granted that this American home is always a woman's home: a man may build and decorate a beautiful house, but it remains for a woman to make a home of it for him. It is the personality of the mistress that the house expresses. Men are forever guests in our homes no matter how much happiness they may find there.[11]

de Wolfe's choice of words reveals her ambition to legitimate women's cultural and social position more broadly and more specifically in relation to the home and its decoration; an endeavor she, among others, deemed worthy of recognition. At the same time, de Wolfe's insistence that men are "guests" displaces their (then current or potential) involvement in interior design altogether as well as a stable relationship to the decoration of its spaces. Two years later, Frank Alvah Parsons declared in *Interior Decoration: Its Principles and Practice*, that

> [t]he house is but the externalized man; himself expressed in colour, form, line and texture. To be sure, he is usually limited in means, hampered by a contrary and penurious landlord or by family heirlooms, and often he cannot find just what he wants in the trade; but still the house is his house. It is *he*.[12]

For Parsons the home is an external materialization of identity, the very foundation of subjectivity itself; more explicitly it *is* man himself, *tout court*.

Parsons' gendered associations unwittingly moves him into murky and dubious territory, when he claims that "colour, form, line and texture" express the contours of the man-house he proposes, aspects which point to the "artifice" of decoration long associated with women. Throughout the twentieth century, key attributes purposefully stood in sharp contrast to and as a means to distinguish virile modernist architects from the artifice, effeminacy, and fey touch of the decorator.[13] In a lengthy article published in *The Upholsterer and Interior Decorator*, "*the measure of a man*" came down to a rather simple, standardized equation: "personality + industry + dependability," at least according to John W. Stephenson who provided the opening talk for an assembled group of men from the editorial and advertising departments of Clifford & Lawton. The proposed equation "constitutes a threefold man – the man as seen by others, plus the man as he sees himself, plus the man as he really is."[14] In 1918, with the United States sending men to the Western front for the first time, the "threefold man" was the sum of a sedimentation of various well-established and still developing processes of social perception.

As a critical voice within and for the industry, *The Upholsterer and Interior Decorator* had a vested interest in the development of the profession and eagerly reported on the various early attempts to organize and professionalize, especially given its seemingly duplicitous mandate of catering to both upholsterers and interior decorators. Published by Clifford and Lawton in New York, the periodical "devoted" itself to all "the home furnishing arts." Originally titled *The Upholsterer* when it was founded in 1888, the magazine changed its name in 1916 to be more inclusive, acknowledging the growing prominence of decorators in the American marketplace. The first union to loosely represent decorators' interests was the Brotherhood of Painters and Decorators of America, originally founded in 1877. Decorators formed a small, if not insignificant, portion of the various trades and laborers associated with the union, which held local chapters throughout the United States and Canada and boasted 7,000 members within its first year. The "the conspicuous entrance of women" together with "the shift away from manual labor" meant that men's roles within interior decorating also shifted significantly.[15] It was not until 1917 when the men's Society of Decorators was formed, three years after its sister organization, The Decorators' Club of New York, was founded.

Despite these initial steps toward aggregation, *The New York Times* in 1920 reported that recent attempts at forming a new society would both "Standardize and Dignify." For *The New York Times*, all 36 members of The Decorators' Club were assumed to be women. Decorating and women were so compatible that, according to the article, it was not simply a case of it being part of a woman's domain, but the other side of the coin of a woman's sexuality. In short, she was either married or a

Designing the gender contest ■

decorator. In the quest to form the "Society of Decorators," standardization was deemed essential as a means to

> raise aesthetic standards; to write a code of ethics, similar to that under which the architects work; to gain for decorators the right to show their work in various exhibitions of the art world – in short, to organize as a profession instead of as a business.

Visibility and a standardization of practice akin to architects' work were key facets to gain legitimacy. According to the author, many so-called professionals were erroneously calling themselves decorators; amongst them male furniture dealers, "the antique furniture man" and even "the upholsterer."[16] Three years earlier, on the eve of the formation of the new men's society, *The Upholsterer and Interior Decorator* lamented that "the decorating business is easy to get into and many irresponsible people presume to be decorators and figure upon a job with no comprehension of the expense of execution."[17] The eagerness to forge a clear, concise and constitutional identity pervaded countless press reports throughout the 1910s and 1920s.

In an era of few educational options and sparse institutional support, the definition of a decorator became an ever-increasingly important task, particularly in light of myriad dubious characters claiming the title for themselves. Posing the simple, yet slightly provocative question, "What is an interior decorator?" as part of their efforts toward raising the awareness and need for professionalization, *The Upholsterer and Interior Decorator*, set out to determine what constituted a genuine interior decorator, regardless of sex. For the magazine, or in its own words "[w]e in the trade," the interior decorator is "the man or woman who, with skill, training, and artistic sensibility, is capable of assembling, furniture, rugs, draperies, walls coverings etc in such a way as to create the harmonious interior of a home."[18] Suppliers of goods, for example, are advised from refraining from the term when referring to themselves. The interior decorator, after all, is more than a mere assembler or collector of *objets*; for, to be a decorator, one "requires an historical and artistic knowledge covering all branches of the decorative trade, which the average supply man who now sometimes calls himself an interior decorator does not possess, nor pretend to possess."[19] Accordingly, the profession necessitates, nay demands, "specialized knowledge; it can be obtained only by a man of artistic temperament and of a studious mind."[20] The quest to define and standardize speaks to a move toward self-actualizing a coherent identity as much as it does an impulse to expand and consolidate a stronger footing in an ever-growing market.

The monthly periodical's position was at once a response to erroneous ideas filtering through the public and a reaction against the flooding of amateur (largely female) decorators into the market as much as it was compelled by a desire for professional standing and the social cachet and dignity that such a designation portends. The byline for a 1918 article on "Decoration and the Woman" from the same magazine reads: "The Vocation of Decoration is Not Exclusive to Either Sex not to Any Station in Life, but There Is no Royal Road to Success. It requires Diligent Study and Thorough Experience to be Able to Deliver a Real Service." According to the article's author

> Women have had always the reputation of being clever in decoration, and as professionals, there are many of them who are as clever as the men. But as between a poorly equipped woman and the poorly equipped man,

John Potvin ■

the man will make fewer mistakes because more conservative [. . .] The woman is responsible for so many atrocities in house decoration that there lingers with many people a feeling of prejudice against the sex.[21]

Although the sexism of the article is made abundantly apparent, it also insinuates growing concerns of women taking over men's roles. As feminist scholars have shown, amateur enterprises particularly popular amongst or largely associated with women have long tended to be dismissed or trivialized.[22]

The concern for the so-called "feminine drift" occurring in the profession did not simply speak to fears over interloping amateurs but the lack of promoting professions like upholstery as a viable option for the new generation of young men; the "upholstery business, as a business, is not properly presented to the male youth of the country." Here, again, the profession, broadly understood, was faced with a concern of public perception or perhaps more aptly a lack of public awareness. For, "as one buyer puts it [. . .] 'the industry as it is talked about, does not occupy a large enough place in public thought to be appreciated at its proper value'. What then be done?" Among the numerous possibilities, perhaps the most revealing suggestion made by the magazine was to encourage the profession itself to " 'sell' their profession to the rising generation for the natural drift, as indicated at present, is against the upholstery business remaining a masculine calling."[23]

The perceptions swirling around the so-called "natural drift" was also inadvertently highlighted in another brief article in *The Upholsterer and Interior Decorator*, outlining the steps needed to becoming an interior decorator. The anonymous author characterizes what *type* is best suited to a profession that "appeals to many people who have an inclination for the artistic, and it will appeal to many others who think they see in it possibilities of easily acquiring the ability to produce an income by a genteel vocation."[24] By 1923, terms like "artistic" and "genteel," especially when placed together and within a context of decoration and design could only really designate two types of people, women and effeminate men. Indeed, the lack of "selling" itself on the part of certain facets of the field coupled with the growing gendered and sexual implications circulating within the profession itself and within a broad segment of the mass media, it can be no wonder that by the post-World War II era, the cliché of the gay decorator was firmly entrenched within the American cultural and socio-political landscape.

INTERIOR DESECRATION

According to Pat Kirkham and Penny Sparke, Billy Baldwin along with many "other male decorators may have been considered effeminate by association with the feminized world of 'lady decorators,' but they were never denigrated as were de Wolfe and Dorothy Draper."[25] Yet, we would do well to remember the (dis)placed role effeminacy plays within North American culture, particularly throughout the twentieth century. Queer theorist David Halperin emphatically reminds us that "effeminacy deserves to be treated independently because it was for a long time defined as a symptom of an excess of what we would call *heterosexual* as well as homosexual desire. It is therefore a category unto itself."[26] By calling attention to the differences between effeminacy and homosexuality Halperin parses how the two have been conflated over the past 100 or so years. It is the effeminacy attributed to homosexuality that proves problematic in a cultural context that ensures and sanctions preferred and hegemonic ideals of masculinity as distinct

Figure 4.1
Dorothy Rothschild, "Interior Desecration," *Vogue (USA)* 49, no. 8 (1917).

from its (feminine) other. The gay decorator's "effeminate manners and voice hinted [and] provided a foil for the 'real' man – productive, reproductive, and resolutely heterosexual."[27] In fact, the effeminate male decorator quickly became a menacing figure for he threatened the implied intimacy of the domestic realm defined by compulsory heterosexuality, companionate marriage, and the nuclear family.

Dorothy Rothschild's (Parker), cheekily, yet revealingly titled article "Interior Desecration" for *Vogue* recounts an afternoon spent with a fictional friend, Alistair St. Cloud, whom she refers to as "one of our most talented interior decorators" (see Figure 4.1].[28] His physiognomy, burdened by a Victorian paradigm, becomes a critical aspect of her story as much as his work and identity. A tenacious and

John Potvin ■

unmitigated allusion to the ephebic Wildean Aesthete of the late nineteenth century, St. Cloud is described as

> pale and tall and slim, and he droops a bit, like a wilted lily. He is always just a little weary. He has phenomenally long nervous hands, white and translucent, which are used principally for making languid gestures for though his voice is sweet and low like the wind of the western sea, he speaks but seldom.[29]

As she moves throughout the home he decorated for his client, Mrs. Endicott, in which "the delicate touch of Alistair was visible," Rothschild quickly becomes overwrought, overcome by the sensory and sensational decoration St. Cloud has engineered. The overwhelming sensations Rothschild experiences were previously theorized and vilified at the end of the nineteenth century by physician and social critic Max Nordau who feared the phenomenological and psychological effects of aesthetic decorative objects and spaces in decadent interiors when he claimed that for men like St. Cloud "[e]verything in these houses aims at exciting the nerves and dazzling the senses. The disconnected and antithetical effects in all arrangements, the constant contradiction between form and purpose, the outlandishness of most objects, is intended to be bewildering."[30] So "outlandish," so "dazzling," so "bewildering" were St. Clouds' designs, Rothschild had to "recover." Rothschild, however, was not alone in her need for recovery. Overcome by his own designs and the grand tour he provides his friend, St. Cloud performs the quintessential performative act of the decadent, feeble queer aesthete cum decorator: "I thought at first that he was going to swoon. I rushed to him and managed to get him into a chair, and after a while he was able to speak."[31] The cause of his swooning? "It took me two weeks to arrange that fruit," he said, bitterly, "and now you have upset it. With one touch, you have shattered my dream. Oh, it is too much!"[32] As I have argued elsewhere, the simple and short, yet powerfully suggestive use of "too" has long been deployed as a linguistically charged index of queer decadence and excess.[33]

Rothschild continues: "He paced the floor, one delicate hand on his hip, one pressing his forehead, behind which great thoughts leaped and surged. But inspiration did not come with exercise."[34] Again, the image is made clear, that of the tormented, though "genteel" and "artistic," decorator. Suggesting he leave and steal himself away from his torment and loss of inspiration, St Cloud cries out: "No, no, I can not [sic] leave now, I must toil until the color comes to me even if I work myself into a nervous break-down. Leave me – leave me to my labor."[35] Colour as source of inspiration is after all, as Parsons once claimed, the very thing that helps a man to externalize himself in the interior decoration of his home; it is, in other words, part of 'he'. Indeed, St Cloud appears from another world and time, a seemingly tragic remnant of late nineteenth-century Aestheticism which has long been said to have died in 1900 in that apocryphal battle between Oscar Wilde and his hideous French wallpaper,[36] but continued to serve as a cipher for a certain type masculinity that conflated effeminacy with a budding profession.

By the 1920s, the image of the gasping, overwrought if not slightly nefarious male decorator abounded in the popular press: whether in *Life* where "[a]n unfortunate guest who placed his chair in the wrong position at the interior decorator's house"[37] caused said decorator to cover his eyes in horror and violently throw himself back into a chair or the "interior decorating boys, Francis and Murray [. . .] enthralled over a gilded [Victorian] shoe . . . pincushion . . . They are going to stick a client, who is being done over in Victorian, all of $35 for it!"[38] The condescension of these tableaux of the mincing decorator amounts to nothing more than a thief, a shyster who, in the article, holds the dubious honour to serve as part of a composition image. Together, set in relief to the rational, sobriety of modern, industrial America, these "artistic" and "genteel" decorators form a scathing snapshot of a modern typology, and the perils that professional interior decoration seem to entail.

NOTES

1 Warren, James. "All the Philosopher King's Men." *Harper's Magazine* 300, no. 1797 (February 2000): 22.

2 A note on terminology is needed here. Throughout this essay, I purposefully vacillate and use interior decoration and interior design interchangeably as a means to stave off the all-too-often negative, gendered and condescending attitudes that are leveled at the former. For a fascinating and important recent discussion of professional terminology see for example Matthews, Carl and Caroline Hill. "Gay Until Proven Straight: Exploring Perceptions of Male Interior Designers from Male Practitioner to Student Perspectives." *Journal of Interior Design* Vol. 36, Issue 3 (May 2011): 15-34.

3 Baldwin, Billy and Michael Gardine. *Billy Baldwin: An Autobiography*. Boston: Little, Brown, 1985.

4 In Huyssen, Andreas. *Twilight Memories: Making Time in a Culture of Amnesia*. New York: Routledge, 1995: 1.

5 Castiglia, Christopher and Christopher Reed. " 'Ah, Yes, I Remember it Well': Memory and Queer Culture in Will and Grace." *Cultural Critique* 56 (Winter 2004): 158.

6 Sanders, Joel. "Curtain Wars: Architects, Decorators, and the 20th-Century Domestic Interior" in *From Organization to Decoration: An Interiors Reader*, eds. Graeme Brooker and Sally Stone. New York and London: Routledge, 2013 [2002]): 26.

7 For a parallel discussion on architecture, see for example, Wigley, Mark. *White Walls, Designer Dresses: The Fashioning of Modern Architecture*. Cambridge and London: The MIT Press, 2001.

8 Wheeler, Candace. "Interior Decoration as a Profession for Women." *The Decorator and Furnisher* 26, no. 3 (1895): 88.

9 This chapter is concerned with the figure of the decorator as a professional typology and will focus largely on the decoration for the domestic interior, although I would contend these issues are still relevant for public, commercial commissions. This focus on the domestic is fuelled by its continued feminization and the long history of its vilification, which has meant that men's involvement in the domesticated realm of taste and beauty was deemed suspect, adding layers to already fraught negotiation. I would also suggest that similar attention must be paid to the way men and women negotiated the terrain of corporate and commercial interiors. See Mark Hinchman's essay in this volume, "Modernism's Glass Ceiling: Women in Commercial Design after World War II" and Paula Lupkin's "For Men by Men: Furnishing the YMCA".

10 Vider, Stephen Joshua. " 'A Peculiar Talent': Measuring Masculinity, Diagnosing Decorating," in *No Place Like Home: A Cultural History of Gay Domesticity, 1948–1982*, Dissertation. Cambridge: Harvard University, 2013: 41.

11 de Wolfe, Elsie. *The House of Good Taste*. New York: The Century Company, 1913: 5.

12 Parsons, Frank Alvah. *Interior Design: Its Principles and Practice*. New York: Doubleday, Page & Company, 1915: vii. Parsons' role within the development of interior design has largely been undervalued in the history of field. In 1904, under his direction, the New York School of Fine and Applied Art, which was to become Parsons School of Design, began offering courses in interior decoration. At the New York YMCA he also offered a course in interior design open only to 50 men.

13 Sanders, "Curtain Wars", 28.

14 "The Measure of a Man," *The Upholsterer and Interior Decorator* 59, no. 1 (1918): 49.

15 Vider, " 'A Peculiar Talent'," 45.

16 "Interior Decoration: New Society Will Aim to Standardize and Dignify." *New York Times*, 18 July 1920: 78.

17 "New York Firms Form a Society of Interior Decorators," *The Upholsterer and Interior Decorator* 58, no. 6 (1917): 63.

18 H., J. B. "What Is an Interior Decorator?" *The Upholsterer and Interior Decorator* 73, no. 2 (1924): 82.

19 Ibid.

20 Ibid.

21 "Decoration and the Woman." *The Upholsterer and the Interior Decorator* 60, no. 1 (1918): 53.

22 See for example: Buckley, Cheryl. "Made in Patriarchy: Toward a Feminist Analysis of Women and Design." *Design Issues* 3, no. 2 (Autumn, 1986): 3–14; Sparke, Penny. *As Long as It's Pink: The Sexual Politics of Taste*. London and San Francisco: Pandora, 1994.

23 "The Feminine 'Drift'." *The Upholsterer and Interior Decorator* 65, no. 8 (1920): 74.

24 "How Can I Become a Decorator?" *The Upholsterer and Interior Decorator* 71, no. 1 (1923): 97–98.

25 Kirkham, Pat and Penny Sparke, " 'A Woman's Place. . .?': Women Interior Designers," in *Women Designers in the USA, 1900–2000: Diversity and Difference*, ed. Pat Kirkham New Haven and London: Yale University Press, 2000: 313.

26 Halperin, David M. "How to do the History of Male Homosexuality." *GLQ: The Journal of Lesbian and Gay Studies* 6, no. 1 (2000): 92.

27 Vider, " 'A Peculiar Talent' ", 29–30.

28 Rothschild. Dorothy. "Interior Desecration." *Vogue (USA)* 49, no. 8 (1917): 54.

29 Ibid.

30 Nordau, Max. *Degeneration*. New York: D. Appleton and Company, 1905, 11.

31 Rothschild, "Interior Desecration," 129.

32 Ibid.

33 Potvin, John. *Bachelors of a Different Sort: Queer Aesthetics, Material Culture and the Modern Interior in Britain*. Manchester and New York: Manchester University Press, 2014): 28.

34 Rothschild, "Interior Desecration," 129.

35 Ibid.

36 See Potvin, *Bachelors of a Different Sort*.

37 *Life*. (21 June 1928): 22.

38 Will, W. E. "Among Us Moderns." *Los Angeles Sunday Times* (18 August 1926): n.p.

Chapter 5: For men by men

Furnishing the YMCA

Paula Lupkin

Was interior decoration a job for a woman or a man? In the early twentieth century the question of gender was embedded in the professionalization of an enterprise that was still fluidly defined. Drawing together the arts, design, history, manufactures, sales, and several other disciplines, interiors work took place in the home, the department store, and in the studios of artists and architects. Formal schooling was still in its infancy, as were gate-keeping associations.[1] This fluidity allowed both men and women with a varied range of skills and experience to work as decorators. After World War I, as the market for interior decoration services expanded beyond individual domestic projects, gender and professional status became a vexed topic.[2] Some observers, like Candace Wheeler, advocated interior decoration as an artistic profession perfectly suited to women's domestic backgrounds and inborn talents. By the 1920s, however, those aligned with the male-dominated world of furniture manufacture had begun to question the ability of women to competently manage large-scale interiors work in the public sphere: clubs, restaurants, and office buildings. Now known as "contract interiors," such commissions often required working for business clients who valued efficiency, good management, and, in some cases, a masculine touch.

The Young Men's Christian Association (hereafter referred to as the Y) was such a client. Supported primarily by business leaders, it demanded expertise, economy, and quality as it undertook one of the largest building programs in the United States. This Protestant organization, dedicated since 1851 to developing the mind, body, and spirit of American manhood, viewed its buildings as tools that would attract and positively influence members. Located in the downtown business district, the typical Y housed a parlor, library, gymnasium, classrooms, and other amenities. In the late-nineteenth and early-twentieth centuries the "Y" was responsible for the construction of hundreds of clubhouses across the country and abroad.[3]

By 1915 the scale and complexity of the Y's building program catalyzed the organization of an in-house consultancy, YMCA Building Bureau. Its role was to rationalize the design and construction process for local building committees. From planning, to architect selection, to the preparation of specifications, and construction supervision, the Bureau managed a carefully organized sequence designed to produce an efficient and beautiful building. Soon after the end of World War I, interior decoration was integrated into the process. Influenced by examples from the world of contracting and the furniture trades, the new Furnishings Service modeled interior decoration as a man's

Paula Lupkin ■

profession aligned with architecture, construction, engineering, and accounting. Staffed completely by men, this department undertook interior and furniture design, purchasing, and installation as part of a coordinated process that delivered tasteful "masculine" spaces on time and on budget. The YMCA Furnishings Service pioneered a gendered model of practice that departs from better-known "feminine" and "effeminate" examples, adding nuance to our understanding of gender in the professionalization of interior decoration.[4]

GENDERING INTERIOR DECORATION

American perception of interior decoration as gendered can be traced directly to the rise of industry and consumer culture in the nineteenth century. Once reserved for the wealthy and controlled by male architects and upholsterers, the introduction of mass production placed the decoration of one's home within the reach of the middle classes. By the 1870s the cornucopia of goods available in the new department stores and through mail-order catalogues gave rise to a generation of new consumers, primarily women. The middle class moral geography of separate spheres located women, and women's work, in the domestic realm. Purchasing goods and decorating the parlor and the home in a tasteful, comfortable, uplifting manner was the job of the lady of the house. To some it seemed a natural extension of this role to take on such work for others, evolving from the amateur consumer-decorator to a practiced professional.

One of the earliest and most influential advocates of this position was Candace Wheeler. In 1895 she published an article in *The Decorator and Furnisher*, arguing for interior decoration as a profession for women.[5] A successful textile designer, an advocate for artistic manufactures, and a proponent of education and professions for middle class women, she sought to define the practice of interior work and secure women's place at the helm. As it existed, she argued, the field was fragmented and commercial, divided between paper hanger, painter, cabinetmaker and upholsterer. All sorts of men, including journalists, manufacturers, and merchandisers, vied for the role of expert, competing for the pocketbook and the taste of Americans. She dismissed such "man-decorators," describing them as jumped up "men of trade."[6] She sought a more unified and harmonious process led by an educated, artistic woman who worked in alignment with the architect. She advocated a professional partnership between architecture and interior decoration, with the female decorator responsible for "the thousand and one details of a house after the work of the architect is completed and it stands in effect a finished building."[7] This included everything from painting to lighting fixtures, hardware, to the selection or design of furniture in keeping with the style of the house and function of the room.

In her analysis men were not suited to the role of decorator. In general, they lacked the natural talents of women: good taste, an eye for color, and an appreciation of objects. They also understood, in a way that no man could, the "conveniences of domestic life." She did, however, acknowledge that women often lacked the education and experience to take on a "wider work." For a sphere of work outside the home, and in a professional capacity, they needed broader perspective, the ability to "generalize and not particularize," and to "subordinate things to effects."[8] The answer to this, she felt, was greater opportunities for women in design education, both in the public schools and educational institutions like the Pratt Institute, which admitted women.[9]

For men by men ■

Figure 5.1
William Sloane Coffin, Kautz Family YMCA Archives, University of Minnesota, Minneapolis.

WILLIAM SLOANE COFFIN

At about the same time that Wheeler was promoting women as professional interior decorators, an alternative male model was emerging in New York City, promoted by William Sloane Coffin and the Y. (Figure 5.1) The scion of W. and J. Sloane's, a successful New York furnishings retailer, Coffin was dedicated to improving the quality of artistry of interiors and furnishings. Sloane's got its start as an importer of fine oriental rugs in 1843 and in 1886 expanded, acquiring an upholstery manufacturing and distributing business.[10] The store began to sell furniture, furniture coverings, draperies, fabrics, and decorative objects. In 1891 Sloane's opened an antiques department and in 1904 pioneered one of the first in-house decorating departments to serve its customers. This department not only designed the interiors of private homes; it also worked with commercial "contract" clients like the Waldorf Astoria Hotel, Chase Manhattan Bank, the New York Telephone Company, and multiple railroads and cruise lines.[11]

Moving beyond his own business to a larger cause, Coffin also worked to promote and professionalize the fine and industrial arts in interior design and furnishing. He undertook major efforts to improve the quality and artistry of furniture manufactures and sales across the industry. In 1902 he worked with pioneering educator Frank Alvah Parsons to develop a series of courses to educate those working in the applied arts. Offered through the New York Y's Education Department, these evening courses in line, color, and historic ornament styles were intended to elevate the skills and the artistry of a distinct group: decorators, manufacturers, artists, and salesmen. In 1906, he organized the Arts-in-Trade Club to foster good practices, exchange, and fellowship amongst the same constituency.[12] Through the 1920s it provided education and a context of professionalization for furnishings manufacturers and salesmen, interior decorators, and others in the furnishings trades. It was, in effect, a male design club for the manufacturing community. Membership rolls show that the club was exclusively male, and was housed in a building on 38th Street with a library, display space, and dining and residential services. Beginning in 1919 it sponsored exhibitions by manufacturers, decorators, and department stores. Coffin was committed to demonstrating the increasingly essential role of professional decorators in business and in the public sphere. His activities and ideas about men and furnishings were influential as a male-directed model for professional interior decoration, especially among the leaders of the New York Y.

THE Y AND MANLY INTERIOR DECORATION

The Y was, in its very beginnings, an urban religious organization. In the nineteenth century thousands of young men left their homes on the nation's farms and migrated to the city in search of their fortunes. Freed from the restraint and oversight of their families, many were tempted by the many entertainment options in the city, especially saloons. First English, and then American, business and religious leaders feared for the effect of such activities on their souls, and even more importantly, their work ethic. They rented rooms to create an alternative space and environment that would build, rather than destroy, Christian character.

In the United States, throughout the 1880s and 1890s, the rooms turned into purpose-built structures that grew increasingly elaborate. Across the United States, in big cities and small towns, the Y relied upon its clubhouses to attract members and exert a positive influence. By providing an attractive Christian alternative, they hoped to compete in the marketplace for the free time of young men.[13] They offered an exchange: a warm sociable place where young men could respectably and comfortably enjoy their free time, if they would submit to surveillance and control of their behavior. The goal was to create a comfortable, homelike interior that would promote the proper values in urban young men away from their families. Design thus played an important in the Y's character-building mission; a sort of "environmental evangelism" that preached subtly and continuously.

In the last quarter of the nineteenth century the organization appropriated the domestic moral sphere of women as its model. Envisioned as home substitutes, the Y's social rooms were decorated by ladies' auxiliary organizations with the very limited funds left over from building campaigns. Throughout the 1880s and 1890s Y parlors, especially in smaller cities and towns, were haphazardly furnished with cast-off sofas and chairs, doilies, curtains, and other fripperies. Decorative motifs and objects from the Aesthetic Movement were common. The 1889 parlor in the Milwaukee Y shows a mix of white wicker, an upholstered Victorian chair strewn with an artistically draped shawl, a bamboo fire screen, assorted art pottery, and a lace tablecloth (Figure 5.2).

With the rise of Muscular Christianity and the explosion of commercial entertainments, the feminine ideal of the parlor and the role of women amateurs increasingly came under fire by the early twentieth century.[14] Editorial pieces in the Y's magazine, *Association Men*, called for a strong, vigorous, Christian, manly identity in furnishing and decoration. There was serious concern about the influence of such spaces on young men. In an op-ed titled "Young Men and Prettiness" one critic described the appearance of some Y dormitory rooms with disdain and disgust as "spangled and stuffed with tawdry and trivial prettiness." There were "cosy corners and gay-colored cushions galore, and some rooms reeked with perfume. Everything suggested luxuriousness, fickleness,

For men by men ■

Figure 5.2

Parlor, Milwaukee YMCA, 1890s Kautz Family YMCA Archives, University of Minnesota, Minneapolis.

effeminacy." Not only were these rooms less than manly, they were unchristian, foreign; suggestive of "the disgusting, rotten Turk." Good men were "not bred in such swansdown."[15]

Instead, the Y promoted interiors that projected an appropriate manly image: rooms with hunting trophies, books, noble pictures, and strong furniture. The apartment of Robert McBurney, the director of the New York Y, offered an important model. (Figure 5.3) He decorated his personal quarters atop the 23rd Street clubhouse with a cultured, Christian, and masculine flavor: Piranesi prints of Roman monuments, a large cross, horned sheep heads, native American relics, walls of bookcases, and eighteenth century English chairs. Such surroundings aligned with the ideals of virtue, clean minds, and hardened bodies advocated by President Theodore Roosevelt in *The Strenuous Life* and reformist pastor Charles Wagner in *The Simple Life*.[16]

By 1905, the amateur feminine phase in Y interiors was replaced with what were termed "efficient" interiors. Plans no longer included parlors. Y interiors decorated in this period rejected the fussy doilies of the Victorian parlor and the Orientalism of the Aesthetic Movement in favor of the simple honesty of Arts and Crafts design. Y leaders embraced Craftsman-style furniture for its simple lines and exposed joints, but placed it sparingly in their public rooms. White walls, dark woodwork, and improving religious prints decorated the walls. Few wall hangings, pillows, or other decorative

73

Figure 5.3
Robert McBurney's room, 23rd Street New York YMCA, c. 1895 Kautz Family YMCA Archives, University of Minnesota, Minneapolis

items softened the rooms. This was not a space for lounging, for relaxation or enjoyment, but an upright space, both literally and metaphorically. (Figure 5.4) This message was conveyed in part by the furnishings but also by posted signs that spelled out prohibitions like, "No Profanity," "Please Take Off Your Hat," "Don't Spit on the Floor," and "Have You Written to Mother?"

This shift in style was not only a material manifestation of Muscular Christianity, it was also a reflection of the influence that the emerging discipline of scientific management had on the Y at this time. Pioneered by Frederick Winslow Taylor, this business model employed the analysis of processes and practices to ensure economic efficiency and labor productivity. Y leaders and supporters in the business community began to view the organization through this management lens.[17] Rather than describing their buildings as Christian clubhouses, the adopted the term "manhood factories," first coined by President Roosevelt, was used.[18] In plan and style, they were meant to mass produce young men of good character.

As a result, the typical Y building of the prewar period had a stripped exterior and aseptic interior, designed to grind out young men of character mechanically. Between 1900 and 1915 a few specialist architecture firms methodically produced and reproduced dozens of buildings on the same plan, and with nearly identical exteriors. Their design process was scientific and efficient, but lacked

For men by men ■

Figure 5.4
Parlor, Milwaukee YMCA, 1915 Kautz Family YMCA Archives, University of Minnesota, Minneapolis.

artistic quality. One observer noted that the organization's social rooms were, as a rule, sparsely furnished, dark, scuffed, and poorly kept. Its parlors were worn and unwelcoming. They lacked in atmosphere and appeal. As one report suggested, "most of our Association buildings have the appearance of efficient machines but many lack that air of hospitality and good-fellowship which characterizes many clubs, the modern hotels, and most homes."[19] A less charitable observer noted that many of them looked as though you could turn a hose on them.[20]

Such negative comments about the efficient "manhood factories" were, in part, a response to the horrors of mechanical warfare during World War I. Y leaders were serving on the front lines in France and Belgium, where hundreds of prefabricated huts were constructed as a precursor to the USO. The Y's War Work program catalyzed new thinking about the organization's role and methods and its buildings. One Y leader commented that, "In view of the collapse of civilization in some portions of the world which had come to be highly regarded because of their so-called . . . efficiency standards, we are compelled to seek a different objective in manhood building."[21]

Figure 5.5
Furnishings advertisements from *Association Men*, 1910 Kautz Family YMCA Archives, University of Minnesota, Minneapolis.

In addition to the aesthetic and conceptual problems with the manhood factory model, there were practical concerns about the building process that produced them. The national scale of the building program, budgetary constraints, and the unreliable and fluid state of the design and building trades, had proven to be a complex problem for Y leaders. Expertise and information came from a variety of sources: the specialist architects, manufacturers, journal articles, and word of mouth. Local building committees frequently complained about the ethics and shady business practices of architects and furniture suppliers. One firm, Shattuck and Hussey, was accused of accepting kickbacks from favored companies. Y leaders were also dubious about the motives of furniture sales reps, who offered decorating advice. (Figure 5.5) Too often they lacked expertise they claimed and cared only about selling their products.[22] Inexperienced and dishonest architects, poor planning and construction, cost overruns, and problems with maintenance plagued the organization.

MODELING PROFESSIONALISM

In response, the Y's National Council in New York developed the Building Bureau (later known as the Architectural Bureau), a multifaceted, integrated professional practice combining architecture, planning, and interior decoration, engineering, finance, and purchasing.[23] To develop this service, the National Council hired Neil McMillan as the first director. He received his architectural degree from the University of Illinois in 1904, and worked for four years as a draftsman and superintendent of construction for the architect of the Chicago Board of Education, where he learned a great deal about bureaucratic organization. He had also worked for the Y's International Bureau, purchasing supplies used to build buildings overseas in China. It was his job to shape a unified process that would collect information, harness the experts, and take guiding control of what the organization's anticipated would be a massive building postwar building effort. McMillan spent most of the war collecting information and doing research.

Confronting an increasingly complex and contending set of forces invested both professionally and commercially in building design, he carved out a new form of practice that fused art and business to rationalize and aestheticize the process. Taking in hand the diverse parties, priorities, and processes involved, he broke them down into parts and created work flow diagrams, standard detail drawings, and space planning protocols. McMillan's plan was undoubtedly influenced by the field of scientific management, but seems to have been more specifically aligned with the innovative organizational structure pioneered by a New York-based contracting company: Hoggson Brothers.

HOGGSON BROTHERS

Founded in 1907 and led by brothers with experience in architecture and business management, Hoggson Brothers was a pioneer in general contracting.[24] Known nationally for its work constructing banks, office buildings, industrial plants, public libraries, clubhouses, and custom homes, the firm pioneered the "Single Contract Method." The Hoggsons intended to put the "erection of a building, with its accompanying design and drawings," on a business basis.[25] Comparing the existing state of the building process to the Tower of Babel, its vice president, Noble Hoggson highlighted that "the confusion of ideas, the lack of sympathetic interest and mutual understanding, and the division of responsibility work disaster."[26] With their arrangement, they claimed, the "disastrous results of divided responsibility" would be avoided. All of the varied activities necessary to produce a building, from publicity to design to contracting and supervision, were coordinated and managed under a single agreement with a guaranteed final price.[27]

This reliable outcome, the company claimed, was ensured by business-like organization of distributing, accounting, and executive divisions, each headed by an experienced expert.[28] (Figure 5.6) Hoggson Brothers' scheme is especially notable in its integration of what were then two separate fields, architecture and interiors, under the rubric of "designing." In sequence, decoration occurs when construction is complete, part of a coordinated plan. As the company's brochure suggests

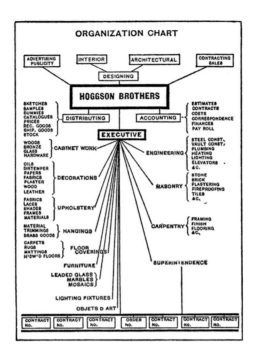

Figure 5.6

Organization Chart, Hoggson Brothers, 1910. From *The Hoggson Building Method* (New York: Hoggson Brothers, 1910).

the color schemes, decorations, hangings, floor coverings and furniture are all studied out and taken up with you before the time arrives to carry them out . . . Each subject is presented to you intelligently and in the proper order, thus giving you a connected mental picture of the work as a whole.[29]

In their scheme design was transformed into a unified and logical process.

The Y Building Bureau followed in Hoggson's footsteps by providing a business-oriented model of coordination and supervision that offered expertise and managed cost. Echoing the Hoggsons, it referred to its building process as "a modern tower of Babel because of its magnitude and its confusion of tongues and ideas: a tower that was in danger of toppling."[30] Conceptually the Bureau emulated the Hoggson Brothers, rationalizing the creative aspects of building and integrating them fully with careful planning, supervision, and financial oversight. Instead of a flow chart of divisions, however, the Y diagramed the building process with a list that focused on each step along the way, indicating the division of responsibility between independent professionals and the in-house experts of the Bureau on the left and right margins with a series of notations. (Figure 5.7) The scheme maintained a certain autonomy for the independent architect, who was responsible for design tasks like sketches, working drawings and details as well as construction superintendence. The majority of interior decoration tasks, however, including furnishing and purchasing, were identified as the province of the Bureau's in-house staff.[31] The YMCA determined that interior decoration, still not professionalized, was in need of closer supervision. McMillan integrated it with administrative tasks like site selection, programming, space budgets and plans, specification writing, architect selection, contract negotiation, bidding and financial statements, construction supervision, and oversight

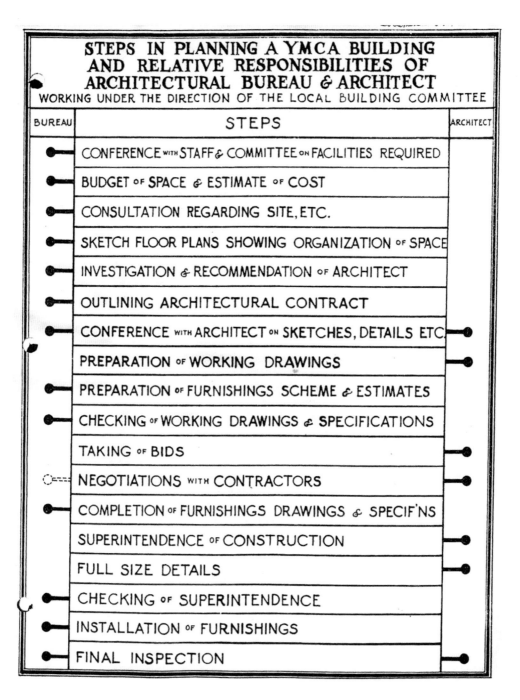

Figure 5.7

Steps in Achieving a YMCA Building, 1925 Kautz Family YMCA Archives.

of plan documents. Integrated amongst these practical matters were what we would think of as "design" tasks like making sketches to show the organization of space, the selection of materials and details, and the preparation of working drawings and details.

In the work-flow diagram of the Bureau, the preparation of a furnishings scheme and estimates is aligned, chronologically, with the preparation of working drawings for the building. The completion of furnishing drawings and specifications falls in between negotiations with contractors and the superintendence of construction. Just before the final inspection of the building by the Bureau, a spot is reserved for the installation of furnishings. Under this system, furnishing and decorating become part of a modern, efficient building process superintended by an integrated team of professionals.

Ironically, as Candace Wheeler proposed, under the Bureau's direction the in-house interior decorator worked with the architect to produce coordinated and harmonious building interiors consistent with Y policy and the architectural scheme of the building. The Bureau, if asked, could make complete room layouts, design furniture, create color schemes, and make selections for upholstery, curtains, lighting, carpets, and all wall treatments. For an additional 4 percent of the cost specialists of the Bureau would also manage the selection of other types of furnishings such as beds, kitchen equipment, bowling alleys, gymnasium apparatus; even janitorial supplies and tools. The Bureau had relationships with manufacturers and jobbers that meant substantial volume discounts. This would include the bidding process, record-keeping, delivery, and installation. Selecting a reputable company with quality products, contracting for the goods, and ensuring they arrived as ordered, when promised, and functioned well required business skills and time that local building committees often did not have. The Building Bureau was a one-stop shop that could take care of the entire process, transforming the Y from spare simplicity to a comfortable, attractive masculinity – at the right price.

STAFFING THE FURNISHINGS SERVICE

Neil McMillan staffed the Building Bureau to complement his own training in bureaucratic architecture with expertise in purchasing, engineering and mechanical system, building management, and business administration. His first hire was R.L. Rayburn, chosen for his experience in purchasing and building management at Ys in Kansas City, Chicago, and Cincinnati. In 1920 Sherman W. Dean, who had helped to supervise real estate development, building projects, and decoration for the Chicago Y came on board, as did Cleveland-based construction engineer Albert M. Allen. The Building Bureau was distinctly masculine. Its employees were men with professional training, technical experience, and in several cases, long service to local Ys. When it came time to hire the director of the Furnishings Service, McMillan wanted similar expertise, experience, and reliability. He needed a team player who was trustworthy and would understand the importance of efficiency and economy in large-scale business of decorating Ys across the country. At the same time the person needed to know how to combine "nice proportion, grace of line, harmony of color, and beauty of texture" to "create that subtle atmosphere that pleases without one's knowing exactly why."[32]

This combination of artistic and business skills raised a key question about gender and decoration. For some in the Y movement women were best suited to the job. McMillan's 1920 proposal notes that "the demand seemed to be to secure those homelike effects which can best be secured thru [sic] the cooperation of a woman."[33] Was a woman, as Candace Wheeler suggested, suited to

For men by men ■

a role as a professional interior decorator? He investigated and found that a woman of "business capacity, artistic ability, and technical experience" was in fact available, perhaps someone like Nancy McClelland, who worked as an interior decorator for Wanamaker's Department Store.[34] Despite her experience, his report expressed concerned about placing this unnamed woman at the head of the Furnishings Service. He closed with a pointed question: Did the job require a man's oversight, particularly in regard to purchasing and management? In doing so he revealed not only his own concerns, but an important outside influence as well.

Although not explicitly mentioned, the perspective provided by William Sloane Coffin was undoubtedly on McMillan's mind as he organized the Furnishings Service. Coffin believed in the Y's mission and had supported it for years, both as a generous donor and active volunteer. He also actively promoted decoration as a career for young men in the Y evening course he organized for young men in 1902 and in his sponsorship of the male-dominated Art-in-Trades Club. To Coffin, the Y was an important part of the growing market for contract interiors. After World War I there was an increasing demand from manufacturers, furniture dealers, and owners of department stores, hotels, and clubs for decorating expertise.[35] Such clients needed a more methodical, commercial, and masculine process, instead of the feminine, personal, intuitive domestic practices of the lady decorators. His model was W & J Sloane's pioneering in-house decorating department, led by Wilson Hungate as manager. Hungate has made his start as a furnishings dealer and eventually became one of the most respected decorators in the country, featured in *Arts and Decoration* as one of eight male decorators "who express our taste." Coffin undoubtedly had a hand in the creation of the Furnishings Service, and it was his view about gender and decorating that ultimately prevailed. Despite the fact that a capable woman was available, Neil McMillan chose a man.

ENTER LAMONT WARNER

To head the Furnishings Service McMillan selected LaMont A. Warner.[36] (Figure 5.8) Warner fit well with the Y in two ways: his religious background and his significant experience in both art and business. As the former Fine Arts Director for the Board of Foreign Missions of the Methodist Episcopal Church, he had already provided art and design consultation to an evangelical Protestant organization. He understood their mission, their goals, and the role of art and design in attracting members to religious life. His educational credentials were also excellent. Warner held a degree from Pratt Institute, where he had studied fine arts with a major in design under Arthur Wesley Dow and Alvan C. Nye, a furniture designer. He burnished this education with travel in Europe and work for several furniture manufacturers, most importantly Thonet and Gustav Stickley. Warner is credited with many of the Craftsmen's most famous chair and table designs.[37] With these employers Warner learned the business side of interior decoration and furniture manufacture and built connections that would serve him well as he secured contracts for the Y.

After gaining business credentials in the furniture manufacture business, Warner attained further professional status through affiliation as a faculty member at Teachers College at Columbia University. There he likely had contact with John Dewey, whose educational philosophy was popular among Y leaders. His responsibilities included courses in Design, Interior Decoration, and Color Harmony. During his tenure there he also wrote and illustrated a textbook, *Design in Line Notan Color*, intended specifically "for students and teachers of household arts, fine arts, house decoration."[38] The drawings included elevations and perspectives based on the collections of the Metropolitan

81 □

Figure 5.8
LaMont A. Warner, Winterthur Library.

Museum of Art. This work creating accurate reproductions aligned him with Coffin, whose Company of Master Craftsman mass-produced replicas of Duncan Phyfe furniture and other museum pieces for those who could not afford antiques. Both men sought to improve the public's taste, the quality of mass-produced furnishings, and the knowledge and skills of decorators.

Warner was well-connected and well-educated, a good Christian, artistic, and well-versed in the business component of design. Most importantly, he was a man who would fit well into the existing office culture and structure of the Building Bureau. McMillan knew this because he had worked with him on several decorating projects for Y buildings in Bayonne, New Jersey, in Oakland, California, and in Lake Geneva, Wisconsin. In 1921 this arrangement was formalized and Warner began work organizing the Furnishings Service at the Y Building Bureau in Manhattan.

FURNISHINGS SERVICE

By 1922 Warner, along with Sherman Dean and R.L. Rayburn, developed a multi-step process to coordinate decoration with architecture, purchasing, and installation. Working from the floorplans provided by the architects at the Building Bureau, they determine the amount and type of furniture needed for each room. After approval from the building committee, they would make a site visit or study detail drawings to create a harmonious scheme for all elements of the interior and determine furniture designs. Warner created paintings to convey the atmosphere of the ensemble. Next, materials samples and sketches for upholstery, hangings, carpets, curtains, lighting fixtures and wall treatments would be submitted. When all had been agreed upon, the Furnishings Service submitted specifications. For an additional fee, the Furnishings Service would handle the ordering, maintain records, and supervise proper installation.[39]

In addition to painting and designing, Warner also set up his own furniture design enterprise within the Building Bureau, hiring in-house furniture designers like Isaac Sanger, who trained with him at Columbia's Teacher's College. Together they made full-size working drawings, sketches, and blueprints to their own specifications, which were put out to bid to numerous mass-production period furniture companies, including Warner's former employer, Thonet, and W & J Sloane's own subsidiary, Oneidacraft. This ensured the quality and functionality that the Y required and also saved money through volume discounts and the elimination of dealers.

The impact of the Furnishings Service could be seen in the consistent design of YMCA interiors of the 1920s. Within ten years, the design of new YMCA buildings, especially their interiors and furnishings, was fundamentally transformed with "harmonious colors, furniture distinct in line and form, improved design and placement of lighting fixtures."[40] Departing from the heroic and progressive Arts and Crafts interiors that he designed for Gustav Stickley, Warner embraced what many manufacturers and decorators did in the postwar period: Early English and Spanish revival period styles.

After promoting the revival of reproduction eighteenth century English styles through the Company of Master Craftsmen, in the middle 1920s W & J Sloane and many other department stores, furniture manufacturers, lifestyle journals, and decorators embraced "the Spanish Motif" and the "Elizabethan Motif."[41] (Figure 5.9) First introduced in London in the years before World War I, the trend towards what became known as the "International Renaissance" took off in the United States around 1922, mixing various seventeenth century motifs: oak furniture with chip carving, gate-leg

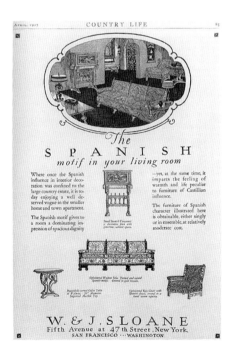

Figure 5.9
"The Spanish Motif in Your Living Room" W & J Sloane advertisement, *Country Life*, April 1922, Winterthur Library.

tables, leather upholstery fastened with copper headed nails, tapestries, hammered metal sconces, carved and painted timber-beamed ceilings, tile floors and stucco walls. Articles introduced the style in decoration and arts magazines, and it grew popular in country houses, executive offices, and public spaces including major hotels and clubs.[42]

Warner's design scrapbook was filled with articles and brochures that chronicled his enthusiasm for the International Renaissance.[43] In keeping with the Arts and Crafts tradition that the Y had previous embraced, the new English/Spanish motif offered a "rugged strength and simplicity, a delightful and winning naivete, and a quaintness which refreshes the modern taste." It also provided a "quiet richness, restraint, and reticence" in keeping with the Y mission.[44] Warner and the Furnishings Service worked with Sloane's and other to produce and use pieces that would fill Y rooms. (Figure 5.10) At the New York West Side Y on 63rd Street these pieces were used to create a harmonious, artistic effect that swept the Y building program nationwide. (Figure 5.11) Across the country, from San Pedro California, to New York to Harrisburg, Pennsylvania to Little Rock, Arkansas, the lobbies and public rooms of the YMCA were furnished in an eclectic and fashionable period revival style that fused Spanish and English Renaissance motifs. The choice of this style, like the Craftsman style, was masculine and rustic, yet refined. Not "expensive brocades and taffetas and luxurious silks and satins" instead, a "study of proportions and lines that

Figure 5.10
Building Bureau table design, c. 1927 Kautz Family YMCA Archives, University of Minnesota, Minneapolis.

Figure 5.11
West Side YMCA, New York, 1927, Kautz Family YMCA Archives, University of Minnesota, Minneapolis.

are vigorous but beautiful, and the use of colors that suggest harmony in their subtleties and intensities."[45] As one observer noted, the social spaces in these new buildings have gotten away from the influence of the old dingy hotel lobby with its unbreakable, unscratchable furniture and impersonal atmosphere. Now they were intimate living rooms. "The new furniture . . . has color and variety and its arrangement tends to acquantainceship."[46] The similarities of buildings designed by the Furnishings Bureau were so striking that it is hard to tell the buildings apart. It seems certain that the same craftsmen and designs were used from building to building, from New York to California.

Warner worked for the Bureau from 1921 to 1925, and established the artistic pedigree that would characterize Y buildings before the Depression. He also firmly anchored the Y amidst a particular sphere of furniture manufacture, period reproduction, revival style, and professional decoration that was distinctly masculine, both in personnel and in organization.

CONCLUSION

The definition of the profession of interior decoration, its context and values, its processes and practices, was and still is intimately tied up with gender issues. The Y was a leader in the development of modern interior design practice, and its story offers us an important missing piece of its early history. Most work has been done on residential practice. Less well integrated into the narrative of the field's professional history are the early business structures that provided work and identity for designers outside of the residential sphere. The story of the Y's Buildings Bureau and Furnishings Service is an early chapter in the history of interior decoration and interior design. This decidedly masculine design firm developed a complex, carefully articulated series of interrelated processes and services for a fee, organizing the amorphous, complex and costly and interrelated jobs needed to produce buildings and their interiors.

NOTES

1 See Burton Bledstein, *The Culture of Professionalism: The Middle Class and the Development of Higher Education in America* (New York: W.W. Norton, 1976) and Grace Lees-Maffei's guest-edited issue "Professionalizing Interior Design, 1870–1970," especially her "Introduction: Professionalization as a Focus in Interior Design History," *Journal of Design History* 21, no. 1 (Spring 2008): 1–18.

2 For a discussion of gender issues and identity in interior decoration see Penny Sparke "Elsie de Wolfe: A Professional Interior Decorator" and John Potvin "Designing the Gender Contest: (Re)Locating the Gay Decorator in the History of Interior Design" in this volume.

3 Paula Lupkin, *Manhood Factories: YMCA Architecture and the Making of Modern Urban Culture* (Minneapolis: University of Minnesota Press, 2010).

4 See John Potvin's essay, "Designing the Gender Contest," in this volume.

5 Candace Wheeler, "Interior Decoration as a Profession for Women," *The Decorator and Furnisher* 26 (June 1895): 87–89.

6 *Op.cit.*, 88.

7 Ibid.

8 Ibid.

9 On the early history of interior decoration education see Mary Anne Beecher, "Interiors: Between Art and Practicality," in Joan Ockman, ed. *Architecture School: Three Centuries of Educating Architects in North America* (Cambridge, MA: MIT Press, 2012), 347–350.

10 W. and J. Sloane, *The Story of Sloane's* (New York, W. and J. Sloane, 1950), 21–30.

11 *Op.cit.*, 30.

12 See Patricia Edmonson, "The Art in Trades Club: Selling Style," in this volume for a discussion of the overlap of the New York YMCA and Art-in-Trades Club.

13 Lupkin, 12–13.

14 Clifford Putney, *Muscular Christianity: Manhood and Sports in Protestant America, 1880–1920* (Cambridge, MA: Harvard University Press, 2001), Brooks McNamara, *The New York Concert Saloon: The Devil's Own Nights* (New York: Cambridge University Press, 2002); Lewis A. Erenberg, *Steppin' Out: New York Nightlife and the Transformation of American Culture, 1890–1930* (Chicago: University of Chicago Press, 1981) Gregory A. Waller, *Main Street Amusements: Movies and Commercial Entertainment in a Southern City, 1896–1930* (Washington, DC: Smithsonian University Press, 1995); David Nasaw, *Going Out: The Rise and Fall of Public Amusements* (New York: Basic Books, 1993).

15 "Young Men and Prettiness," *Association Men* (December 1904): 125.

16 Theodore Roosevelt, *The Strenuous Life* (New York: The Century Co. 1904), Charles Wagner, *The Simple Life* (New York: McClure and Company, 1904).

17 "The Business of Developing Men and Boys to Higher Efficiency," *Association Men* 34 (January 1909): 155; C. M. Wonacott, "Scientific Association Management," *Association Men* 37 (May 1912): 398–399; Charles R. Towson, "Engineers of Environment: A New Evangelism in the Industrial World," *Association Men* 34 (September 1909): 580–581.

18 William McKinley and Theodore Roosevelt, "The Association: A National Defense" and "For More Manhood Factories," *Association Men* 34 (February 1909): 234–236.

For men by men ■

19 "Statement Regarding a Proposed Extension of the Service of the Building Bureau of the International Committee," 22 October 1920. Buildings and Furnishings Services/Property Management Records, Administrative Records, Kautz Family YMCA Archives, University of Minnesota Libraries, Minneapolis.

20 Quoted by Neil McMillan in "Buildings That Express Ideals," *Association Men* 48 (May 1923): 232.

21 George B. Hodge, "Efficiency at Too High a Price," *Association Men* 41 (July 1916): 560–561.

22 Lupkin, 148.

23 Charles C. May, "A Post-War Construction Program: The Building Bureau of the International Committee of the Y.M.C.A.," *Architectural Record* 45 (March and April 1919): 216–241, 325–342.

24 *The Hoggson Building Method: Described and Illustrated for Those Who Contemplate Building, Remodeling, Decorating or Furnishing* (New York: Hoggson Brothers, 1910); "Economy and Efficiency in Building," *Literary Digest* (31 May 1913): 1245; Alfred Willis, "Design-Build and Building Efficiency in the Early Twentieth Century United States," *Proceedings of the First International Congress on Construction History*, Madrid, 20–24 January 2003. Ed. S. Huerta Madrid, S. Juan de Herrera, SEdHC, ETSAM, A.E. Benevuto, COAM, F. Dragados, 2003, pp. 2121–2124; Abigail Van Slyck, *Free to All: Carnegie Libraries and American Culture, 1890–1920* (Chicago: University of Chicago Press, 1995), 58; Jeffrey W. Cody, "Erecting Monuments to the God of Business and Trade: The Fuller Construction Company of the Orient," *Construction History* 12 (1996): 76.

25 Frederick Winslow Taylor, *Scientific Management*, 1911; "Story of a Unique Organization," *Coast Banker* 16 no. 3 (March 1916): 285.

26 "The Tower of Babel and Modern Bank Construction," *Trust Companies* 22, no. 2 (February 1916): 162.

27 *The Hoggson Building Method: For Those Who Contemplate Building, Remodeling, Decorating, or Furnishing*, (New York: Hoggson Brothers, 1910), 7.

28 *The Hoggson Building Method*, 35.

29 *The Hoggson Building Method*, 18.

30 Sherman Dean, "Putting Character into Buildings," *Association Men* 53 (January 1928): 215.

31 A copy of "The Hoggson Building Method," published in *Architectural Record*, is in the papers of LaMont Warner, the early director of the Furnishings Service. Lamont Adelbert Warner Collection, Col. 647, Winterthur Library.

32 "Outline of the Furnishings Service," The Building Bureau of the International Committee of the Young Men's Christian Associations, 15 April 1921, box 1, Buildings and Furnishings Materials, Administrative Records, Kautz Family YMCA Archives, University of Minnesota Libraries, Minneapolis.

33 "Story of a Unique Organization," *Coast Banker* 16 (January 1916): 285.

34 Bridget May, "Nancy Vincent McClelland (1877–1959): Professionalizing Interior Decoration in the Early Twentieth Century," *Journal of Design History* 21, no. 1 (Spring 2008): 59–74.

35 "Outline of the Furnishings Service" The Building Bureau of the International Committee of the Young Men's Christian Associations, 15 April 1922, box 1, Buildings and Furnishings Materials, Administrative Records, Kautz Family YMCA Archives, University of Minnesota Libraries, Minneapolis.

36 LaMont Adelbert Warner Collection, Col. 647, The Winterthur Library.

37 Kevin Tucker, "LaMont Warner," in *Gustav Stickley and the American Arts and Crafts Movement* (New Haven: Yale University Press for the Dallas Museum of Art, 2010).

38 LaMont Warner, *Design in Line, Notan, Color* (New York: Macmillan, 1918).

39 "Outline of the Furnishings Service" The Building Bureau of the International Committee of the Young Men's Christian Associations, 15 April 1922, box 1, Buildings and Furnishings Materials, Administrative Records, Kautz Family YMCA Archives, University of Minnesota Libraries, Minneapolis.

40 "Some Gains to the Association Movement From the Service of the Architectural Bureau" 8 September 1927, 2. Buildings and Furnishings Materials, Administrative Records, Kautz Family YMCA Archives, University of Minnesota Libraries, Minneapolis.

41 "The Spanish Motif in Your Living Room," W. and J. Sloane advertisement, *Country Life* 51 (April 1927): 85; "The Elizabethan Motif in your Dining Room," W. and J. Sloane advertisement, *Country Life* 51

(March 1927): 81; "Old English Decorations & Furniture," W. & J. Sloane advertisement, *The House Beautiful* 44 (November 1917): 334.

42 One example is the main lounge in the newly redecorated Elks Club, Newark, NJ, *The Decorative Furnisher* 58, no. 6 (September 1925): 90.

43 LaMont Adelebert Warner Collection, Winterthur Library. The contents of Warner's papers and scrapbook includes: *Replicas of Old English Furniture* (London: Story and Triggs Ltd., 1912); Robert L. Ames, "Planning and Furnishing in the Early Spanish Style," *The House Beautiful* 53, no. 1 (January 1923): 17–20; William Laurel Harris, "Spanish Furniture: What We Really Know About It," *Good Furniture Magazine* 12 (April 1919): 24–29.

44 Ames, 19.

45 Sherman Dean, "Putting Character Into Buildings," *Association Men* 48 (January 1928): 236.

46 Neil McMillan, Jr. "Are We Getting Better Buildings?" *Association Men* 50 (January 1926): 228.

Chapter 6: The Art-in-Trades Club

Selling style

Patricia Edmonson

"We are a great industrial nation, but have no industrial art."[1] With this sentiment, decorator William Laurel Harris highlighted early twentieth-century America's search for a design identity that led to the formation of professional associations like the Art-in-Trades Club of New York. Working in the nation's design capital during a time of growth in options for design education, design educator Frank Alvah Parsons and furniture manufacturer William Sloane Coffin set out to empower and connect members of the furnishings trades by founding this organization in 1906.[2] They felt that designers needed a support network and that the identities of manufacturing and retail employees – who wanted to be seen not only as businessmen, but as decorating experts – were especially in crisis. Their roles fell into a liminal state between the production of fine art and commercial art, and many struggled to define and value their work in the trade.[3] By the 1920s, some American designers felt especially lost in the face of changes spurred by European Modernism and the lack of US representation at the 1925 Parisian Exposition. With this in mind, Parsons and Coffin believed that designers could create better products, manufacturers could produce these designs without fear of commercial failure, and that decorators and salesmen could help improve and expand public taste. By bringing together men from all areas of the field they hoped to "harmonize commercial activity with the growing art tendencies of the present time," in other words to find success in times of great stylistic change.[4] To achieve these lofty goals, the Art-in-Trades Club created a wide professional network, educational opportunities, and, by 1924, exhibitions of Club members' work, all of which helped them navigate the defining of an American style. With so many major players in the early 1920s design trade investing in its membership, the Art-in-Trades Club both represented and shaped the field at large and how they sought to legitimize their work. This chapter will explore the ways in which the Club armed designers, interior decorators, and businessmen with tools to convince a buying public to trust the trade's knowledge and authority.

Club co-founder William Sloane Coffin was well positioned to assist the trade. He directed his family business, the retail giant W. & J. Sloane, founding a subsidiary called the Company of Master Craftsmen, which manufactured colonial revival furniture.[5] As a board member, Coffin worked closely with staff at the Metropolitan Museum of Art, supporting education for design students and members of the trade through the development of the museum's department of industrial relations.[6] In 1902, he invited Frank Alvah Parsons to lecture on color, form, historic ornament, and period decoration at the YMCA with the intent to educate both designers and salesmen.[7] Parsons was a leader in the establishment of formal design education, introducing new coursework to the New York School of Art (now the Parsons School of Design) in 1904.[8] He grounded his methodology with the historical periods, arguing that they were an integral part of the language of design.[9] High attendance of these YMCA lectures encouraged Parsons and Coffin to form the Art-in-Trades Club in 1906.[10]

By the nineteen-teens the Club was an established organization in the public eye. In 1914, the *New York Times* published an excerpt from their mission statement:

> To bring into association men engaged in or interested in the Arts and Art Trades for mutual advancement and study; to study the principles of art as applied to trades connected with the decoration and furnishing of buildings; to harmonize commercial activity with the growing art tendencies of the present time; to foster feeling and taste for art expression in general; and to strengthen the natural bond between those thus allied by fellowship and a community of interests.[11]

Most of these allies were either influential men in the museum and design fields or employed by well-known retail and manufacturing firms, and their names appear in design publications consistently during the nineteen-teens and twenties.[12] The Club's roster is significant, and in this context list-worthy, because it demonstrates that prominent figures in the field saw the value of membership, and seized the opportunity to create this professional community. Designers and decorators – for example, Paul Frankl, Jules Bouy, Walter Kantack, Kneeland Green, Louis Rorimer, and Harry Pray Worster of Tiffany Studios – all belonged to the Club. Educators and administrators from New York University, Pratt Institute, Columbia University, and the Metropolitan Museum of Art also joined the Club. The largest group of members worked in manufacturing and retail, including Roger Brunschwig, T. Atkins Tout, Sidney Blumenthal, Frederick Carder, Harry Brown of Lenox, Michael Friedsam of B. Altman, and Donald Porteus of Macy's, as well as those responsible for disseminating trade knowledge such as James P. Rome and Thomas A. Cawthra of *Good Furniture* and *The Decorative Furnisher*, and Leonard Barron, editor of *The Garden Magazine*. The organization's roots at the YMCA first created an all-male membership, but the founders may also have believed that, despite the number of successful female decorators, men were more suited for the business of design.

Club members provided their colleagues with expert information and behind-the-scenes access. The Metropolitan Museum of Art's head of Industrial Relations, Richard F. Bach, allowed the Club to use collections during decorative arts talks.[13] The museum's *Bulletin* touted that only experts hosted these museum lectures and demonstrations on topics such as "Historic Ornament in Textiles" by historian George Leland Hunter and "The Historic Styles" by architect and author C. Howard Walker.[14] Decorative arts curator Wilhelm Rudolph Valentiner hosted Saturday evening meetings at the museum, offering a rare opportunity for men who were usually busy designing and selling industrial arts during working hours.[15] Upon visiting, Club members could use equipment, facilities, a full library, and the collection, for study. Industrial designers had long been using museums as educational and design resources, and the Club exposed their members to the opportunities available at the Metropolitan and other museums.[16]

Members of the Art-in-Trades Club believed in the intellectual and artistic importance of museums, which was tied to their commercial value. In 1919 and 1920, Richard F. Bach wrote about the Metropolitan's industrial arts exhibitions, arguing that museum collections were commercially useful.[17] He described a museum employee charged with visiting shops and workrooms in order to

The Art-in-Trades Club ■

help manufacturers best use the museum to their advantage. In order to soften any negative connotations of the word "commercial," he argued that the museum's department of industrial arts was in a "definitely acceptable phase of its educational service to the public."[18] Equating industrial objects with museum-quality art, Bach believed that recent exhibitions had demonstrated a high level of quality from American designers.[19] The museum approved of manufacturers "cashing in on the museum's influence" to establish artistic credibility when they authorized W. & J. Sloane to copy nineteenth-century Duncan Phyfe furniture for a new line which Sloane's "exhibited," using the museum's name.[20] In this case, the company and the museum advertised for one another – the fellowship between Club members like Bach and William Sloane Coffin was mutually beneficial. Singling out the Club for their ability to wed art and industry, a 1921 editorial in *Good Furniture* stated:

> America's house furnishing activities must be built upon a perfect coordination of her artistic and industrial forces. . . . The Art in Trades Club is unique in being the only considerable group of men in trade who have been drawn together by an admiration for beauty and who have desired an increasing knowledge of art as a necessary part of their business education. Their enthusiasm for fine things has been strengthened because this knowledge of art has been used profitably in their everyday occupations as businessmen.[21]

Lectures and discussion continued outside the museum, on field trips, and at weekly round table meetings, which began in 1916.[22] At these meetings, leading figures across the field offered advice and mentorship. Representatives of furnishing companies, antiques dealers, retailers, and homeowners opened their doors for behind-the-scenes tours highlighting industry concerns. Club events took place at manufacturing establishments, such as the cabinetmaking demonstration and lecture held at the Schmieg and Company furniture factory.[23] On other occasions members visited showrooms, such as Charles of London's, where they discussed an exhibition of antiques and furniture.[24] In addition to studying the production and display of objects, access to interiors played a large role in their activities. Groups visited hotels, such as the Plaza in New York City, and private homes, such as Louis Comfort Tiffany's Laurelton Hall, in order to increase awareness about what was considered *good design*.[25] During these visits, Club members could learn firsthand about materials, techniques, shop display, the history of design, and contemporary decoration.

The Art-in-Trades Club hoped to marry artistic and commercial aspects of the trade by connecting men from different fields. They armed salesmen with the historical periods, and decorators with the details of textile production, but the trade was also connected with design history through publications. Publishing connections and a collective academic prowess allowed the Club to disseminate knowledge and strengthen the relationship between these two areas of the field. Club members, Chandler Robbins Clifford and George Leland Hunter, in particular, authored texts about historical furnishings and contemporary interior decoration that served as references for their peers. Both authors partnered with contemporary manufacturers in order to supplement the available images of historical furnishings. F. Schumacher & Co.'s reproduction textiles illustrate Hunter's 1918 *Decorative Textiles* and Clifford included historically-inspired modern furniture in his "Colonial Styles" chapter in *Period Furnishings: An Encyclopedia of Ornament*.[26] The use of modern reproductions demonstrates a relationship between the trade and academia that existed during the period, often facilitated by the Club. Historians and manufacturers were useful to one another, and were often, unabashedly, one and the same. During the early 1920s, historians, museums, and manufacturers were important resources for one another, and the Art-in-Trades Club helped connect this community.

Beginning in 1922, the Art-in-Trades Club's annual exhibitions offered members further avenues for collaboration, visibility, and subtle methods for connecting with their buyers.[27] On 23 September, the Art-in-Trades Club opened their first exhibition of decoration on the rooftop of the Waldorf Astoria Hotel. The show lasted one month, and admission was 50 cents.[28] Comprised primarily of pasteboard room settings, the show also included single objects, craft displays such as a weaving workshop, and an exhibit of historical textiles.[29] A jury vetted Club members' room designs and chose 36 for display. The Club published an exhibition catalogue (called a yearbook) for trade members and the public alike, with images of the rooms, notable work in the field, a list of club members, and advertisements.[30] The yearbook explained that the Club attempted to respond to the public's need for comfort, personality, and information about interior decoration and home furnishings. After their first exhibition, a writer for *The Decorative Furnisher* proclaimed:

> The time has come for someone to speak with authority on the subject of home decoration and teach by precept. The Art-in-Trades Club, numbering as it does among its members the leaders in the interior decorative arts in New York City, was the logical organization to assume the dual role.[31]

The exhibitions also gave members across the country an opportunity to increase Club participation. The minority of members from other cities, such as Philadelphia and Cleveland, had fewer opportunities to attend meetings and lectures, but they were able to showcase their work, often partnering with locals, in these new exhibitions.

Decorators and home furnishing firms collaborated to create the room settings, which, as reviewers explained, helped to reduce commercial implications. Without the limitation of sourcing from one manufacturer or retailer, each room was created to show an "actual example of what is right and proper in the sphere of home furnishing and not to sell particular products."[32] For example, the Philadelphia decorator E. A. Belmont combined products from William H. Jackson & Co., the Shaw Furniture Co., W. & J. Sloane, Edgewater Tapestry Looms, Maison LaFee, Edwin F. Caldwell & Co., The Bristol Company, and Edward Maag, Inc. for his Queen Anne lacquered room in the first exhibition.[33] Without price lists, company literature, or salesmen, the exhibitions were intended to feel like a museum – an educational experience for visitors. The Art-in-Trades Club exhibited decoration that they believed held "high artistic worth" (a phrase used twice in *The Decorative Furnisher's* review), demonstrating how objects could be incorporated into the home in good taste, and empowering visitors with a wealth of knowledge.[34]

The Club imbued their exhibitions with academic authority through cultural and historical installations. Just as their members could learn about manufacturing during factory visits, exhibition visitors received a firsthand look at techniques. In 1922, Edgewater Tapestry Looms showcased a loom and needlework demonstration beside their finished tapestries and in 1923 the Club displayed techniques such as woodcarving, weaving, and embroidery in a workshop setting.[35] One reviewer wrote, "a revival of ancient skill and learning was noted," recalling sentiments of nineteenth-century design reformers and later Arts and Crafts idealists. As early as the 1840s, British design reformer Henry Cole – called the first great propagandist for design – sought to combine "the best Art with familiar objects in daily use."[36] Decades later, proponents of the Arts and Crafts Movement reacted to industrialization, believing that by bringing art to industry one could "reclaim the unity and beauty believed to have been lost through the degradation of work."[37] The Club's desire for craft demonstrations and historical installations highlights the tension between artistic and industrial production, reminding us that these categories remained in flux even during the twenties.

For their 1923 exhibition, The Art-in-Trades Club partnered with the Eastern Association of Indian Affairs (EAIA) to create an exhibit of art from the American southwest.[38] For this display, a group of men gathered textiles from Arizona and New Mexico, as well as Pueblo ceramics. By the 1920s, Native American Pueblo communities became American tourist destinations and Navajo weavers were producing textiles for a wide and eager market.[39] Designers like the Club's William Laurel Harris fueled interest in these textiles, and he worked with traders and dealers to create new designs.[40] In addition to the EAIA's display of American-made objects, Harris decorated his own exhibition rooms with fashionable Native American rugs and ceramics, creating the most celebrated interiors of the 1923 show.[41] He combined antiques with the work of twentieth-century Pueblo potters such as Maria Martinez, who revived the San Ildefenso coiled blackware pots during the 1920s.[42] Several of these austere glistening forms punctuate his otherwise busy, tapestried interiors (Figure 6.1). Reviewers described these native objects as pure, rooted in tradition, and perfectly suited as "ornamental features for modern homes."[43] Although their long history became a selling point, the vessels were primarily twentieth-century interpretations of historical objects.[44] The glossy surface and minimal decoration was in keeping with the aesthetics associated with what was then termed *modernistic* interiors and, by 1941, work like this was on view at the Museum of Modern Art.[45] In a decorating climate that likened antique pudding molds to contemporary sculpture, using chic collectibles in interior decoration allowed one to stay tied to a respected history, however

Figure 6.1

View of Spanish Colonial Reception Room by William Laurel Harris Shown in the Second Annual Exhibition of the Art-in-Trades Club – 1923. **The Art-in-Trades Club of New York.** *Year Book.* **New York: The Club: 1924. Author's collection.**

constructed.[46] Club members could use these lessons to help their customers explore contemporary aesthetics in safe, respectable ways.

Club president and textile designer Harry Wearne created another museum-like environment by loaning his collection of toile de Jouy, complete with proof of authenticity, for the 1924 exhibition.[47] In his *New York Times* review, Walter Rendell Storey used as much real estate providing a history of Wearne's textiles as he did reviewing the contemporary interiors. He wrote:

> It is truly a capital idea to show these beautiful old prints, toned by time but unfaded, with their naïve histories, their informing evidence of past events, their decorative value, their reserved schemes of color: but it would be far better to extend the exhibition to include some of the modern cottons designed by Mr. Wearne himself in the spirit of the past, fused amazingly with the spirit of the present. Then one could see that virtue has not gone out of original work.[48]

Wearne's textile design *Sixteenth Century Ships* was satisfying, stimulating, and freed from the "self-consciousness of imitation," and Storey wanted more (Figure 6.2).[49] Those who attended the exhibition a year earlier would have seen Wearne's *Old Vauxhall*, another design that transformed a historical source into a lively twentieth century textile. Like the Pueblo ceramics, these textiles were forward-thinking in spirit, but safely steeped in tradition.[50] Wearne and his peers collected museum-worthy chintz and toile de Jouy as these textiles experienced a renewed popularity during the 1920s.[51] In *Arts & Decoration*, Winifred Willson described the rising interest in both the new interpretations and exhibitions of the antiques.[52] The latest aesthetic trends fueled the demand for historical printed textiles with a youthful sense of movement and rhythm. At the Club's 1924 exhibition, the textile display served as a resource for study but also to link this long history to contemporary design – bridging art and industry. Club members working for textile and wallpaper companies took a similar approach, and in 1928, the W. H. S. Lloyd Company published a wallpaper catalogue disguised as a history of toile de Jouy.[53] The catalogue contains samples of over 20 designs, including two modern adaptations depicting contemporary figures in landscapes, using the same formula as the antique textiles that inspired them. This grounding in history helped the design field promote new adaptations, and it gave the furnishings industry credibility by connecting it to museum-quality objects.[54]

With so many educational resources, the exhibitions armed visitors with the language they needed in order to buy and sell furnishings. One review described a visitor's revelation as she learned the word for the correct period of a particular style she admired, and that she "had never dared ask for it because she was not sure of its name or period."[55] Design education was founded on an understanding of the historical periods and the Art-in-Trades Club labeled exhibition rooms as Spanish Colonial, Sheraton, Chippendale, Tudor, and Louis XVI, providing the proper terminology as well as an instructive format of the ensemble.[56] A 1923 exhibition reviewer argued that the room format was also a great help to those working in the shops:

> A salesman may know all about printed linens, know how they are designed and manufactured, and yet may not know the various purposes to which they are put by a decorator who purchases them. By showing how goods are used in completed schemes the exhibition is of tremendous assistance to those who handle decorative furnishings as single units day by day.[57]

The Art-in-Trades Club

Figure 6.2

Sixteenth Century Ships. **Harry Wearne.** *Harry Wearne, a Short Account of His Life and Work.* New York, Thomsen-Ellis Company, 1933. Author's collection.

During the 1920s, the contextual grouping of objects in room settings became a popular tactic for selling goods, as well as presenting museum collections.[58] In 1924 the Metropolitan Museum of Art debuted their American Wing period rooms, imbuing this display technique with the ultimate authority.[59] That same year, *The Decorative Furnisher* begged its readers, "Don't Neglect the Period Styles," stressing that the knowledge needed to arrange a period room was vital to the field of interior decoration.[60] In another article that year, *The Decorative Furnisher* reviewed the Club's exhibition, stating:

> And so, with the Art-in-Trades Club Show showing how furnishings are to be used properly, and with the Metropolitan Museum putting the stamp of approval upon interior furnishings as art objects, is it any wonder that some in the home furnishings trade hear opportunity knocking very definitely at the door?[61]

The ability to categorize the past would help designers understand their present and future. Chronological compartmentalization helped Americans navigate style during the twenties as Modern design made waves in the press. *Modernistic* became the newest historical period, and so became more understandable. With their exhibitions, the Club sought to help the public feel at ease with interior decoration, which in turn would help manufacturers cope with the enormous pressures of stylistic changes in store.

The Art-in-Trades Club presented their expertise of historical styles, and within the safe space of their exhibitions, members could also tackle widespread skepticism of modern style – with the same sense of authority. Club members watched their field rapidly change during the 1920s, and they looked for ways to maintain profits without taking risks on trends that, for many, felt temporary. In their exhibitions, the Club offered visual lessons that provided the trade with methods to help their conservative customers subtly combine old and new aesthetics. The shows taught salesmen principles of design that could be applied to any style or era, such as "how various colors are keyed, one with each other, and how fabrics are used in connection with other appointments such as furniture, lamps, art objects, and so forth."[62] Club members used rugs, metalwork, and other decorative accessories to change the feeling of a room. No matter the style of the setting, objects with a modern look would show visitors that a homeowner had varied tastes, they understood new aesthetics, and that they possessed individuality.[63] A 1923 exhibition at the Anderson Galleries had attempted to demonstrate how contemporary art could be styled with period furniture, and numerous magazine articles showed that objects such as Hunt Diederich's fire screens with lithe animals could live happily alongside reproduction or antique furniture.[64]

The Art-in-Trades Club exhibitors did the same, in their own quiet way. Oscar Bach exhibited a number of objects that might freshen up a room, including work that looked to European modernists for inspiration. The decorating firm R. J. Haddock Inc. assembled a "Sheraton" dining room, against a backdrop of shining gold and black wallpaper by W. H. S. Lloyd, which highlighted silver by Georg Jensen. Art-in-Trades Club members used the comforting language of historical periods to quell their visitors' nerves as they demonstrated how to infuse tradition with modernity. Their exhibition rooms reflected the coming years, when, as *Vogue* declared in 1930, "We are violent antiquers and at the same time fanatic modernists . . . We mix bakelite with lustre, modern paintings with hooked rugs, chromium with flowered serge. Restless, if you will, but never self-satisfied, for us the game of decorating goes on forever."[65] The *New York Times* review of the 1924 exhibition explained that there were "signs of healthy change, although the signs are made with a certain carefulness that hardly attracts attention."[66] For manufacturers and retailers, attracting attention might have seemed like a smart publicity move, but it did not necessarily have a positive effect on sales. During the late twenties stores like Lord & Taylor reported, at best, equal sales in modern and period furniture, and the modern lines of companies like Steuben and F. Schumacher never sold well, despite the amount of advertising and press they received.[67] At the show, visitors from the trade could learn how to find originality through combining multiple periods or that a Colonial interior could be streamlined to feel new.[68]

The exhibitions also demonstrated that decorators and homemakers could use color to make changes without taking the risk of wholly "going modern." During the late 1920s, Club members used trade literature to discuss these methods of venturing into new stylistic territory without losing customers.[69] Some argued that manufacturers of textiles and wall coverings should take risks first because consumers were more likely to update a room with soft furnishings than to make an investment in new furniture.[70] At the 1924 exhibition, the decorator E. A. Belmont's use of bright red toile de Jouy felt "vivid and engaging," and rather too bold to be considered guilty of pure ancestor worship.[71] In its black and white photograph, the interior appears traditional, but Belmont used bold color to create a more contemporary mood, outfitting a room entirely in red toile de Jouy, from walls to window hangings, to upholstery (Figure 6.3). Club members, like Belmont, made traditional interiors feel current through color. This tactic became more common with the rising number of color guides, systems, and forecasts that fueled an entire field of color management.[72] Companies like Stroheim & Romann explained in their advertisements that bright colors would never ruin period

Figure 6.3

French Sitting Room. E. A. Belmont. 1924 Exhibition. **The Art-in-Trades Club of New York.** *Year Book*. **New York: The Club: 1926. Author's collection.**

style and many manufacturers promoted their traditional products in daring colors, introducing new colorways each year as a means to freshen and move stock.[73]

Current events, like the 1925 *L'Exposition Internationale des Arts Décoratifs et Industriels Modernes*, influenced colors, and each new trend allowed manufacturers to change without producing new forms or patterns.[74] By 1927, *Times* critic Walter Rendell Storey argued against previously stylish faded colors, explaining that the latest brocades "would seem too delicate and faint if reproduced with the exact tone of color of the time of Louis XV or XIV."[75] The following year, he described a bedroom papered in toile de Jouy, saying, "the new feeling for color is apparent even in designs that have been inspired by Colonial types. Many patterns originated 150 years ago and influenced by the French toile de Jouy fabric designs are today reproduced in the hues and color intensity of the modern vogue."[76] Storey and other authors argued that the supposedly pale colors of old textiles should be abandoned for apple green, lavender, cardinal, orange-yellow, and rust-blue because well-lit contemporary interiors called for these brighter hues – one even announced that "the drab era is definitely done."[77] Club members showed that modern colors were tied to the latest edicts of taste, they reflected the spirit of reinvention and individual expression, and they could be used to compose stylish interiors and help Americans begin to digest a new look.

Despite these subtle methods and praise for the first exhibitions, the press soon critiqued the Club for their historical approach to design. Many designers and decorators were guilty of ancestor worship, and during the early 1920s the Club joined the furnishings field in a discourse about the value of new European designs, wondering how they might profit from adaptations.[78] The Club's importance lies not just in its stylistic stance, but in the support system it sought to create for designers and manufacturers. Using trade periodicals such as *Good Furniture* and *The Decorative Furnisher*, they debated whether they could or should incorporate modernistic furnishings into American interiors, and some attempted to do so in the Club's exhibitions. The Club offered designers and decorators a safe environment to debut their work in the modernist vein. With financial backing from the Rockefeller Foundation, the Club put their annual exhibition on hold; instead, they challenged members to design two rooms, banning direct copies of old styles.[79] In order to avoid what they considered extreme designs, they encouraged work that, "while recognizing our present traditions, will carry forward the expression of these traditions into new and pleasing forms suited to American homes."[80] The call for entries was advertised in magazines and newspapers, and meanwhile, three of the Club's members joined publicity guru Edward Bernays as President Hoover's Commissioners, visiting the Paris Exposition in order to see what the latest international furnishings looked like.[81] However, that December, the Club announced that no entrants had fully satisfied their specifications of original design or stayed within the outlined budget, but that two members, Paul Zimmerman and Lorentz Kleiser, would receive prize money.[82] Zimmerman's bedroom and Kleiser's tapestry commemorating Newark, New Jersey appeared a year later in the Club exhibition's "20th century Gallery."

Although the Club had hoped to organize an exhibition entirely of new work in 1925, it, instead, presented a wide variety of styles at its 1926 exhibition. In addition to both positive and negative reactions, reviewers recognized that the underlying theme of the show was contrast, and that the transition between different styles was surprisingly smooth.[83] Elisabeth L. Cary wrote that the exhibition represented American taste, or at least what it would be in its best form. She noted that although Paul Zimmerman's room was French in inspiration, it was an "American translation of the modern idiom" (Figure 6.4).[84] In between Colonial and Jacobean rooms, W. & J. Sloane

The Art-in-Trades Club

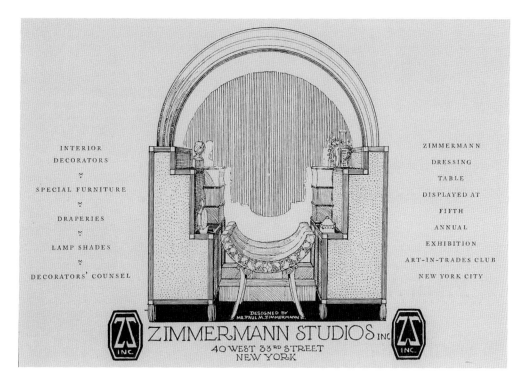

Figure 6.4
Zimmermann Studios Inc. Advertisement. The Art-in-Trades Club of New York. *Year Book*. New York: The Club: 1926. Author's collection.

presented their interpretation of Jacques Emile Ruhlmann's work, Walter Kantack exhibited a French-inspired wall sconce, table, and mirror, and Paul Frankl arranged a modernist room, with his famous D-shaped chair (Figure 6.5). Some of the work displayed, especially Paul Frankl's designs, would become symbolic for American modernism. Paul Zimmerman's dressing table hit the pages of *Vogue* and was offered for sale at the Park Avenue Galleries in 1928, and Paul Frankl illustrated Walter Kantack's mirror and console table in his February 1927 article for *House & Garden*, "Furniture of the Fourth Dimension."[85]

After 1926, the Club stopped organizing its own shows and many members chose to turn their efforts to the department store exhibitions of modern design. Kantack and Frankl took their work from the Club's show right into Macy's Exposition of Art and Trade in May of 1927, and other members, such as several Cheney Brothers employees, joined them.[86] Club members from large retailers like Macy's and B. Altman offered their friends a wider reach and an existing customer base, ready and willing to be educated. The end of the Club's exhibitions marks a shift from a time when its members needed a venue that offered multiple styles with an intentional "carefulness that hardly attracts attention," into a period of sweeping statement-making, publicity-seeking work during the second half of the decade.[87] Historians have explored the department store exhibitions of the late 1920s with careful attention, but the Art-in-Trades Club provides an important precedent.[88] Although their modern experiment ultimately failed, the same men involved with the Club and their

Patricia Edmonson ■

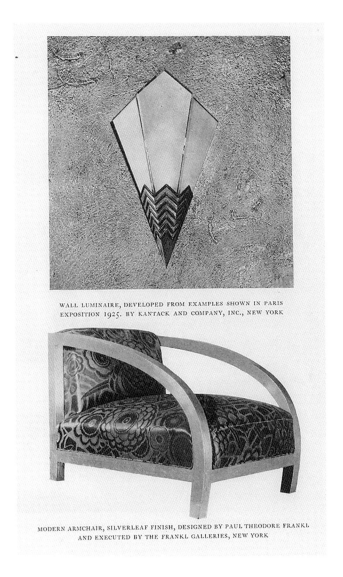

Figure 6.5

Wall Luminaire and Modern Armchair. 1926 Exhibition. The Art-in-Trades Club of New York. *Year Book.* New York: The Club: 1926. Author's collection.

exhibitions helped make the department store shows a reality. At the Club's exhibitions, members tested the waters and generated excitement about stylistic change, as well as its commercial viability. They found the motivation and resources to make modern exhibitions in commercial spaces, in a full-scale attempt at wedding art to industry.

The 1930s brought change for the Art-in-Trades Club and its members. Adventurous modernists had ever-increasing opportunities to show and sell their new work, and many of the Club's older members faded from the design scene. In addition to the department store exhibitions, the

Metropolitan Museum of Art resumed their industrial design exhibitions in 1929 with *The Architect and the Industrial Arts*.[89] Club members exhibited work there and comprised a large percentage of the exhibition's Advisory Committee.[90] During these years, Club activity slowed immensely, and, as a seeming last gasp in 1932, the Metropolitan Museum's Richard Bach worked with the Club to organize a series of lectures and study hours at the museum on the basics of design using museum objects and items from department stores.[91] This may have been the last series of formal lectures sponsored jointly by the museum and the Club. With the death of important figures such as Harry Wearne in 1929, Frank Alvah Parsons in 1930, and William Sloane Coffin in 1933, the Club faded from the spotlight.[92] By 1934, activities were moved to the Lombardy Hotel at 111 East 56th Street, indicating the loss of their clubhouse on East 38th Street, which they auctioned the following year.[93] Both businesses and museums suffered after the crash of the stock market in 1929, and it is likely that, along with the deaths of its leaders and the rise of department stores as the ultimate exhibition venues, the weakened American economy contributed to the disappearance of the Art-in-Trades Club.

The Club's conservatism and ultimate demise should not overshadow its contribution to the furnishings trade. Its meetings, educational offerings, and exhibitions were conceived to give the trade tactics for communicating with one another and the public. The trade needed these tools when they felt exceeding pressure to adapt and explore new styles, just as they were finding their professional footing. As styles changed, members of the trade knew that many of its customers would hold on to old furnishings and buy only what fit in their homes. Club members used exhibitions to showcase ways in which customers could adapt to new decorating ideas at a comfortable pace. These displays provided transparency about the field's adjustment and experiments – members showed consumers that they were in the same predicament when it came to new styles. Whether or not this was a reality, it served as a model for how the furnishings trade could relate to its customers. The Club's combination of periods and styles reflects the industry at large, and the addition of the modern period to a long line of established periods that manufacturers would continue to offer – and still do, today. Above all, the Art-in-Trades Club reminds us that design was a business. Professional networks connected collaborators; historians and museums offered design inspiration and sales techniques; design education could prove crucial to a firm or individual's public image; and within the trade, stylistic change was not a simple matter of principle.

NOTES

1 As quoted in Jay Cantor, "Art and Industry: Reflections on the Role of the American Museum in Encouraging Innovation in the Decorative Arts," in *Technological Innovation and the Decorative Arts*, eds. Ian M. G. Quimby and Polly Anne Earl (Charlottesville, VA: University of Virginia Press, 1974), 342.
2 Portions of this essay were first thought out in my 2008 MA thesis: Patricia Edmonson, The Tension Between Art and Industry: The Art-in-Trades Club of New York, 1906–1935 (MA Thesis, University of Delaware, 2008), 13–16. In 1876, the Commonwealth of Pennsylvania chartered a Museum and School of Industrial Art, by 1916, author and architect Sherrill Whiton founded the New York School of Interior Design, and in 1926, New York University added six courses in art instruction, including one in furniture design. "N. Y. U. Plans to Add Six Courses in Art," *New York Times*, 16 April 1926.
3 For further exploration of the struggles to define design and decorative arts, see Isabelle Frank, ed., *The Theory of Decorative Art: An Anthology of European and American Writings, 1750–1940* (New Haven, CT: Yale University Press, 2000), 1–9.

4 The Art-in-Trades Club of New York, *Year Book*, Annual Exhibition, 1923 (New York: The Club, 1923), 2–4.

5 *The Story of Sloane's* (New York: W. & J. Sloane, 1950), 42; 11.

6 Ella S. Siple, Burlington Magazine for Connoisseurs, February 1933, 84; 87–88; "Wm. S. Coffin Dies; Art Museum Head," *New York Times*, 17 December 1933. Coffin was also involved with Oneidacraft, Inc. and Creekfront Realty Company. He was made honorary vice president of the Museum of the City of New York and was a trustee of the Provident Loan Society.

7 The Art-in-Trades Club, *Year Book*, 1923, 2–4.

8 Anna-Maria and Stephen Kellen Archives Center for Parsons The New School for Design, "Frank Alvah Parsons," http://library.newschool.edu/speccoll/findingaids/KA0037.html.

9 Frank Alvah Parsons, *Interior Design: Its Principles and Practice* (New York: Doubleday, Page & Company, 1916), 128–129.

10 The Art-in-Trades Club of New York, *Constitution* (New York: The Club, 1913), 12–13; The Art-in-Trades Club of New York, *Year Book*, Annual Exhibition, 1924 (New York: The Club, 1924), 1; "Art in Trades Club," *Metropolitan Museum of Art Bulletin* 6, no. 6 (June 1911): 141.

11 "Art at Home and Abroad: News and Comment," *New York Times*, 1 November 1914.

12 For sample membership lists, see The Art-in-Trades Club, *Constitution*, 34–39; The Art-in-Trades Club of New York, *Year Book*, Annual Exhibition, 1926 (New York: The Club, 1926), 39–45.

13 The Art-in-Trades Club, *Year Book*, Annual Exhibition, 1924, 1; "Art in Trades Club," Metropolitan Museum of Art Bulletin, 6, no. 6 (June 1911): 141.

14 Hunter was an authority on American decorative art, and was widely published in both popular and trade periodicals, as well as the author of many texts. Walker was a painter and an architect, and played an important role in the founding of the Architectural League of New York. "Recent Accessions and Notes," Metropolitan Museum of Art Bulletin, 6, no. 6 (June 1911): 141; Art-in-Trades Club New York, *Constitution* (New York: The Club, 1913), 12–13.

15 That year (1911), the first electric light was installed in the museum's decorative arts galleries, allowing for evening access. "Recent Accessions and Notes," 141; Dr. Valentiner left the MMA staff in 1917, when he returned to Germany, "Valentiner Quits Museum Here," *New York Times*, 24 February 1917.

16 "The Textile Collection and Its Use," Metropolitan Museum of Art Bulletin 10, no. 5 Supplement (May 1915): 2; Cantor, "Art and Industry," 331–354; Calvin Tomkins, *Merchants and Masterpieces: The Story of the Metropolitan Museum of Art* (New York: Henry Holt and Company, 1989).

17 Richard F. Bach, "The Museum as Laboratory," *Metropolitan Museum of Art Bulletin* 14, no. 1 (January 1919): 2–3.

18 Bach, "The Museum as Laboratory," 3; For a discussion of the ICA Boston's department of Design in Industry and how they assisted manufacturers, see Richard Meyer, *What Was Contemporary Art?* (Cambridge, MA: MIT University Press, 2013): 230–234.

19 Richard F. Bach, "Exhibition of Work by Manufacturers and Designers," *Metropolitan Museum of Art Bulletin* 15, no. 2 (February 1920): 35.

20 "The Art Museum and the Store," *Good Furniture* (March 1925), 142.

21 "How Live Wire Organizations, Industrial and Artistic, are Making the Most of the Contact Idea," *Good Furniture* (July 1921), 19.

22 The Art-in-Trades Club, *Year Book*, Annual Exhibition 1924, 1.

23 The Art-in-Trades Club, *Constitution*, 11.

24 The Art-in-Trades Club, *Constitution*, 11.

25 The Art-in-Trades Club, *Constitution*, 10–11. See also Alice Cooney Frelinghuysen, Louis *Comfort Tiffany and Laurelton Hall: An Artist's Country Estate* (New York: Metropolitan Museum of Art, 2006).

26 See, for example, textiles on p. 44, credited to Schumacher on p. 53 in George Leland Hunter, *Decorative textiles; an illustrated book on coverings for furniture, walls and floors, including damasks, brocades and velvets, tapestries, laces, embroideries, chintzes, cretonnes, drapery and furniture trimmings, wall papers,*

The Art-in-Trades Club ■

carpets and rugs, tooled and illuminated leathers (Philadelphia: J. B. Lippincott Company, 1918); Chandler R. Clifford, *Period Furnishings: An Encyclopedia of Historic Furniture, Decorations, and Furnishings* (New York: Clifford and Lawton, 1922), 208. Clifford owned Clifford & Lawton publishing house, which published text books and trade journals such as *The American Silk Journal* and *The Interior Decorator*. "C. R. Clifford Dies; Long a Publisher," *New York Times*, 24 March 1935.

27 The Club first became involved in exhibitions in 1915 when they co-organized a show at the Metropolitan Museum of Art with the American Federation of Arts. William Sloane Coffin, Frank Alvah Parsons, and NYU professor William MacDougal Odom curated a collection of sketches, photographs, and objects related to interior decoration and industrial arts. Beginning in 1917, members of the Club participated in the Metropolitan's own industrial design exhibitions. Not only did representatives from companies such as Edgewater Tapestry Looms and the Kensington Company exhibit their museum-inspired work, but they also comprised the museum's organizing committee. "Accessions and Notes," *Metropolitan Museum of Art Bulletin* 10, no. 4 (April 1915): 82; "Color Effects at the Museum," *New York Times*, 19 April 1915; "Accessions and Notes," *Metropolitan Museum*, 82; "Exhibit of Manufactured Objects," *Metropolitan Museum of Art Bulletin* 13, no. 2 (February 1918): 34; Christine Wallace Laidlaw, "The Metropolitan Museum of Art and Modern Design: 1917–1929," *The Journal of Decorative and Propaganda Arts* 8 (Spring 1988): 92, 98. Laidlaw's list can be cross-referenced with Club membership lists in their exhibition catalogues.

28 "Home Decorations Show," *New York Times*, 23 September 1922. Fifty cents in 1922 has the buying power of $7.06 in 2016, Bureau of Labor Statistics Inflation Calculator, http://data.bls.gov/cgi-bin/cpicalc.pl.

29 "New Ideas at the Art-in-Trades Club Exhibition," *Good Furniture* (November 1923), 207.

30 "An Exhibition of Decoration," *Decorative Furnisher* (October 1922): 70.

31 "An Exhibition of Decoration," 70.

32 "An Exhibition of Decoration," 69.

33 Decorators were not the only entrants in need of collaboration; companies such as P. W. French & Co. worked with Kent-Costikyan Trading Co., Inc. and Edwin F. Caldwell & Co. on a room, and several other partnerships were formed for the exhibitions. "An Exhibition of Decoration," 68–70.

34 "An Exhibition of Decoration," 70.

35 "Art-in-Trades Exhibition a Success," *Decorative Furnisher* (November 1922), 88.

36 Fiona MacCarthy, *All Things Bright and Beautiful: Design in Britain 1830 to Today* (Toronto: University of Toronto Press, 1972), 14.

37 Nicolas Maffei, "John Cotton Dana and the Politics of Exhibiting Industrial Art in the US, 1909–1929," *Journal of Design History* 13, no. 4 (2000): 303; "New Ideas at the Art-in-Trades Club Exhibition," 208.

38 "New Ideas at the Art-in-Trades Club Exhibition," 208.

39 Marian E. Rodee, *Old Navajo Rugs: Their Development From 1900 to 1940* (Albuquerque: University of New Mexico Press, 1981), 1–6.

40 Nancy J. Blomberg, *Navajo Textiles The Collection of William Randolph Hearst* (Tuscon: University of Arizona Press, 1988), 5–6.

41 "New Ideas at the Art-in-Trades Club Exhibition," 209–210.

42 W. Jackson Rushing III, *Native American Art in the Twentieth Century: Makers, Meanings, Histories* (New York: Routledge, 2013): 34.

43 Carl E. Guthrie, *Pueblo Pottery Making: A Study at the Village of San Ildefonso* (New Haven: Yale University Press): 1925; "New Ideas at the Art-in-Trades Club Exhibition," 209–210; John Stuart Gordon, *A Modern World: American Design From the Yale University Art Gallery, 1920–1950* (New Haven, CT: Yale University Press, 2011), 213.

44 Rushing III, *Native American Art in the Twentieth Century*, 57–58.

45 The Museum of Modern Art, "Exhibition of Indian Art of the United States Opens at the Museum of Modern Art," Press Release, 20 January 1941, www.moma.org/momaorg/shared/pdfs/docs/press_archives/665/

releases/MOMA_1941_0004_1941-01-20_41120-4.pdf?2010. For a discussion of early twentieth-century exhibitions of Native American art, see Elizabeth Hutchinson, *The Indian Craze: Primitivism, Modernism, and Transculturation in American Art, 1890–1915* (Durham, NC: Duke University Press, 2009), 118–129.

46 Derek Patmore, "The Accolade of the Pudding Mold," *House & Garden* (August 1928), 57; Helen Appleton Read, "Twentieth-Century Decoration: The Modern Mode as Exemplified by American Craftsmen," *Vogue* (1 September 1928): 77; Pierre Dutel, "Combining the Old and New," *The American Home* (July 1930): 418–420, 440, 442.

47 "The World of Art: "To Harmonize Commercial Activities With the Growing art Tendencies," *New York Times*, 2 November 1924.

48 "The World of Art".

49 "The World of Art".

50 John Stuart Gordon discusses "historical modernism" in chapter seven of A Modern World.

51 Much of Wearne's collection is now at the Royal Ontario Museum.

52 Winifred Willson, "Famous Eighteenth Century Toiles De Jouy," *Arts & Decoration* (April 1925), 48.

53 William T. Tucker, *History and Development of Toile de Jouy Wallpapers* (New York: W. H. S. Lloyd Co., Inc., 1928).

54 As early as 1920, Raoul Dufy had done much the same when he partnered with first Paul Poiret and then Bianchini et Ferrier to make textiles with contemporary imagery in a technique reminiscent of toile de Jouy. A decade later W. & J. Sloane produced Ruth Reeves' work in the same vein. Times critic Elisabeth L. Cary described Reeves work, which depicted historic American icons as "a modern and thoroughly American variant of the toile de Jouy of France." William D. Moore, "You'd Swear They Were Modern: Ruth Reeves, the Index of American Design, and the Canonization of Shaker Material Culture," *Winterthur Portfolio* 47 (Spring 2013): 5–6.

55 "Art-in-Trades Exhibition a Success," *Decorative Furnisher* (November 1922), 76.

56 "The Second Exhibition of the Art-in-Trades Club," *Decorative Furnisher* (October 1923), 71.

57 "The Second Exhibition," 71–72.

58 Roland Marchand, *Advertising the American Dream: Making Way for Modernity 1920–1940* (Berkeley, CA: University of California Press, 1985), 133.

59 Mr. and Mrs. G. Glen Gould, "The American Wing of the Metropolitan Museum of Art," *Good Furniture* (December 1924), 296–303.

60 "Don't Neglect the Period Styles: A plea for deeper interest in classical design and an attempt to show that knowledge is the decorator's greatest requirement," *Decorative Furnisher* (June 1924), 59.

61 "Art-in-Trades Exhibition," *Decorative Furnisher* (November 1924), 69.

62 "The Second Exhibition of the Art-in-Trades Club," *Decorative Furnisher* (October 1923), 72.

63 Helen Koues, *How to be Your Own Decorator* (New York: Good Housekeeping, 1926), 10–11; "The New Mingles with the Old," *House & Garden* (June 1929), 98–99; "Vogue's-Eye View of the Mode," *Vogue* (2 August 1930), 25.

64 Guy Pene du Bois, "Modern Art and Antique Furniture in Harmony," *Vogue* (15 September 1923), 92–93; "The Art of Hanging Pictures," *House & Garden* (September 1919), 24–25.

65 "Vogue's Eye View of the Mode," *Vogue* (2 August 1930), 25.

66 "The World of Art: "To Harmonize Commercial Activities With the Growing art Tendencies."

67 "A New Merchandising Problem," *Good Furniture* (June 1928), 279; "The Modern Manner," *Good Furniture & Decoration* (October 1929), 219; Meyer, *What was Contemporary Art?*, 234; Richard E. Slavin, *Opulent Textiles: The Shumacher Collection* (New York: Crown Publishers, Inc., 1992), 132.

68 "The World of Art:

69 "Is Modernism a Passing Fancy or a Fact?" *Good Furniture* (March 1928), 111; "A New Merchandising Problem," *Good Furniture* (June 1928), 279; "Commercializing Art Moderne Furniture: Macy's Merchandising Plan is Practical and Successful," *Good Furniture* (January 1928), 30–31.

The Art-in-Trades Club ∎

70 "A New Merchandising Problem;" Paul T. Frankl, "Furniture of the Fourth Dimension," *House & Garden* (February 1927), 76–77, 140; F. Schumacher & Co., *Fabrics: The Key to Successful Decoration* (New York: The Company, 1928), n.p.

71 "The World of Art:

72 For a full picture of color management and forecasting, see Regina Lee Blaszczyk, *The Color Revolution* (Cambridge, MA: The MIT Press, 2012), 139–162.

73 Frank Alvah Parsons, "An Analysis of Modernism," *House & Garden* (February 1926), 134; Stroheim Romann, Advertisement, *Good Furniture* (November 1927), 21; "A Silk Brocade in the 'Plein-Air' Brilliance of Modern Color," F. Schumacher & Co. Advertisement, *Vogue* (1 April 1925), 113; "A Tapestry Inspired Linen," F. Schumacher & Co. Advertisement, *The Decorative Furnisher* (March 1926), 17.

74 F. Shumacher & Co. Advertisement, *Arts & Decoration* (March 1926), 30.

75 Walter Rendell Storey, "Brocades Come Back in Brighter Hues," *New York Times*, 20 March 1927.

76 Walter Rendell Storey, "Modernizing the Walls of Our Homes," *New York Times*, 14 October 1928.

77 Walter Rendell Storey, "Home Draperies in the New American Manner," *New York Times*, 18 December 1927; Storey, "Brocades Come Back;" "Bright Color and Striking Design in the Textiles for Spring," *House & Garden* (February 1928), 105–108; Charles Matlack Price, "Color in Furniture," *Country Life* (September 1927), 34–39; Walter Rendell Storey, "New Color and Sparkle for the Table," *New York Times*, 24 June 1928; Dorothy Bent, "Autumn Decorating a Fascinating Adventure," *Arts & Decoration* (August 1927), 68; "Textiles in Retrospect and Prospect: Color, Modernism, and Bold Design are the Features," *Good Furniture* (January 1928), 51–54.

78 "Is Modernism a Passing Fancy or a Fact?" *Good Furniture* (March 1928), 111; "A New Merchandising Problem," *Good Furniture* (June 1928), 279; "Commercializing Art Moderne Furniture: Macy's Merchandising Plan is Practical and Successful," *Good Furniture* (January 1928), 30–31.

79 "Of Trade Interest," *Good Furniture* (May 1925): 222–223.

80 "Of Trade Interest," 223.

81 26 of the Commission's delegates were also members of the Art-in-Trades Club. "Names Delegates to Paris Exposition," *New York Times*, 19 April 1925; The Art-in-Trades Club of New York, *Year Book*, Annual Exhibition, 1926.

82 "Art-in-Trades Club Withdraws Prize Offer," *The Decorative Furnisher* (December 1925), 102.

83 Elizabeth L. Cary, "Modes: Old and New," *New York Times*, 3 October 1926; Walter Rendell Storey, "Modern Art Adapted to the Home," *New York Times*, 10 October 1926; "Marvelous Reproductions at Art-in-Trades Show," *Arts & Decoration* (November 1926), 64–65, 100.

84 Cary, "Modes: Old and New."

85 "New Dressing Tables Reflect the Modern Point of View," *Vogue* (1 May 1928), 87; Paul T. Frankl, "Furniture of the Fourth Dimension," *House & Garden* (February 1927), 76–77, 140.

86 Marilyn F. Friedman, *Selling Good Design: Promoting the Early Modern Interior* (New York: Rizzoli, 2003), 29.

87 "The World of Art:

88 See, in particular, the work of Marilyn Friedman and Christine Wallace Laidlaw.

89 Christine Wallace Laidlaw, "The Metropolitan Museum of Art and Modern Design: 1917–1929," *The Journal of Decorative and Propaganda Arts* 8 (Spring 1988): 103.

90 Metropolitan Museum of Art, *The Architect and the Industrial Arts: An Exhibition of Contemporary American Design* (New York: The Museum, 1929).

91 Huger Elliott, "Educational Activities 1932–1933," *Metropolitan Museum of Art Bulletin* 27, no. 9 (September 1932): 213.

92 "Harry Wearne Dies in Paris," *New York Times*, 6 September 1929; "Wm. S. Coffin Dies; Art Museum Head," *New York Times*, 17 December 1933.

93 "Art Brevities," *New York Times*, 8 March 1934; "What Is Going On This Week," *New York Times*, 24 February 1935; "Large Properties Go Under Hammer," *New York Times*, 20 December 1934; The AITC owed $54,249.00 and $3,380.00 in taxes. Their property at 34 East 38th Street was auctioned for $50,000.00.

BIBLIOGRAPHY

The Art-in-Trades Club of New York. *Year Book*. New York: The Club, 1922–1924, 1926.

The Art-in-Trades Club of New York. *Constitution*. New York: The Club, 1913.

Blaszczyk, Regina Lee. *The Color Revolution*. Cambridge, MA: The MIT Press, 2012.

The Decorative Furnisher (see Notes above for specific issues).

Edmonson, Patricia. "The Tension Between Art and Industry: The Art-in-Trades Club of New York, 1906–1935." MA Thesis, University of Delaware, 2008.

Friedman, Marilyn F. *Selling Good Design: Promoting the Early Modern Interior*. New York: Rizzoli, 2003.

Good Furniture (see Notes above for specific issues).

Gordon, John. *A Modern World: American Design From the Yale University Art Gallery 1920–1950*. New Haven, CT: Yale University Press, 2011.

House and Garden.

Hutchinson, Elizabeth. *The Indian Craze: Primitivism, Modernism, and Transculturation in American Art, 1890–1915*. Durham, NC: Duke University Press, 2009.

Laidlaw, Christine Wallace. "The Metropolitan Museum of Art and Modern Design: 1917–1929." *The Journal of Decorative and Propaganda Arts* 8 (Spring 1988): 88–103.

Long, Christopher. *Paul T. Frankl and Modern American Design*. New Haven, CT: Yale University Press, 2007.

Maffei, Nicolas. "John Cotton Dana and the Politics of Exhibiting Industrial Art in the US, 1909–1929." *Journal of Design History* 13, no. 4 (2000): 301–317.

Metropolitan Museum of Art Bulletin (see Notes above for specific issues).

Meyer, Richard. *What Was Contemporary Art?* Cambridge, MA: MIT University Press, 2013.

New York Times (see Notes above for specific issues).

Parsons, Frank Alvah. *Interior Design: Its Principles and Practice*. New York: Doubleday, Page & Company, 1916.

Quimby, Ian M. G. and Polly Anne Earl, eds. *Technological Innovation and the Decorative Arts*. Charlottesville, VA: University of Virginia Press, 1974.

Rushing III, W. Jackson. *Native American Art in the Twentieth Century: Makers, Meanings, Histories*. New York: Routledge, 2013.

Vogue (see Notes above for specific issues).

Wearne, Harry. *Harry Wearne, a Short Account of His Life and Work*. New York: Thomsen-Ellis Company, 1933.

Chapter 7: Demonstrating the profession

Interior decorating instruction on early television

Danielle Charlap

When the Radio Corporation of America (RCA) introduced television to the US market at the 1939 New York World's Fair, Americans could not have anticipated the future influx of television programming.[1] Although it would take several years for television to develop into a widespread household commodity, savvy individuals recognized television for what it was and could be: a new medium through which to share their expertise with a popular audience. Indeed, in its first decade on the market, television became a novel stage for professionals, including interior decorators.[2] Television's inherently visual nature made it a promising, if sometimes challenging, platform for promulgating the profession. It could showcase interior decorators as experts and educators, introducing them to a large audience that might otherwise have had little contact with the field. Presenting the profession on the air enabled new modes of instruction, while demanding consideration of how to make the interior decorator's role telegenic.

This chapter explores the early history of interior decorating instruction on television through the career of interior decorator Paul MacAlister. With the founding of his own practice in 1926, MacAlister made a living fashioning domestic and commercial spaces. He decorated the homes of wealthy men like George Vanderbilt and the interiors of yachts, assisted department stores with their merchandise displays, and dispensed interior decorating advice to budget-minded housewives.[3] In 1931, MacAlister established the Permanent Exhibition of Decorative Arts and Crafts (PEDAC), which took over the entire tenth floor of the RCA building in Rockefeller Center.[4] PEDAC served as a showroom for the display of various companies' interior wares, presented as ensembles for members of the trade. As the owner of PEDAC, MacAlister constantly had to consider both the larger arrangement of the space and the individual displays of each firm.[5] His ample experience with interior decoration display surely informed and helped him conceive of Plan-a-Room, a kit of miniaturized furniture pieces that would become central to his on-air interior decorating instruction. By 1941, MacAlister had pivoted from PEDAC to focus on Plan-a-Room and its use across multiple platforms, especially television.

Since "interior decorator" and "interior designer" were titles applied interchangeably to MacAlister throughout his career, a distinction is not made between them in this chapter. MacAlister's training reflects the challenge of categorizing him neatly. He was neither defined by the idea of inherent taste as was the case with many "lady decorators" nor simply considered a modernist architect.[6] Rather, MacAlister received a certificate in architecture from Yale's School of Fine Arts in

1926, but with a focus in interior decoration – a degree he claimed none had received before.[7] The unchartered nature of his training reflected a field in which experience could be acquired through numerous channels, whether on-the-job apprenticeships or formal academic training within departments of home economics, architecture, or fine arts.[8] MacAlister would take advantage of this flexibility to pursue diverse interior decorating projects over the course of his career.

In 1941, MacAlister broke new ground in the interior decorating field by venturing into television. Looking at MacAlister's shows, I document the numerous techniques he developed in the 1940s and 1950s to expand the mode of communicating interior decorating instruction and make it suitable for television demonstration. Many of his methods involved the on-air use of his Plan-a-Room kit, providing a fresh mode of popular instruction. These methods would change as technology improved and as color possibilities altered considerations of how and what to show on television. Yet throughout this period, MacAlister used his airtime to promote his own expertise and interior decorating's relevance to a growing audience of popular viewers, whom he encouraged to consider their own domestic spaces.

POPULAR INTERIOR DECORATING INSTRUCTION

Television's emergence by no means marked the first time interior decorators shared their skills with the public. The American field of professional interior decorating had already begun to take form in the late nineteenth century, when Candace Wheeler wrote her 1895 "Interior Decoration as Profession for Women."[9] Elsie de Wolfe, moreover, had established a public persona as an interior decorator in the early decades of the twentieth century, followed by a generation of diverse decorators like Dorothy Draper and Eleanor McMillen Brown.[10] These interior decorators were renowned for both the prestige of their clientele and the rarified homes and institutions they decorated.

But interior decorators insisted on their relevance far beyond the traditional circle of élite private clients. De Wolfe, for example, reached out to a broader audience through her articles in mainstream magazines like *Good Housekeeping* and her 1913 book *The House in Good Taste*. Her work for popular audiences often straddled the line between instructional advice and fodder for aspirational fantasy, inviting readers to consider the relevance of interior decorating to their lives.[11] In the 1930s, moreover, Draper became an increasingly commercial presence, attaching her name to numerous items available on the popular market.[12] She published her advice book *Decorating is Fun! How to Be Your Own Decorator* in 1939, its popularity evidenced in the rapid publishing of her follow-up book, the 1941 *Entertaining is Fun! How to Be a Popular Hostess*.[13] Interior decorating experts also found stages at institutions like the Metropolitan Museum of Art (MMA), which organized free interior decorating lectures. One program, "Study-Hours on Practical Subjects Conducted by Grace Cornell," included instruction from decorator Mrs. Frederick Lee Ackerman and Nancy McClelland, who lectured on wallpaper using the MMA's historic wallpaper collection.[14] Such involvement with popular outreach reflected attempts among interior decorators to build and capitalize on a broader market fascination for interior decorating and home planning.[15]

Interior decorators realized that educating the public about the need for quality interior decoration – while simultaneously arming it with the knowledge and the tools to begin its own decorating projects – helped these experts expand the audience for their professional skills. This approach allowed them to showcase themselves and encouraged the public to appreciate interior decoration's

Demonstrating the profession ■

value. By the time television became a viable educational platform, there was already a popular audience long familiar with the idea of interior decorating instruction.

By the 1930s, moreover, the interior decorating field – like many others before it – was becoming increasingly professionalized. Following the professionalization of related fields like Home Economics, practitioners formalized their credentials not only through degree programs like MacAlister's, but also through the creation of professional organizations.[16] Decorators such as Nancy McClelland helped establish and nurture organizations like the American Institute of Decorators, of which MacAlister was a charter member.[17] These organizations justified to the public the benefits of working with an interior decorator while seeking recognition for their members' skills. They also strove to define the parameters of the title "interior decorator," hoping to standardize and regulate the use of the term to elevate it as a marker of professional expertise. MacAlister would lean on his identity as a professional to justify his relevance as the televised face of interior decorating instruction.

PLAN-A-ROOM AND INTERIOR DECORATING'S TELEVISION DEBUT

Eager to participate in the instructional interior decorating market, MacAlister turned his attention to popular instruction in 1941. To this audience – or at least a subset that had the means and time to redecorate their houses – MacAlister presented his Plan-a-Room kit.[18] Devised to assist

Figure 7.1
Plan-a-Room kit, created by Paul MacAlister, c. 1941. Courtesy Hampton C. Wayt.

with organizing room arrangements and color schemes, the Plan-a-Room kit served as an experimental space where people could conceive their ideal room designs in miniature. The earliest kits contained 76 wooden pieces in the diminutive shapes of common household furniture, scaled a half-inch to a foot (Figure 7.1). These pieces were referred to as "symbols," given their abstract and non-specified style.[19] In addition to furniture symbols, the kits included a rectangular wooden base meant to represent the floor of any given room. The wooden base had a grid of incised squares that allowed one to insert thin walls, thus defining the perimeter of the room and providing an opportunity to consider window treatments and wall colors. MacAlister used the Plan-a-Room kit in department store presentations in 1941 and sold it commercially.[20] With this popular-minded, entrepreneurial approach, MacAlister entered the market for instructional interior decorating.

Despite the nascent state of the television medium, MacAlister found himself poised to take the interior decorating profession on the air in 1941. The location of PEDAC, his furniture showroom company, in the Rockefeller Center RCA building brought him close to the physical hub of television production in New York City.[21] Perhaps because of his proximity to the NBC studio, he began hosting interior decorating television segments, seizing the opportunity to reach would-be do-it-yourself decorators. His first foray was a segment called *America Redecorates*, which utilized his Plan-a-Room miniature furniture. Beginning in 1941, it aired from the NBC-Live Talent Studio, 3-H, from Radio City, in New York.[22]

The show was billed as "eight minutes of informal, entertaining, highly instructive, discussion of home arrangement problems with solutions demonstrated visually."[23] Employing the Plan-a-Room kit as a demonstration tool, the show focused on furniture placement but also included topics such as carpeting, window treatments, mirrors, and walls.[24] MacAlister embraced television for its essential role in his interior decorating instruction, boldly claiming, "[t]here is no better medium with which to produce a convincing decorating program than through television."[25] With such sentiments and actions, he planted interior decorating in the fertile ground of television programming.

To appreciate just how early interior decorating arrived on television, one need only look to the medium's early history. While talk of television had already begun in the 1920s, Americans' first real encounter with commercial television occurred in 1939, at the New York World's Fair.[26] Building on publicity generated at the fair, manufacturers began to sell television sets to the general public. But by the end of 1939, only around 3,000 people had purchased sets in the United States.[27] Originally ranging in price from $199 to $600, television sets remained expensive during the prewar years and a rarefied luxury at the end of the Depression.[28] Programming during this era was minimal, as the Federal Communications Commission (FCC) only approved commercial telecasts in 1941 and broadcasts were generally confined to the late afternoon and evening.[29] Production conditions were also far from ideal in the prewar years. The infant technology of television created unbearably hot studios and relied on cameras with restricted mobility. These conditions limited cooking shows to demonstrations such as salad mixing.[30]

A 1941 premier date, therefore, meant *America Redecorates* belonged to the very first television programming in the United States. Curtailed television production during World War II and MacAlister's 1943 Naval Reserve enlistment took him off air entirely.[31] But the show continued, with producer Edward McDougal taking on hosting duties while MacAlister finished his service.[32] When MacAlister moved to Chicago in 1946 to become the Director of Interior Decoration and

Industrial Design at Montgomery Ward, he brought his experience in instructional interior decorating television to a new city.[33] In 1948, he left his job at Montgomery Ward and remanufactured his Plan-a-Room kit, returning to television in 1949 with two new shows for the local Chicago market: *Plan-a-Room* and *Interior Decoration*, followed in 1952 by *Rooms for Improvement*.[34] His audience only grew when, in 1954, both MacAlister and interior decorating made inroads into a national broadcast show: *HOME*. *HOME*, an important benchmark in American television, aired daily as an hour-long show comprised of numerous segments, including occasional appearances by MacAlister. Combined, these segments were billed as an "electronic magazine" for women.[35]

MacAlister's shows consistently targeted a female homemaker audience. As stated in 1946 advertising material for *America Redecorates*, the show "present[ed] unique opportunities for commercial presentation of any product [. . .] in any field where the American Woman is the backbone of the market," highlighting its intended audience.[36] By the time MacAlister aired his shows in Chicago, his female audience became an explicit consideration for show times. *Plan-a-Room*, a 15-minute-long weekly show that began in January 1949, first aired at a prime 8:30 p.m. time slot popular for wrestling.[37] The show moved around the television schedule until, in the fall of 1949, it became part of an afternoon block the station publicly billed as aimed at women and children.[38]

The growth of television production in the postwar years ushered in increased daytime programming geared specifically to women, whom advertisers appreciated as a lucrative television market.[39] The *HOME* show, meant to "[fill] *specific known needs* of the American homemaker," belonged to this phenomenon and included interior decorating segments (emphasis in original).[40] In spending airtime and advertising on instructional interior decorating, the network showed its confidence in the subject to boost its ratings.

THE ON-AIR PROFESSIONAL

Not all instructional television figures had professional backgrounds in the subject they hosted. Rather, many connected with audiences via a telegenic personality and a relatable "every woman" or "every man" demeanor.[41] On air, MacAlister presented his instruction "informally and amusingly," but he blazed his path to airtime by touting his interior decorating credentials.[42] He considered television a stage for professionals and sold himself as the consummate expert.[43] Promotional materials for *America Redecorates* explicitly notified advertisers of the professional molding episode content. Materials from 1946 – when the show was temporarily helmed by McDougal while MacAlister was on active duty – made clear that McDougal was only "pinchhitting" and providing "informal running comment," while "MacAlister retains active supervision of the show as far as his duties will permit – and indicates all decorating solutions which are used on the air."[44] This description followed MacAlister's billing as a "distinguished architect and interior designer."[45] The same promotional booklet dedicated an entire page to MacAlister's credentials, pinning his relevance as television host precisely on his professional pedigree.

Illuminating behind-the-scenes correspondence reveals how deliberately the MacAlister team encouraged hiring professional television personalities. In a memo from July 13, 1954, Flolydia Etting, MacAlister's right-hand associate, wrote him with her concerns about the *HOME* show's first few months. From Etting's perspective, the show needed a "change of direction and the inclusion of a 'name authority' in the picture."[46] The MacAlister team directly benefitted from this shift, for it allowed MacAlister to move from a behind-the-scenes *HOME* show consultant to a *HOME* on-air personality. But, in pushing for this change, Etting's language indicated that there were other experts to be found in the interior decorating field, professionals with a public face.

By advocating for "name authorities" like MacAlister, Etting also made the case for television as an ideal platform for professionals at large, whether in interior decorating or other fields. According to her, "[t]his precedent might stand the HOME Show management in good stead, if the business of 'name authorities' is expanded into other portions of the show."[47] In her words, these changes would provide a "professional twist" and "a general raising of the standard of the segment and the addition of a sound professional approach to the service show idea."[48] For the "service show" to work, Etting argued, one needed to respect the credentials of the person imparting the valuable advice.

By August 1954, the *HOME* show developed along these lines, and a brochure for potential marketers makes the emphasis on expertise clear. Indeed, the brochure referred to the show's regularly scheduled on-air guests as "*guest-experts* on new developments in all fields of home interest" (emphasis in original).[49] The promotional pamphlet included a full page of these guest experts' biographies, with MacAlister listed as "President of the Industrial Designers League" and "creator of the famous PLAN-A-ROOM kit."[50] He had convinced the *HOME* team of the value of his interior decorating expertise.

THE EXPANDING FIELD OF INSTRUCTIONAL INTERIOR DECORATION: MAKING THE FIELD TELEGENIC

How, then, to portray interior decorating as an established discipline on the air? Authoritative language was one way to signal the professional nature of the instruction. MacAlister's shows' scripts assertively referenced well-established interior decorating standards. In an *America Redecorates* episode from 22 May 1946, for example, the host prompted his audience:

> There are several errors in the present furniture arrangement, but one of them is a particularly glaring one, and I'd like to see if you can spot it. Look the room over carefully for a second. [Pause] . . . Yes, the bed is facing the windows! This arrangement violates one of the first principles of bedroom furniture arrangement.[51]

This language of "errors" and "principles," with its implication of a learned set of decorating fundamentals, impressed upon the lay viewer that she should heed closely the host's advice. As such language insisted, interior decorating had rules, guidelines that could benefit viewers' lives and homes with the help of a well-informed instructor.

Given the visual nature of television, this authoritative tone alone would not suffice. MacAlister needed to find methods to make his professional expertise visibly demonstrable on television. His primary solution entailed using his Plan-a-Room kit. The Plan-a-Room's miniature furniture suited the detail-capturing television camera. Using these forms not only enabled MacAlister to furnish an entire room quickly and economically, but it also allowed for the visualization of a room that might

Demonstrating the profession ■

Figure 7.2
Chicago's WGN-TV's *Plan-a-Room* studio. Courtesy Hampton C. Wayt.

otherwise be too large to capture on camera. The Plan-a-Room kit became a miniature television studio, standing in for a life-size room.

A photograph of the *Plan-a-Room* show's studio indicates how MacAlister used the miniatures as a proxy set [Figure 7.2]. In this photograph, he sits propped on a stool reviewing a document, while Etting points to a form in a model room. Given the studio's starkness and the placement of the camera in front of the kits on the table, it appears the camera filmed closely. Indeed, the Plan-a-Room's small-scale pieces would be rendered illegible if they were not the primary focus of the shot. The scripts reflected this with the regular inclusion of the simple stage direction "close-up of model."[52]

As seen in a photograph that accompanied a 1946 *America Redecorates* script, MacAlister painstakingly decorated the symbolic Plan-a-Room forms to give the impression of specific and stylized furniture (Figure 7.3). He fashioned new decorated pieces as needed to match the content of a given episode. A rare photograph of a television screen airing miniatures – albeit non-Plan-a-Room

Figure 7.3

Painted Plan-a-Room pieces. This photograph accompanied a 22 May 1946, *America Redecorates* script. Courtesy Hampton C. Wayt.

pieces – helps us understand how all miniatures would have appeared to home audiences (Figure 7.4).[53] By its very nature, television shrinks the filmed object to the scale of the television screen. Filling the television screen with miniatures, as in this photograph, effectively presented the pieces in similar proportions to full-size furniture in a regular room, thus obscuring their original size.

MacAlister considered verisimilitude the key to Plan-a-Room's success. For him, the kit transformed a blueprint – a two-dimensional visualization – into a visceral experience. In MacAlister's words, Plan-a-Room enabled "three-dimensional reality."[54] He labeled the use of Plan-a-Room as "visual education" and promoted his kit as a new tool whose three-dimensionality made it both practical and novel.[55] While one can point to earlier interior decorating instructional models with similar three-dimensionality, television made the use of such tools newly relevant and effective.[56]

According to MacAlister, three-dimensional interior decorating tools like Plan-a-Room were most immersive when viewed at eye-level. Writing about the Plan-a-Room kit, MacAlister exclaimed: "[t]o see the true view of your room, hold the box-top planner at eye-level. The accuracy of your miniature room will amaze you."[57] Later instructional material even encouraged the kit user to "[p]ut yourself 'in scale' with the room plan . . . Place Mrs. American Planner No. 19 in room and view it at eye level."[58] Television facilitated MacAlister's enforcement of this perspective with unprecedented ease. The television screen invited viewers to consider the camera's vantage point as their

Demonstrating the profession ■

Figure 7.4

Photograph of television screen airing a 1954 episode of the *Today* show, featuring Paul MacAlister-designed miniatures. Courtesy Hampton C. Wayt.

own, shaping audiences' visual experience through filming choices. By placing the camera squarely in front of the Plan-a-Room kit, as if at eye-level, MacAlister employed television's capacity to structure an audiences' view in accordance with his ideal perspective.

The camera, however, did not focus exclusively on the kit, sometimes panning out to include the host and other objects on the set (Figure 7.5).[59] Zooming the camera on the host presented him as the face of professional expertise, a role MacAlister relished. It also allowed him to highlight a stand-alone piece of actual furniture, particularly useful for sponsorship tie-ins from home furnishing companies.[60] This style of filming provided additional commercial value to his instructional lessons.

At first, MacAlister favored a "right" and "wrong" instructional technique, pitting a well-designed Plan-a-Room set against a poorly designed one.[61] Technologically, the camera captured this comparison by the mere rotation of a turntable, making it an ideal demonstration technique during the early years of television when camera mobility was severely limited.[62] Comparing rooms

Figure 7.5
Paul MacAlister holding Plan-a-Room pieces at Chicago's WGN-TV's *Plan-a-Room* studio. Courtesy Hampton C. Wayt.

visually, with the addition of MacAlister's verbal explanation, kept the decorating advice stimulating and transformative.

Given the manageable scale of the pieces, MacAlister also held individual pieces and moved them around as he spoke, as well as indicated items in the rooms with a pencil-sized pointer. Early scripts help us imagine what this entailed. On an episode from 1946, pinch-hitting host McDougal exclaimed, "To show you what we mean, let's remove these draperies and hang up these instead," words presumably followed by a hand lifting the existing miniature draperies and replacing them with new ones.[63] At other times in the script, a dash was used to reflect a physical action on the part of the host, for example when it states, "But why don't we see how this actually looks. There – – -," indicating that the host had just changed his words from an abstract idea to a visible reality.[64]

A 1949 script, moreover, indicates that MacAlister constructed ideal rooms from the ground up, explaining his logic as he developed the room piece by piece.[65] As his promotional newsletter explained, he dealt with arrangement problems "clearly and entertainingly . . . by building the desired room before the television audience."[66] MacAlister seemed to recognize the camera's suitability to movement, providing constant changes throughout the episode. By doing so, he could captivatingly demonstrate his interior decorating instruction.

The ability to alter rooms or develop them from scratch on the air made television an ideal medium for highlighting process and change over time – reflecting the reality of interior decoration as a series of gradual modifications rather than instantaneous transformations. Television offered up the labor of interior decorating as both instructional and entertaining, albeit in a still limited and representational fashion. Using the Plan-a-Room kit as he did, MacAlister underscored formative choices, shifting the focus away from the mere results of interior decoration. Television enabled him to couple dynamic on-air visual change with simultaneous verbal explanation, furnishing audiences with a new model of at-home interior decorating instruction.

Other tools for televising interior decorating principles included blackboards and drawings, which provided visual representations of the host's recommendations. As Etting insisted, "heavy

Demonstrating the profession

reliance [should] be placed on the miniature room technique, sketch pad and black board gimmicks – in order to prove the solution to the given problem."[67] The act of "proving" was essential to the show's instructional premise; without proof, the show merely provided a survey of idealized rooms without imparting applicable lessons.

In spite of their authoritative approach, the shows accommodated individual preference. Episodes often included multiple approved resolutions to the same problem. In one 1946 episode, for example, the host stated, "That's one solution for the spinster window, but we have another one for you."[68] He offered the viewer an active participatory role by emphasizing "the choice between the two methods should depend solely upon the personal taste of the individual."[69] The shows underscored the host's role as an authority, but by including numerous solutions to a given situation, they anticipated the audience's needs and desire for customization. Through this strategy, MacAlister could reassert his professional expertise while actively encouraging homemakers to embrace their role as do-it-yourself decorators.

TELEVISION TECHNOLOGY DEVELOPS

Yet the desire to instruct viewers had limitations on early television. Given that television only aired in black and white until 1953, MacAlister's early shows could not contend visually with color schemes.[70] MacAlister recognized this technological shortcoming and promoted his preparedness for black and white television.[71] He deftly painted Plan-a-Room pieces in black, white, and gray, making them telegenic to a camera that only captured colors in gray scale.

After the National Television Systems Committee set color standards in 1953, the NBC network began broadcasting color segments and permitted MacAlister to include color in a *HOME* appearance in late 1954.[72] But even then, almost no one owned color televisions.[73] Moreover, not all color patterns telecasted equally. As Etting recounted to MacAlister, the NBC art department advised him to focus the camera on one item at a time and to choose patterns that were not too busy for the camera.[74] Technological bounds hampered MacAlister's ability to engage fully with interior decorating color instruction.

Despite these limitations, televised interior decorating segments continued to become more diverse. In 1954, the *HOME* show began to include "on the road" telecasting at locations like furniture showrooms, such as Chicago's Merchandise Mart, which had small filming studios created for this purpose.[75] MacAlister used his access to these professional showrooms to showcase the exhibited furniture to audiences at home. Such developments granted MacAlister's television audiences the behind-the-scenes privileges of a professional, opening further the inner-workings of the interior decorating field. Through television, MacAlister could serve as their professional tour guide.

CONCLUSION

From the medium's earliest days, instructional interior decorating had found a home on television. While the state of early television technology limited what could be shown on air, much was already possible. The profession's arrival on television built upon the growing awareness of interior decoration as a popular pastime. MacAlister understood television's potential, and he leaned on his professional pedigree to assert his interior decorating expertise in a field that was simultaneously professionalizing around him.

MacAlister entered the television realm with his Plan-a-Room kit and an acute sensitivity to his new medium of choice, taking full advantage of the Plan-a-Room qualities inherently suited for television. He developed numerous techniques, many of which used the miniature and three-dimensional nature of the kit to bypass technological constraints and small budgets. Television offered MacAlister the possibility of choreographing his audience's visual experience within the frame of the screen, empowering him to insist on his ideal eye-level perspective.

The opportunity to couple visual movement and verbal instruction enabled MacAlister to present interior decorating as a progression of adjustments over time. In effect, he encouraged viewers to conceive of interior decorating as a process. As such, some episodes stressed the act of interior decorating rather than the final results alone, bringing this mode of instructional demonstration into a growing number of American homes. Through his programs, MacAlister helped create a new television genre—one that has served as a professional outlet for interior decorators ever since.

NOTES

1 In the late 1920s, Charles Francis Jenkins created and sold a mechanical television in the United States with incredibly limited technology and matching sales. But the 1939 World's Fair served as electronic television's national debut. James Von Schilling, *The Magic Window: American Television, 1939–1953* (New York: Haworth Press, 2003), 2–4; Gary R. Edgerton, *The Columbia History of American Television* (New York: Columbia University Press, 2007), 14–16.

2 For example, in 1941, the CBS network aired Arthur Murray instructors teaching two beginners to dance. James Beard and Dione Lucas, two professional chefs, also had television segments in the 1940s. Von Schilling, *Magic Window*, 39; Lori F. Brost, "Television Cooking Shows: Defining the Genre" (PhD diss., Indiana University, 2000), 77–80.

3 MacAlister, for example, wrote a book titled *Display* in 1954, a compilation of his industry articles on in-store ware display, which also utilized the Plan-a-Room kit. According to his resume, he also "developed home furnishings display pattern for the WEIBOLDT STORES [and] color engineered all new BUTLER BROTHERS retail stores throughout the country." Paul MacAlister, *Display: Home Furnishings Display Techniques* (Chicago: Seng Publications, 1954). "Summarization" resume, Paul MacAlister Papers (PMA Papers), Collection of Hampton C. Wayt.

4 "Biography," PMA Papers.

5 According to PEDAC promotional material, the PEDAC team could provide individual companies with assistance in "designing, supervising, and all installations, if so desired." "Permanent Exhibition of Decorative Arts & Crafts: What is PEDAC," PEDAC scrapbook, PMA Papers.

6 For more on the complicated gendering and degradation of interior decorating, the relationship between taste and formal training, and the term "lady decorators," see Pat Kirkham and Penny Sparke, "'A Woman's Place. . .'? Women Interior Designers, Part One: 1900–1950," in *Women Designers in the USA: 1900–2000, Diversity and Difference*, ed. Pat Kirkham (New York: Bard Graduate Center, 2000), 305–316. For the post-World War II divide between lady decorators and modernist architects, see Penny Sparke, *Elsie de Wolfe: The Birth of Modern Interior Decoration* (New York: Acanthus Press, 2005), 21, 23.

7 According to Judith Ann Schiff, Chief Research Archivist at Yale University Library, MacAlister was "officially entered in the Catalogue of Yale University Alumni 1925–1954 as Yale School of the Fine Arts Certificate Holder in Architecture, 1926. At that time the Department of Architecture was in the Yale School

Demonstrating the profession ∎

of the Fine Arts." In the 1926–1927 art school catalog, "MacAlister is listed under architecture, Students of Interior Decoration, as the only fourth year class student." This notice of specialization correlates with MacAlister's resume, in which he states that he "holds the first degree ever awarded in Interior Design and Architecture." Judith Ann Schiff, Yale University Library, e-mail message to author, 2 February 2014; Untitled biography, 1, PMA Papers.

8 Bridget May, "Lessons in Diversity: Origins of Interior Decoration Education in the United States, 1870–1930," *Journal of Interior Design* 42, no. 3 (September 2017): 5–28.

9 Bridget May, "Nancy Vincent McClelland (1877–1959): Professionalizing Interior Decoration in the Early Twentieth Century," *Journal of Design History* 21, no. 1 (20 March 2008): 63.

10 Kirkham and Sparke, "A Women's Place," 307–311.

11 Penny Sparke, "The 'Ideal' and the 'Real' Interior in Elsie de Wolfe's 'The House in Good Taste' of 1913," *Journal of Design History* 16, no. 1 (January 2003): 63–76.

12 Carleton Varney, *In the Pink: Dorothy Draper – America's Most Fabulous Decorator* (New York: Shannongrove Press, 2012), 74, 77.

13 Ibid, 73.

14 Study-Hours on Practical Subjects, Conducted by Grace Cornell: Arthur Gillender Lectures (New York: Metropolitan Museum of Art, 1924), accessed 4 February 2018, http://libmma.contentdm.oclc.org/cdm/ref/collection/p15324coll10/id/1295; "Metropolitan Museum Tells of Fall Talks," Retailing, New York City, 23 September 1940, Box 115, Folder 3, Clippings Collection, The Metropolitan Museum of Art Archives.

15 By the late 1930s, as the country emerged from the Great Depression, the government took active steps to encourage home ownership. The National Housing Act of 1934 established the Federal Housing Administration, which helped facilitate home purchases in the late 1930s by encouraging high percentage loans. The year 1939 saw the introduction of the personal income tax deduction for home mortgages. Even during the war years – when housing starts were low as resources were channeled into the war effort and personnel housing – the country continued planning for its not-too-distant postwar future. Gwendolyn Wright, *Building the Dream: A Social History of Housing in America* (Cambridge, MA: MIT Press, 1993), 240–242; Dolores Hayden, *Redesigning the American Dream: The Future of Housing, Work, and Family Life* (New York: Norton & Company, 1984), 34; Andrew Michael Shanken, *194X: Architecture, Planning, and Consumer Culture on the American Home Front* (Minneapolis: University of Minnesota Press, 2009), 16; Donald Albrecht, Margaret Crawford, and National Building Museum [Donald Albrecht, Margaret Crawford, and National Building Museum] *World War II and the American Dream* (Washington, DC; Cambridge, MA: National Building Museum; MIT Press, 1995), xxii–xxiii.

16 For more on professionalization in general, see B. A. Kimball, *America: A History* The "True Professional Ideal" in *America: A History* (Lanham, MD: Rowman & Littlefield Publishers, 1996) and Samuel Haber, *The Quest for Authority and Honor in the American Professions, 1750–1900* (Chicago: University of Chicago, 1991). For more on the professionalization of the interior decorating field, see Grace Lees-Maffei, "Introduction: Professionalization as a Focus in Interior Design History," *Journal of Design History* 21, no. 1 (1 March 2008): 1–18; Peter McNeil, "Designing Women: Gender, Sexuality and the Interior Decorator, c. 1890–1940," *Art History* 17, no. 4 (December 1994), 638–639; and May, "Nancy Vincent McClelland," 61–68.

17 May, "Nancy Vincent McClelland," 59–74; "Summarization."

18 In 1941, the kits cost $5, in 1948 they cost $7, and by 1964 they sold for $14. Individuals in the finance, insurance, and real estate field earned only $1,777 annually in 1941, implying a target kit audience of some means. "Display Ad 50: Gimbels Plan-a-Room Forums Start Tomorrow at 2 P.M.," *New York Herald Tribune*, 2 March 1941, 38; Mary Roche, "New Ideas and Inventions," *New York Times*, 26 December 1948; *Plan-a-Room Instruction Book*, c. 1964, PMA Papers, 7; Scott Derks and Tony Smith, *The Value of the Dollar: 1860–2004*, Third Edition (Millerton, NY: Grey House Publishing, 2004), 254.

19 *Plan-a-Room Instruction Book*, c. 1941, 5, PMA Papers.

20 For example, see "Gimbel's Launch Plan-a-Room," *Retailing*, 24 February 1941, Plan-A-Room scrapbook (PAR scrapbook), PMA Papers; Betty Ann, "Compact Kit Helps Women Plan Room Arrangements," *Milwaukee Journal*, 28 March 1941, PAR scrapbook; "Living and Leisure: Doll's House," *New York Times Magazine*, 23 March 1941, PAR scrapbook.

21 RCA moved to Rockefeller Center in 1932 and was a television market leader in the pre- and postwar years, not only manufacturing some of the first televisions on the market, but also owning one of the main broadcasting stations, NBC. "Biography," 2; Erik Barnouw, *Tube of Plenty: The Evolution of American Television* (New York: Oxford University Press, 1990), 70, 76–77, 96.

22 According to a newsletter in MacAlister's files, *America Redecorates* appeared on television in 1941. A resume lists MacAlister on air by that year as well. The date of the first episode of *America Redecorates* remains unknown, but by 1942 other sources reference *America Redecorates* on television. It aired as a weekly segment on Tuesday evenings, as part of the *Radio City Matinee* television show. Promotional material for a later iteration of the show in the mid-1940s states that the show began in 1942 and now aired weekly as a segment on Friday evening's *For You and Yours*. "Plan-a-Room News," newsletter, c. 1949, PMA Papers; "Summarization"; "Radio Today," *New York Times*, 10 February 1942, sec. Business Financial; "Home Furnishings Get Televised" newspaper clipping, unknown newspaper, c. 1941–42, in *America Redecorates* scrapbook (AR scrapbook), c. 1946, PMA Papers; "Plan-Room Used at Metropolitan: Nancy McClelland Lectures with MacAlister Kit," *New York Sun*, 6 March 1942, in "Visual Education" Plan-a-Room pamphlet, PMA Papers; *America Redecorates* promotional material, AR scrapbook.

23 *America Redecorates* promotional material.

24 Ibid.

25 "Home Furnishings."

26 Edgerton, *Columbia*, 14–16.

27 Ibid., 15.

28 The number of sold televisions increased more rapidly after World War II. In 1946, RCA produced their "model T" television – the 630-TS – which sold 10,000 units. The next year, 250,000 televisions were sold in the United States. By 1950, "9 percent of the nation, or an estimated 3,875,000 television households, now owned TVs." Edgerton, *Columbia*, 77, 90; Barnouw, *Tube of Plenty*, 90.

29 Until 1941, broadcasters could not sell airtime and could only accept sponsorship to cover costs, limiting the financial resources supporting the growth of television. The FCC would maintain a stronghold on television production, regulating the growth of the industry through its decisions over the course of the 1940s. Barnouw, *Tube of Plenty*, 92, 99; Edgerton, *Columbia*, 76–78.

30 Barnouw, *Tube of Plenty*, 90.

31 Television broadcasters and manufacturers quickly supported wartime production, with the head of RCA, David Sarnoff, serving during the war. In May 1942, the War Production Board also put an end to any additional television expansion. Edgerton, *Columbia*, 67–68, 73–74; "Paul R. MacAlister Joins United States Naval Reserve," *New York Herald Tribune*, 24 January 1943, C2.

32 It is unlikely the show aired consistently during the war. According to promotional materials, however, the show "remained on air," and sources definitively place the show back on television in 1946. *America Redecorates* promotional material; Unknown title, *Television*, Frederick A. Kugel Company, 3, 1946: 34.

33 Untitled biography.

34 The kit had been discontinued for six years, presumably because of wartime production restrictions and Mac Alister's Naval Reserve service. See S. Oliver Goodman, "Who's Who Today," *Washington Post*, 2 November 1948, 16; Roche, "New Ideas and Inventions"; Biography.

35 For more on the *HOME* show, see Inger L. Stole, "There Is No Place Like Home: NBC's Search for a Daytime Audience, 1954–1957," *The Communication Review* 2, no. 2 (1 August 1997): 135–161; *Housewives are Sold at HOME*, promotional booklet, August 1954, PMA Papers.

36 *America Redecorates* promotional material.

Demonstrating the profession ■

37 In the first years of commercial television, sporting events were one of the most popular types of programming. Barnouw, *Tube of Plenty*, 102; Edgerton, *Columbia*, 96; "New Television Show to Give Pointers on Decorating of Homes," *Chicago Daily Tribune*, 4 January 1949, sec. Part 2.

38 See "WGN-TV to Send Boxing Shows to East Coast," *Chicago Daily Tribune*, 8 September 1949, sec. Part 2; "Other 12: Television," *Chicago Daily Tribune*, 20 September 1949, 16; Larry Wolters, "WGN-TV Revises P. M. Schedule to Add Variety: Action Expands Shows for Women, Children," *Chicago Daily Tribune*, 2 January 1950, sec. Part 6.

39 For more on early television and women's programming, see Lynn Spigel, *Make Room for TV: Television and the Family Ideal in Postwar America* (Chicago: University of Chicago Press, 1992); Edgerton, *Columbia*, 97–99.

40 *Housewives are Sold*, 6.

41 Borst, "Television Cooking," 66–67.

42 *America Redecorates* promotional material.

43 MacAlister also generally appeared on television wearing a suit – adding an air of professionalism to his role as host (see Figures 7.2 and 7.5).

44 *America Redecorates* promotional material.

45 Ibid.

46 Flolydia Etting to Paul MacAlister, 13 July 1954, "NBC . . . Show Ideas" folder, PMA Papers.

47 Ibid.

48 Ibid.

49 *Housewives are Sold*, 8.

50 Ibid., 13.

51 *America Redecorates* script, 22 May 1946, AR scrapbook, 1–2.

52 For example, *America Redecorates* script, 12 June 1946, AR scrapbook, 1.

53 MacAlister and Etting were talented model makers. In 1954, the Libbey-Owens-Ford Glass Company commissioned MacAlister to craft refined miniatures, paying $6,000 for two sets. June Cabot, a representative of the company, used these models in demonstrations and on television, appearing with the miniatures on Dave Garroway's *Today* show in 1954. "Miniatures Aid Decorator with Home Problems," *St. Louis Post-Dispatch*, 26 September 1954, 10-J; "Mirror Promotion Pulls Traffic to Lasalle & Koch," *Retailing* (18 February 1954), 16.

54 "Visual Education."

55 *Plan-a-Room News*.

56 For example, see Marion Post Wolcott, *Miniature rooms constructed by students in home economics class, where home planning is studied through model house. Ashwood Plantations, South Carolina*, May 1939. Farm Security Administration - Office of War Information Photograph Collection, Library of Congress, LC-USF34-051666-D (b&w film neg.), accessed 4 February 2018, http://www.loc.gov/pictures/item/2017800888/; New York School of Interior Decoration, *Devoe Career Set Interior Decoration*, 1939, Library of Congress, LOT 3203 (G) [P&P], accessed 4 February 2018, http://www.loc.gov/pictures/item/2005688218/>.

57 *Plan-a-Room Instruction Book*, 1948, PMA Papers, 5.

58 Mrs. American Planner No. 19 was a Plan-a-Room symbol meant to represent a human figure. *Plan-a-Room Instruction Book*, 1964, 5.

59 For example, see *America Redecorates* script, 5 June 1946, AR Scrapbook, 5.

60 For example, the Stiffle-Bradley company had their "Stiffle-Switch" light switch featured on MacAlister's *Plan-a-Room* show in 1949. "Gleams," *Retailing* (29 July 1949), PAR scrapbook.

61 The use of this technique on *America Redecorates* would change in 1946. Unknown title, *Television*; *America Redecorates* promotional material; "Good, and Bad, Rooms," PAR scrapbook; "*Plan-a-Room News*."

62 *America Redecorates* script, 5 June 1946, 4.

63 Ibid., 2.
64 Ibid., 3.
65 "Plan-a-Room with Paul MacAlister, WGN-TV" script, 9 March 1949, PAR scrapbook.
66 "*Plan-a-Room News.*"
67 Flolydia Etting to Paul MacAlister, 13 July 1954.
68 *America Redecorates* script, 5 June 1946, 4.
69 Ibid., 3.
70 See David F. Donnelly, "Color Television," in *Encyclopedia of Television*, ed. Horace Newcomb (Chicago: Fitzroy Dearborn Publishers, 1997), 396–397.
71 "*Plan-a-Room News.*"
72 Flolydia Etting to Paul MacAlister, 31 August 1954, "NBC HOME – 9/24/54 *COLOR* How to Plan a Color Sch." folder, PMA Papers.
73 Television stations continued to broadcast very few color programs through the mid-1960s. By 1965, only 19 percent of American homes owned a color television. Donnelly, "Color Television," 397.
74 Flolydia Etting to Paul MacAlister, 31 August 1954.
75 Filming in the NBC studio at the Merchandise Mart, MacAlister presented furniture from the American Furniture Mart. "NBC Program to Show Market, Retailing, in "NBC HOME – 6/28/55 – Market A. F.M." folder, PMA papers.

BIBLIOGRAPHY

Albrecht, Donald, Margaret Crawford, and National Building Museum. *World War II and the American Dream*. Washington, DC; Cambridge, MA: National Building Museum; MIT Press, 1995.

Barnouw, Erik. *Tube of Plenty: The Evolution of American Television*. New York: Oxford University Press, 1990.

Box 115, Folder 3, Clippings Collection, The Metropolitan Museum of Art Archives.

Brost, Lori F. "Television Cooking Shows: Defining the Genre." PhD diss., Indiana University, 2000.

Derks, Scott and Tony Smith. *The Value of the Dollar: 1860–2004, Third Edition*. Millerton, NY: Grey House Publishing, 2004.

"Display Ad 50: Gimbels Plan-a-Room Forums Start Tomorrow at 2 P.M." *New York Herald Tribune*. 2 March 1941, 38.

Donnelly, David F. "Color Television," in *Encyclopedia of Television*, ed. Horace Newcomb. Chicago: Fitzroy Dearborn Publishers, 1997.

Edgerton, Gary R. *The Columbia History of American Television*. New York: Columbia University Press, 2007.

Goodman, S. Oliver. "Who's Who Today." *Washington Post*. 2 November 1948, 16.

Hayden, Dolores. *Redesigning the American Dream: The Future of Housing, Work, and Family Life*. New York: Norton & Company, 1984.

Kirkham, Pat, and Penny Sparke. " 'A Woman's Place. . .'? Women Interior Designers, Part One: 1900–1950," in *Women Designers in the USA: 1900–2000, Diversity and Difference*, ed. Pat Kirkham. New York: Bard Graduate Center, 2000: 305–316.

Lees-Maffei, Grace. "Introduction: Professionalization as a Focus in Interior Design History." *Journal of Design History* 21, no. 1 (1 March 2008): 1–18.

MacAlister, Paul. *Display: Home Furnishings Display Techniques*. Chicago: Seng Publications, 1954.

Paul MacAlister Papers. Collection of Hampton C. Wayt. Aiken, South Carolina.

May, Bridget. "Lessons in Diversity: Origins of Interior Decoration Education in the United States, 1870–1930." *Journal of Interior Design* 42, no.3 (September 2017): 5–28.

"Nancy Vincent McClelland (1877–1959): Professionalizing Interior Decoration in the Early Twentieth Century." *Journal of Design History* 21, no. 1 (20 March 2008): 59–74.

Demonstrating the profession ∎

McNeil, Peter. "Designing Women: Gender, Sexuality and the Interior Decorator, c. 1890–1940." *Art History* 17, no. 4 (December 1994): 638–639.

"Miniatures Aid Decorator with Home Problems." *St. Louis Post-Dispatch*. 26 September 1954, 10-J.

"Mirror Promotion Pulls Traffic to Lasalle & Koch." *Retailing* 18 February 1954, 16.

"New Television Show to Give Pointers on Decorating of Homes." *Chicago Daily Tribune*. 4 January 1949, sec. Part 2.

"Other 12: Television." *Chicago Daily Tribune*. 20 September 1949, 16.

"Paul R. MacAlister Joins United States Naval Reserve." *New York Herald Tribune*. 24 January 1943, C2.

"Radio Today." *New York Times*. 10 February 1942, sec. Business Financial.

Roche, Mary. "New Ideas and Inventions." *New York Times*. 26 December 1948, 16.

Shanken, Andrew Michael. *194X: Architecture, Planning, and Consumer Culture on the American Home Front*. Minneapolis: University of Minnesota Press, 2009.

Sparke, Penny. *Elsie de Wolfe: The Birth of Modern Interior Decoration*. New York: Acanthus Press, 2005.

Sparke, Penny. "The 'Ideal' and the 'Real' Interior in Elsie de Wolfe's 'The House in Good Taste' of 1913." *Journal of Design History* 16, no. 1 (January 2003): 63–76.

Spigel, Lynn. *Make Room for TV: Television and the Family Ideal in Postwar America*. Chicago: University of Chicago Press, 1992.

Stole, Inger L. "There Is No Place Like Home: NBC's Search for a Daytime Audience, 1954–1957." *The Communication Review* 2, no. 2 (August 1, 1997): 135–161.

Study-Hours on Practical Subjects, Conducted by Grace Cornell: Arthur Gillender Lectures. New York: Metropolitan Museum of Art, 1924. Accessed 4 February 2018 at http://libmma.contentdm.oclc.org/cdm/ref/collection/p15324coll10/id/1295.

Varney, Carleton. *In the Pink: Dorothy Draper – America's Most Fabulous Decorator*. New York: Shannongrove Press, 2012.

Von Schilling, James. *The Magic Window: American Television, 1939–1953*. New York: Haworth Press, 2003.

"WGN-TV to Send Boxing Shows to East Coast." *Chicago Daily Tribune*. 8 September 1949, sec. Part 2.

Who's Who in the Midwest. 7th Edition. Chicago: Marquis, 1960.

Wolters, Larry. "WGN-TV Revises P. M. Schedule to Add Variety: Action Expands Shows for Women, Children." *Chicago Daily Tribune*. 2 January 1950, sec. Part 6.

Wright, Gwendolyn. *Building the Dream: A Social History of Housing in America*. Cambridge, MA: MIT Press, 1993.

Chapter 8: Coeds and t-squares

Interior design education and home economics

Patrick Lee Lucas

Home economics, a distinctive and historically important discipline long hidden from view, deserves a place within the history of interior design education. Women educators from wide-ranging disciplines carried the mantle of approaches to the design of the home that placed humans at the center of that work. Most of this work unfolded at land-grant institutions with extension missions to assist a rapidly developing American nation in two seminal periods. At the turn of the twentieth-century, home economics (and interior design along with it) in its infancy, connected the domestic economy and professionalized, resulting in the establishment of programs in colleges and universities to teach (largely) women the basic principles of managing a home. At the mid-twentieth century, when home economics perhaps was at its zenith in the decades of the postwar period, co-eds took up their t-squares and activated the practice of design bringing their education to the dream house suburban landscape of the mid-century, where houses served as laboratories for scientific approaches to home economy and students explored social and cultural dimensions of the practice of design in greater depth. In this period, interior design education – institutionalized on more than a dozen campuses in home economics departments and colleges – became increasingly disciplined and professionalized. Theory turned to practice for some interior design programs and approaches, including the establishment of home management houses located on or near college campuses for students to experiment in the real world. Despite these important contributions to the development of both discipline and profession, design departments with home economics legacies find themselves often swept into a hidden aspect of institutional culture, underscoring the greater challenge in seeing home economics as a legitimate birthright for the disciplined places that those studying, researching, and practicing interior design find themselves.[1]

Developed in the late nineteenth and early twentieth centuries, home economics emerged in the curricula of colleges and universities as institutions admitted more women. With the premise of applying science to the management of the home, home economics units arose largely at land-grant universities established by the Morrill Act of 1862, which established home economics as one mechanism to achieve the land-grant mission through extension programs and other initiatives. The profession of home economics, formalized during the Lake Placid Conferences held yearly from 1899 to 1909, evolved throughout the first half of the twentieth century, spawning programs, departments, schools, and colleges.[2] At first, home economics embraced traditional areas in housing and interior design, textiles and clothing, home management and consumer studies, foods and nutrition, and child development and family studies. As faculty and administrators institutionalized courses and formalized curricula beginning in the early twentieth century, the content shifted to include changing family patterns, emerging roles for women in the work force and at home, an increase of men in the field, and the demand for research agendas in keeping with the professionalizing universities.[3] Regardless, training of teachers in domestic science took shape with the Lake Placid meetings and thus whole new generations of academics learned and shared the varied approaches of the constellation of professions, among them interior design.

From its inception, home economics struggled with perceptions and notions about mission and purpose, so much so that authors like Marjorie East stated, "A good way to start an argument among home economists is to ask the simple question 'What is home economics?' "[4] And in this way, among others, interior design shares its DNA with home economics in struggling to define itself in the context of other professions and initiatives in higher education.[5] Moreover, women who trained in home economics placed humans at the center of their work – and for this approach, they often experienced a significant devaluing of their discipline and its "applied" research within the academy, particularly alongside men studying some of these same issues in architecture and engineering. According to Megan Elias, "the strongest criticism of the movement came not in the popular press, however, but from other academics . . . who felt that home economics threatened progress that had been hard to win," championing a field that "seemed to advocate a pre-feminist view of womanhood."[6] Home economics educators advocated that, since the domestic environment was a site for change and personal transformation, it merited placement and prominence in the academy.[7] Such education took myriad forms, everything from coursework to Future Homemakers of America and 4-H clubwork, robust extension programs tied to the land grant institutions and research in funding streams related to housing and the environment sponsored by the US Department of Housing and Urban Development. Throughout all these forms, the educated student (and thus the educated consumer) took center stage. The linkage between student and consumer represents an important issue in that home economics instruction resulted in an educated consumer rather than as a distinct design profession, roots that make home economics different than architecture, for instance. Keeping in mind the post-World War I consumer cultural context in which these programs unfolded, tracing the legacies of some of the home economics units helps to better understand the place of design within them as well as the attitudes towards the emerging interior design profession seen through the home economics lens at these institutions.

FROM DOMESTIC ECONOMY TO INTERIOR ARCHITECTURE

Institutions in Iowa, Kansas, and Illinois were among the first to offer courses in what was then called "domestic economy." Iowa State University, which opened in 1869, adopted the Mt. Holyoke plan, requiring service by students in the dining rooms, pantries, and kitchens of the institution. This led to more formal instruction for students by the mid-1870s with training in "cooking, house furnishing, care of children, care of the sick, management of help, dress physiology, and domestic chemistry."[8] Mary deBaca, a graduate of the home management program at Iowa State University, indicated the value of home economics: "This was the first time women had access to higher education," she says. "Women were beginning to see aspects of home economics as career possibilities, as well as being homemakers."[9] Kansas State Agricultural College, founded in 1863, admitted both women and men with blended instruction in agriculture and the liberal arts for its coeducational student population. During the 1870s, Kansas State pioneered the academic teaching of home economics for women, one of the first colleges to offer such a program of study, encouraging women to "prepare for self-supporting careers as well as traditional roles," including courses in home furnishing.[10] The Illinois Industrial University admitted women in 1870 with an announcement a year later that the institution would open a school of Domestic Science and Domestic Art. University Regent John Gregory recommended to the board that a "lady of broad cultural background, wide experience, and high character" be hired to direct the new school.[11] Gregory thus gave shape to a description for the kind of women faculty sought for so many programs in human ecology, domestic science, and home economics: inter-disciplinary and multi-talented individuals to teach applied courses and approaches for the emerging field. The wide experience and broad cultural background of these professionals gave distinctive voice to the early years of the up-and-coming profession – scholars who applied scientific methods to the home – on college campuses across regions in the eastern half of the United States.

In the latter nineteenth century, regents in the University of North Carolina system divided the land grant mission between North Carolina State University in Raleigh and the North Carolina College for Woman in Greensboro. Though they placed the larger share of programs in Raleigh, notably the education and home economics programs found their way to the Greensboro campus, including the founding of the School of Home Economics there in 1911. The interiors program emerged from courses offered in both art and home economics. In 1948, a heated debate opened between then Chairman of the Department of Art, Gregory Ivy, and Naomi Albanese, Dean of the School of Home Economics (later the School of Human Environmental Sciences) regarding the interior design major. Albanese won out, establishing the Department of Housing and Management in Home Economics. Through the department's 50-year history, changes within the interior design industry prompted changes in departmental focus, which in turn prompted three changes in department name – from Housing and Management (1958–1975), to Interior Design (1975–1981), to Housing and Interior Design (1981–2001), and finally Interior Architecture (2001 to present). In 2007, university leadership dissolved the School of Home Economics and Interior Architecture moved to its present home in the College of Arts & Sciences. Carolina's evolution of departments within schools and universities reflects the mercurial tendency for the study interiors to be institutionally housed in a variety of places over time.[12] Doubly, the housing birthright of the design program there, emphasized twice in its history, speaks to the intertwined nature of housing and interior design as one aspect of the profession.

In the upper Midwest, the Wisconsin legislature responded to public demand and founded a Department for Home Economics in 1903, which the land grant university transferred in 1908 from College of Letters and Science to the College of Agriculture. In 1951, the university elevated the department to a School of Home Economics, renamed in 1968 by the university faculty as the School of Family Resources and Consumer Sciences. The faculty affirmed four program areas of study: Home Economics Education and Extension, Home Management and Family Living, Related Art, and Textiles and Clothing. In 1973, the school stood as an autonomous unit in the University of Wisconsin system with Departments of Community and Non-Profit Leadership, Human Development and Family Studies, Interior Architecture, Personal Finance, Retailing and Consumer Behavior, and Textiles and Fashion Design. In 1996, the university renamed it the School of Human Ecology. The Department of Interior Architecture espouses that students combine "the art of design with social science to create revolutionary spaces and environments for people."[13]

In 1907, Cornell University established the first four-year home economics program in the Northeast with its first graduates matriculating in 1911. By 1912, the Cornell faculty named Martha Van Rensselaer and Flora Rose co-directors of the Department of Home Economics in the College of Agriculture. In 1919, the department became the School of Home Economics within the New York State College of Agriculture, morphing into the New York State College of Home Economics established at Cornell in 1925. By 1949, the College of Home Economics became one of 32 constituent units of the State University of New York (SUNY). Throughout the subsequent decades and changes, faculty offered interior design courses and, in 1984, Cornell granted interior design its own department. The current name of the unit, Design and Environmental Analysis, reflects the Department's commitment "to innovative research, design and strategic planning of the built environment to improve people's lives."[14] The department represents one of seven units housed within the College of Human Ecology, distinct from the College of Architecture, Art, and Planning, where disciplines in the title of the latter college – architecture, art, and urban planning – can be found.

In the upland South, the University of Kentucky (UK) College of Design reflects a similar range of programs and approaches from varied units over a 100-year history of design studies on the campus. The institution offered an architectural option in the College of Engineering in the 1920s and a residential design program in the College of Home Economics (eventually the College of Human Environmental Sciences) by the 1950s. In the early 1970s, Dean of Home Economics Marjorie Stewart hired noted educator Richard Rankin to establish a degree program in interior design, responding to a national movement for professionalization. Rankin and others put UK's program in place in 1975, with the first graduating class earning degrees in 1979. The Foundation of Interior Design Education and Research (now the Council of Interior Design Accreditation or CIDA) accredited the program in 1981. UK established the College of Design in 2002, bringing together the disciplines of architecture and interior design. This scattershot approach for design disciplines in the Bluegrass State, not at all uncommon in foundation years of land grant institutions, reflects the disciplinary fluidity of study, later concretized or synthesized in the university.

Kansas State University currently houses two programs in the study of interiors, reflecting its own evolving institutional culture. Under its program founder, Jack C. Durgan, K-State's Department of Interior Architecture and Product Design traces its roots to the Department of Architecture and Allied Arts (within the School of Engineering) at Kansas State College. In 1963, the University established the College of Architecture and Design and formed the Department of Interior Architecture in 1964. 1972 marked the first year to offer the Bachelor of Interior Architecture degree and the program achieved accreditation the following year. Faculty voted an additional name change to the Department of Interior Architecture and Product Design in 2002 and the Kansas Board of Regents approved a new accredited degree offering for Master of Interior Architecture and Product Design in 2006. Across campus, an additional interiors program finds a home in the Department of Apparel, Textiles, and Interior Design within the College of Human Ecology. This Department indicates the focus on a human ecological framework in the classroom and beyond, setting forth a goal to improve the human condition through teaching and scholarship, leaning on the home economics roots of the greater unit. The department targets students seeking the Bachelor of Science as the first professional degree to prepare graduates to practice in the field.[15]

In looking at interior design within home economics paradigms, no clear pattern in history emerges for an approach to study the interior. Though it is important to understand the roots of the profession born within integrated and interdisciplinary approach of the home economist, what happened as programs evolved helps us to see how and why designers of the mid-twentieth century received their education, fundamental knowledge resistant to recovery with poor or non-existent records from this sector of the academy. Interior design education, when viewed as a humanist endeavor, takes on layers of significance in helping to see the mindsets of coeds training as designers at the mid twentieth century. As is clear by the institutional histories, before licensure expectations, accreditation, and disciplinary standards, approaches to design education varied widely. By the 1940s, coeds learned about interior design within home economics paradigms that focused on social and domestic aspects of the home interior. With the postwar suburban building boom resulting from economic investment across the nation, the design of the dream house became a focus of professional and consumer education within home economics.

THE DREAM HOUSE CONTEXT

While all designed buildings, spaces and objects signify the human condition in tangible, three-dimensional form, the design of houses, particularly, carries extra and often personal layers of meaning. The tremendous housing boom of the twentieth century, especially in the two decades following the end of World War II, wrought fundamental changes in cities and in family life throughout the United States, particularly in the explosion of the consumer economy driven largely by the quest for home ownership. In all areas of the country, residents turned outward from the core to land at the edges of urban settlements, fashioning new ways of occupying the landscape in predominately horizontal houses on sprawling lots resulting in corresponding shifts in gender roles and mobility, and compartmentalization in both class and race.[16] In a period of roughly 20 years, what people wanted in houses, how they were designed, how designers furnished and modified them, how residents lived in them, and how homeowners paid for them all dramatically shifted in this suburban milieu. Education in home economics shifted as well to absorb these changes and to confront them with hard evidence and science so that American homeowners would wisely invest in the democratic cause.

Though changes in houses had beginnings much earlier than the mid-century, what drove such powerful transformation to domestic space and place related to the aspiration for single-family home ownership. The "dream house" ideal in retail marketing, architectural design, media programming, home economics education, and many other aspects of American culture resulted in a raised awareness and multiple expectations of what homeowners thought they should have in their houses. Families, young and old, having survived a significant economic depression and two world wars, increasingly found themselves freed from the strictures of the Victorian world of their parents and grandparents.[17] In spreading one-story homes, one encountered flexible public spaces, representing social and physical mobility, support spaces like kitchens, outfitted with the latest appliances, a family or recreation rooms at the center of which often stood the suburban citizen's viewfinder to the world, the television, and private areas with storage space for the accumulation of consumer goods. Home economics programs helped shaped the agendas for both public and support spaces and framed media attention through careful scientific research and studies of consumer behavior.

But what of the political and social import of this "dream house" at mid-century? How did home economics programs frame the ideologies imbedded in the suburban landscape? In the midst of the cold war, the United States government feared that its middle class citizens would embrace alternatives to capitalism. The single family home helped each American to secure economic prosperity and an investment in the future, thus preventing the communist threat.[18] Countering the ever-moving American, the suburban residence symbolized financial and political stability and permanence, hovering in the landscape as an anecdote to the high mobility of its citizens and to urban ills, instead focusing on spaciousness.[19] In locating their own politics within the study of the home, home economics programs bought into these deeply political and social cultural influences. Many of these changes stemmed from images of ideal homes in magazines, in newspapers, on television, and in the landscape.[20] Design magazines, particularly, provided a location for easily attained and copied floor plans, sometimes with designers providing owner-directed amendment. These magazines, too, contained a plethora of advertisements for the latest materials and technologies within the building arts. Side by side, these innovations could be seen with visual advertisements for furnishings, equipment, and finishes espoused by a growing industry centered on the construction of the single-family home. Home economics programs utilized these same periodicals as major sources for class projects, study, and debate.[21]

Students pursuing interior design through home economics in college also learned about the "dream house" through instructional materials. Design represents one of a dozen inter-related subjects in the short film, *Why Study Home Economics?*, where the narrator explains home economics and its value.[22] In the promotional film, Hill explains home economics and the value it has in society and to a student who might pursue study in the field. Interior design garners a mention about halfway through the piece where the narrator declares "whether trailer or dream home, a student studying home economics makes it more attractive and suitable for a healthy family." With the suggestion that students gain practical skills in recognizing furniture styles, combining fabrics, colors, and textures, and understanding house design, the film situates design within the context of good family relationships, money management, social situations, democratic practices, and an attitude for students to "be active in community affairs." In other words, design takes a position along with other disciplines centered on the home and like the dream home ideal, design (among other related topics) helped shape the American spirit, the domestic environment standing as a site for change and personal transformation.[23]

Cooley and Kinne suggest that the study of interiors as part of the home economics approach finds its roots in earlier theories of the ideal woman in the home:

> The house is the place where the homemaker surrounds herself with artistic and harmonious furnishings and
> where she tries to work out the ideals and standards of the home that will create the real home atmosphere

and bring about the development of all the members of the family. The material things of the home express the real spirit of the family and exert an untold influence on its moral and intellectual life.[24]

Following the nineteenth-century theorists who espoused simplicity and rusticity in the home, home economics faculty adopted approaches in the design curriculum to include surveys of architectural styles, contemporary furnishings, and knowledge about topics like color theory and material science to insure that household matrons would not be taken by salesmen who espoused attributes to products and finishes not based on research. The home economics approach mixed the art and science of design (and other interdisciplinary topics) in a way that made it possible for students to be responsible consumers not based merely on the surface of what something looked like but on the craft and care and longevity of furniture, finishes, and equipment in the home. Moreover, students learned about the "moral and health dimensions of topics like wallpaper and paint so that they would make appropriate decisions in decorating in their houses they would occupy once married."[25] Home economics students studying interior design learned that design unfolded with purpose and intention rather than being dictated by fashion. The science part of home economics helped provide the solid evidence for design decisions rather than whims of fancy – substance over surface, as expressed in the early twentieth century by home economist and faculty member Kate Watson, who indicated "decoration should never be purposely constructed."[26] As a work rather than a leisure environment, the home and the home economist functioned to help the individual and the family unit to reach their greatest solo and collective potential:

> Despite the reality that most students would not have the opportunity to design their own house, domestic architecture courses taught them to think of the house as a variable and controllable environment, something that existed to serve its users rather than the other way around.[27]

And yet, some women did have the opportunity to flex their design skills and help design and build a "dream house" as part of their curriculum.

COMMENCEMENT HOUSES

In 1957, architect Edward Loewenstein began teaching an innovative course in architectural design at Woman's College of North Carolina in Greensboro. Twenty-three students took the year-long course open to both home economics and art majors, a course that gave "students a real working knowledge of the problems they would face in making homes for themselves and their families," a home economics-centric view of the academic offering. Students achieved "working knowledge" of design as many opportunities and problems arose, such as a design based on load-bearing construction, material qualities, and the challenges posed by new, state-of-the-art technology "such as dishwashers, garbage disposals, and aluminum wiring, which cut down wiring cost for the project by over twenty percent."[28] Under Loewenstein's guidance, students grounded all design decisions in consumer behavior and material science, underscoring the home economics orientation in design. Loewenstein "felt that there was a lack of interest in platform lecturing and that the students needed something to spark their interest," visualizing that if the student could "design something

Patrick Lee Lucas ■

Figure 8.1
The design students of the Woman's College of the University of North Carolina in the studio working with faculty member Edward Loewenstein, Architect, on early iterations of the 1958 Commencement House in Greensboro, NC. Photograph courtesy of Photograph Collections UNCG University Archives.

and see it carried out in the form of an actual home," they would "have a feeling of solid creativeness," an idea they went after "tooth and nail."[29]

Following the interdisciplinary, experiential, and practical tenets of home economics education, the students designed a house, oversaw its construction and decorated the resulting structure, dubbed the "Commencement House" by the university's public relations office. Acclaim for the structure came from local and national sources.[30] *McCall's Magazine* reported on the first house, *Living for Young Homemakers Magazine* on the second, and *Brides Magazine* on the third. These national periodicals provide evidence to suggest that the home economics story unfolding in Greensboro had a national reach. Each publication profiled the students who helped design the houses and spoke to the collaborative nature of the design team and the home economics and consumer products based approach for the structures. The result of their efforts, according to *McCall's*: a "real honey of a home." The reality was that many of the design decisions were based on scientific approaches to each of the areas of the design. Writers in *Bride's Magazine* suggested

Figure 8.2

The co-eds pose at the groundbreaking ceremonies for the 1958 Commencement House. Photograph courtesy of Photograph Collections UNCG University Archives.

class members "were determined that the décor should be an integral part of the house itself, and not superimposed 'like a mink stole over a tennis dress'," noting that their goal of quiet neutrals in the permanent interior scheme "allowed brilliant, rich colors in paintings, accessories, and upholstery."[31]

Apparently, the house met the needs of the market and was made possible by the confluence of all of its partners, who contributed to the success of the venture. The students alone did not achieve the building and furnishing the houses as they cemented partnerships with local building supply companies and house furnishing concerns, including Duke Power Company, which awarded the house a gold medallion for electrical excellence, as well as numerous local and regional businesses. Loewenstein and the house's contractor, Eugene Gulledge (Superior Contracting Company of Greensboro), placed two restrictions on the students as they designed, the first relating to the number of people to live in the house, and the second to design a house that could sell in Greensboro. According to Gulledge, "while the house should contain pioneering ideas of layout and design, it

Figure 8.3
Nancy Smith, hostess of the WUNC public television program, Potpourri, interviews a member of the 1958 Commencement House design team about the features of the home. University officials and Mr. Loewenstein look on. Photograph courtesy of Photograph Collections UNCG University Archives.

should not be so radical as to make it unmarketable." Working in the architecture firm, John Taylor, Walter J. Moran, and then Gregory Ivy served as interior designers, with Loewenstein coordinating student efforts in the studio and on site. Though built on speculation with a budget of $30,000, the house sold to the Squires family for $45,000 less than two months after its completion. And before that contract was signed, at the dedication of the first house, Ivy and Loewenstein conceived of a second project, continuing to work in partnership with Superior Contracting. "The only real drawback in this venture," agreed Ivy and Gulledge, "is that we didn't start in time. Ten weeks ago, this was a vacant lot. We expect to overcome that handicap in the future."[32] Loewenstein, Ivy, and Gulledge in fact continued in partnership and achieved their goal for a house built the next year, less than a mile to the west. The second house had a slightly more modest budget at $24,000 but continued to be built on speculation and purchased at the budget price by the Kenneth Hinsdale family. Loewenstein and his student-led design team conceived, built, and furnished the third house in 1965 in nearby Sedgefield in a single semester for clients Herbert and Nancy Smith. Why there was a six-year hiatus between commencement houses is debatable, but one reason could be due

Figure 8.4
A rear view of the two-story 1958 Commencement House, as constructed. The design features of the house and all aspects of the interior resulted from student coursework centered in the community. Photograph courtesy of Photograph Collections UNCG University Archives.

to turmoil in the Department of Art at the Woman's College that resulted in Chairman Gregory Ivy's departure (and subsequent employment in Loewenstein's firm), including heated conversations about the place of the interior design program and the courses within its curriculum.

Some common design themes emerged among the three houses echoing basic tenets of home economics instruction: efficiency, evidence, and practicality. The students divided the houses into public and private zones, orienting the public rooms with large glass walls aimed toward wooded lots. The private parts of the house, for quiet and personal retreat, included bedrooms and typically en suite baths. According to the aims of the course, students considered: areas zoned for family activity, a step saving traffic pattern, visual spaciousness beyond actual square footage, easy maintenance, dramatic lighting, and climate conditioning – all aspects of a home economics approach centered in the consumer economy and based on scientific evidence. In each house, dramatic entry sequences and living rooms views permitted "a borrowing and lending of space and light, with each area maintaining an independence and formality of its own." The electric lighting in each plan unified formal spaces, the furnishings wove in texture and color, underscored by layered textiles on curtain walls. In the private areas of the house, students made the most of the space in the framework of a strict decorating budget, incorporating gently-hued draperies, hardwood floors, and multi-functional bathrooms that could be open or closed when entertaining in the public part of the house.[33] All of these design suggestions from the clients echoed what students were hearing in the studio and in lectures – strong themes about mid-century living that so shaped houses and their interiors.

These three so-called "commencement houses" stand as evidence of a hands-on learning experience grounded in a home economics curriculum. In scale and scope when compared to other home economics programs, the Greensboro example does suggest the evolving pedagogies and the experimental methods attempted by some faculty and administrators as design evolved from home economics foundations. But far more typical than designing and building a dwelling was practice in a home management house, an idealized environment that simulated real-world conditions.

HOME MANAGEMENT HOUSES

Home economics faculty believed students should learn about the effective management of the home according to modern principles of efficiency and economics. Home economics faculty and programs educated the public through various means: outreach programs in public schools, extension services through the land-grant universities, articles in popular and scholarly publications, and practical experience in home economics higher education. For example, home management experts evolved time and motion studies with consumer products to streamline household tasks such as food preparation, dishwashing, and laundry. Academic approaches involved careful study as homemakers went about their work, quantifying productivity and making recommendations for better organized and more efficiently run household work and living spaces. Home management faculty helped homemakers to make the best use of limited financial resources. As more women entered the paid workforce with less time available for housework, they eagerly sought advice for managing time and resources effectively. Also, as new consumer products such as dishwashers and washing machines came on the market, consumers eagerly sought advice for selecting and using these items, as well as more traditional aspects of the home in the materials, furnishings, and finishes found there. Thus, home economics faculty provided education and counseling on budgeting and spending, seeking to help consumers to make good decisions to achieve the greatest possible level of health and comfort in a particular household.[34] Interior design was one of but a dozen or so aspects of home management taught regularly in many programs.

As early as the first decade of the twentieth century, home economics programs established full-scale rooms and houses in which students could practice real home-making skills. For most programs, students spent a few nights up to a few weeks in order to ground them in home management. The Woman's College of the University of North Carolina erected three such management houses, fondly remembered by many home economics graduates there. In Iowa, a home management house stood on or near campus from the 1924 to 1958. Before graduation, groups of eight students plus a resident advisor formed a single-family household, each of the women taking turns in various roles. During their practicum, the cohort had to clean and supervise the house, host a party, decorate, manage accounts, schedule leisure time, continue their studies, and take care of an actual baby for six weeks. The goal of the domestic economy courses was "The training of mind and hands so that a young woman will be prepared to understand the supervision of her home with the same comprehension and confidence deemed essential to any profession."[35] The Home Management houses program grew over time from its origins in the 1916 practice house until 1958 when the house program was discontinued. The campus dedicated ten homes for use by the program, although six homes were the most in use at any one time.[36] Many additional home economics programs sponsored on- or near-campus houses following an experiential model to give future homemakers and consumers real-life experience in the home setting.

DISCIPLINARITY

Beginning in the twentieth century, interior design, in part, found its home within higher education in academic units associated with home economics and, later, human environmental sciences, or human ecology. In justifying this location for design, one can draw a strong parity with a lineage in home economics that brings to mind apron-clad mothers and grandmothers putting up the perfect preserves, cooking tasty and nutritious meals, making meticulously stitched clothes, selecting serviceable and beautiful home furnishings, and managing well-ordered homes. As design has come to encompass ever greater influence in the world as a way of working and as the design of our interior environments encapsulate and ultimately necessitate ever-increasing data and information, the design discipline has grown more distant from this location in home economics, at the center of which stands the human condition, surrounded by social science rhetoric and practice.[37] By seeing the significance of coeds and t-squares, the human-centered approach that comes to us through this legacy represents at least one distinction from architecture, for example, a sister discipline accused at midcentury of abandoning human connections to designed spaces.[38]

With little opportunity to approach higher education from other entry points in the first half of the twentieth century, women interested in interior design made their way to it through courses in home economics.[39] Within these courses, interior design represented but one multidisciplinary and integrative approach, emphasizing applied research to the real world of the home, families and communities. Sharing a lineage with other feminized service professions, such as teaching and nursing, women in interior design struggled to establish a professional identity, both within and outside higher education. Viewed as faculty who pursued applied research, home economists interested in design found increasing disadvantage in the modern research university, where basic research generated greater status and funding.[40] Moreover, faculty and students in interior design within home economics units faced challenges wrought by increasingly specialized knowledge and the concrete definitions for disciplines demanded by the academy, in strong contrast to the porous boundaries of the home economics approach. Administrators and faculty alike marginalized home economics (and interior design programs with it) because female faculty gained access to programs across the academy not traditionally associated "women's" disciplines. In that women comprised the majority of the students, faculty, and administrators in interiors and in home economics, increasing activity along gendered lines led to reorganization and sometimes dissolution of schools and programs.[41] At a number of institutions, the home economics moniker faded and new names emerged – human environmental sciences or human ecology – to repackage and retool the lineage of five or more

137

decades of important contributions.[42] Interior design's humanist substructure and process became shrouded behind the greater exercise of justification for post-home economics rubrics. In the present, where many laud inter-disciplinary and multidisciplinary approaches, returning to the previous century and investigating the human-centered research and practice in home economics allows us to uncover the politics, the identities, and the relationships among women, unsettling the historical record that has minimized the contribution of these emerging professionals.

As the authors of other essays in this volume illustrate, interior design came to be the discipline that we know from many different sources – architectural practice, antiques firms, materials manufacturers, museum publications, magazines and television – each source bringing life to some aspect of the professionalizing practice surrounding the design of the interior. Coming to encounter interior design through the eyes and minds of thousands of coeds and their teachers who grabbed their t-squares, among other tools, and turned their attention to the design of domestic environments, adds much to an already rich story of design luminaries of the nineteenth and twentieth centuries.

Understanding how and why designers of the mid-twentieth century received their education about the design of the home suggests fundamental knowledge yet to be uncovered.[43] In the two decades after World War II, women entered training in droves for the newly professionalizing field of interior design, often in home economics schools. Thus this 20-year period of curriculum development and first efforts at teaching about interiors provide one way to scrutinize the human condition as understood by educators and students taking up the task of designing houses, cultural artifacts that geographer Peirce Lewis characterizes as our "unwitting biographies," buildings that unconsciously reflect the intentions of their owners.[44] By studying the values embedded in the curricula, we come away knowing the place of women and the education required to put them in that place. As Dolores Hayden implies: the houses of the mid-century sustain the Victorian stereotypes of the home as "woman's place," a haven for human activity shaped around a matriarchal domestic frame.[45] In reality, these homes found women enmeshed in a form of social control – disciplined in another sense – as the unpaid household managers in the patriarchal worlds of their husbands.[46]

NOTES

1 Anne Massey, *Interior Design since 1900*, Third edition (London: Thames & Hudson); John Turpin, "The History of Women in Interior Design: A Review of Literature," *Journal of Interior Design* 33 (2007): 1–15.
2 Marjorie Brown, *What Is Home Economics Education?* (St Paul: University of Minnesota, 1980); Jessie Bernard, *Academic Women* (University Park: Pennsylvania State University Press, 1964).
3 Laura Bailey, Francille Firebaugh, Elizabeth Haley, and Sharon Nickols, "Human Ecology in Higher Education: Surviving Beyond 2000," *Journal of Home Economics* 85 (1993): 3–10.
4 Marjorie East, *Home Economics: Past, Present, and Future* (Boston: Allyn and Bacon, Inc., 1980).
5 Massey, 2008; Turpin, 2007.
6 Megan J. Elias, *Stir It Up: Home Economics in American Culture* (Philadelphia: University of Pennsylvania Press, 2008), 15.
7 Dena Attar, *Wasting Girls' Time: The History and Politics of Home Economics* (London: Virago Press, 1990).
8 Hazel Craig and Blanche Stover, *The History of Home Economics* (New York: Practical Home Economics, 1946), 5.

9 Talk of Iowa Radio Broadcast, http://iowapublicradio.org/post/iowa-states-home-management-houses#stream/0.
10 Virginia Railsback Gunn, "Industrialists Not Butterflies: Women's Higher Education at Kansas State Agricultural College, 1873–1882," *Kansas History* 18 (Spring 1995): 3.
11 Craig and Stover, 6.
12 See the essay by Penelope Dean, "Imaging Interior Design: Beside, Beneath, and Within Architecture," in this volume, where the author traces similar nomenclature changes through titles and sections in professional journals.
13 "University of Wisconsin School of Human Ecology," accessed 15 January 2017, http://sohe.wisc.edu.
14 "Cornell University College of Human Ecology," accessed 15 January 2017, http:// www.human.cornell.edu.
15 "Kansas State University College of Architecture, Planning and Design," accessed 15 January 2017 http://apdesign.k-state.edu and Kansas State University Department of Apparel, Textiles, and Interior Design," accessed 15 January 2017, www.he.k-state.edu/atid/id-ugrad.
16 Postwar suburbanization literature comes from a wide range of sources. John Archer, *Architecture and Suburbia: From English Villa to American Dream House, 1690–2000* (Minneapolis: University of Minnesota Press, 2005); Rosalyn Baxandall and Elizabeth Ewen, *Picture Windows: How the Suburbs Happened* (New York: Basic Books, 2000); Robert A. Beauregard, *When America Became Suburban* (Minneapolis: University of Minnesota Press, 2006); Clifford E. Clark, *The American Family Home, 1800–1960* (Chapel Hill: University of North Carolina Press, 1986); Lizabeth Cohen, "Residence: Inequality in Mass Suburbia," in *A Consumers' Republic: The Politics of Mass Consumption in Postwar America* (New York: Vintage, 2003); Alice Friedman, *Women and the Making of the Modern House* (New Haven: Yale University Press, 2007); Dolores Hayden, *Redesigning the American Dream: Gender Housing, and Family Life*, Second edition (New York City, New York: W. W. Norton & Company, Inc., 2002); Sandy Isenstadt, *The Modern American House: Spaciousness and Middle-Class Identity* (Cambridge: Cambridge University Press, 2006); Karal Ann Marling, *As Seen on TV: The Visual Culture of Everyday Life in the 1950s* (Cambridge: Harvard University Press, 1996); Lynn Spigel, *Welcome to the Dream House: Popular Media and Postwar Suburbs* (Durham: Duke University Press, 2001); George Teyssot, ed., *The American Lawn* (New York: Princeton Architectural Press, 1999); Eleanor Thompson, *The American Home: Material Culture, Domestic Space, and Family Life* (Hanover: University Press of New England, 1988); Gwendolyn Wright, *Building the Dream: A Social History of Housing in America* (New York City, NY: Pantheon Books, 1981).
17 Archer, 2005.
18 Baxandall and Ewen, 2000.
19 Isenstadt, 2006.
20 Marling, 1996.
21 4-H Notebook, from the private collection of Susan Camenisch, accessed 15 July 2016.
22 "Why Study Home Economics?" Centron Corporation (1955). The film was produced by Edna A. Hill, Chair of the Department of Home Economics at the University of Kansas. Downloaded from https://archive.org/details/WhyStudy1955.
23 Elias, 2008.
24 Anna B. Cooley and Helen Kinne, *Shelter and Clothing* (New York: McMillan, 1913), 202.
25 Jan Jennings, "Controlling Passion: The Turn-of-the-Century Wallpaper Dilemma," *Winterthur Portfolio* 31 (1996): 243–264. Helen Brinkerd Young (1877–1959) taught at Cornell University's Department of Home Economics, drawing on her training as an architect and encouraged design principles in home planning and furnishing. Young's notes of 1921 were cited in Elias, 2008, 193. Gwendolyn Wright takes up morality and furnishings in her book on nineteenth-century advice literature, *Moralism and the Model Home* (Chicago: University of Chicago Press, 1980).
26 Kate Heinz Watson, *Textiles and Clothing* (Chicago: American School of Economics, 1907), 203.
27 Elias, 2008, 41.
28 "Designed by 23 College Girls," McCall's, November 1958, 139.

29 *Southern Appliances Magazine*, September 1958.
30 The *Greensboro Daily News* proclaimed the house "as modern as tomorrow," hailing the women who designed it as pioneers, reporting that "they are the first pupils outside the schools of architecture to attempt the complete designing and building of a house." Mereb Mossman, Dean of Instruction at Woman's College, described the project as "an exciting experience in construction," suggesting that the walls of a college building are no longer the boundary lines for a program of learning." Echoing Mossman, Chancellor Gordon W. Blackwell declared that building the house "marks another national 'first' for the college." *Greensboro Daily News*. 30 May 1958, B2.
31 *McCall's Magazine*, November 1958. "Greensboro LBE House Designed by WCUNC Class." *Southern Appliances Magazine* (September 1958) 6–8. "22 Brides Build a House: That is Every Inch a Home," *Brides Magazine* (Spring 1965), 206.
32 *Greensboro Daily News*, 30 May 1958, B2.
33 "A House with a College Diploma," *Living for Young Homemakers* (October 1959), 178–181, 183, 186–187.
34 "Hearth Home Page," http://hearth.library.cornell.edu/h/hearth/home_mgt.html, accessed 15 January 2017.
35 *"Home Management Houses at Iowa State College* 1916-1927." Compiled by Ruth M. Lundquist. RS 12/5/4 box 1, folder 2.
36 "House Babies at Iowa State," https://isuspecialcollections.wordpress.com/2015/01/08/house-babies-at-iowa-state/, accessed 15 January 2017.
37 Tom Kelley, *The Art of Innovation: Lessons in Creativity* (New York: Doubleday, 2001); Henry Petroski, *The Evolution of Useful Things* (New York: Knopf, 1992); Ralph Caplan, *By Design: Why There Are No Locks on the Bathroom Doors in the Hotel Louis XIV and Other Objects Lessons* (New York: Fairchild, 2005).
38 Massey, 2008.
39 John Kurtich and Garrett Eakin, *Interior Architecture* (New York: Van Nostrand Reinhold, 1993); Sarah Stage and Virginia Bramble Vincenti, *Rethinking Home Economics: Women and the History of a Profession* (Ithaca: University of New York Press, 1997); John Turpin, "Omitted, Devalued, Ignored: Reevaluating the Historical Interpretation of Women in the Interior Design Profession," *Journal of Interior Design* 27 (2001): 1–11.
40 "Home Economics Archive—Research, Tradition and History," (2010) Online resource: http://hearth.library.cornell.edu/.
41 Barbara Miller Solomon, *In the Company of Educated Women: A History of Women and Higher Education in America* (New Haven: Yale University Press, 1985).
42 Elias, 2008.
43 Susie McKellar and Penny Sparke, eds., *Interior Design and Identity* (Manchester: Manchester University Press, 2004); Brenda Martin and Penny Sparke, eds., *Women's Places: Architecture and Design, 1860–1960* (London: Routledge, 2003).
44 Peirce A. Lewis, "Common Houses, Cultural Spoor," *Landscape* 19 (1975): 2.
45 Dolores Hayden, 2002.
46 Michel Foucault, *Discipline and Punish: the Birth of the Prison* (New York: Random House, 1975).

BIBLIOGRPAHY

John Archer, *Architecture and Suburbia: From English Villa to American Dream House, 1690–2000* (Minneapolis: University of Minnesota Press, 2005).
Dena Attar, *Wasting Girls' Time: The History and Politics of Home Economics* (London: Virago Press, 1990).
Laura Bailey, Francille Firebaugh, Elizabeth Haley, and Sharon Nickols, "Human Ecology in Higher Education: Surviving Beyond 2000," *Journal of Home Economics* 85 (1993): 3–10.
Rosalyn Baxandall and Elizabeth Ewen, *Picture Windows: How the Suburbs Happened* (New York: Basic Books, 2000).
Robert A. Beauregard, *When America Became Suburban* (Minneapolis: University of Minnesota Press, 2006); Clifford E. Clark, *The American Family Home, 1800–1960* (Chapel Hill: University of North Carolina Press, 1986).

Marjorie Brown, *What Is Home Economics Education?* (St Paul: University of Minnesota, 1980); Jessie Bernard, *Academic Women* (University Park: Pennsylvania State University Press, 1964).

Ralph Caplan, *By Design: Why There Are No Locks on the Bathroom Doors in the Hotel Louis XIV and Other Objects Lessons* (New York: Fairchild, 2005).

Lizabeth Cohen, "Residence: Inequality in Mass Suburbia," in *A Consumers' Republic: The Politics of Mass Consumption in Postwar America* (New York: Vintage, 2003).

Anna B. Cooley and Helen Kinne, *Shelter and Clothing* (New York: McMillan, 1913), 202.

Hazel Craig and Blanche Stover, *The History of Home Economics* (New York: Practical Home Economics, 1946), 5.

Marjorie East, *Home Economics: Past, Present, and Future* (Boston: Allyn and Bacon, Inc., 1980).

Megan J. Elias, *Stir It Up: Home Economics in American Culture* (Philadelphia: University of Pennsylvania Press, 2008), 15.

Michel Foucault, *Discipline and Punish: the Birth of the Prison* (New York: Random House, 1975).

Alice Friedman, *Women and the Making of the Modern House* (New Haven: Yale University Press, 2007).

Virginia Railsback Gunn, "Industrialists Not Butterflies: Women's Higher Education at Kansas State Agricultural College, 1873–1882," *Kansas History* 18 (Spring 1995): 3.

Dolores Hayden, *Redesigning the American Dream: Gender Housing, and Family Life*, Second edition (New York City, New York: W. W. Norton & Company, Inc., 2002),

Sandy Isenstadt, *The Modern American House: Spaciousness and Middle-Class Identity* (Cambridge: Cambridge University Press, 2006).

Jan Jennings, "Controlling Passion: The Turn-of-the-Century Wallpaper Dilemma," *Winterthur Portfolio* 31 (1996): 243–264.

Tom Kelley, *The Art of Innovation: Lessons in Creativity* (New York: Doubleday, 2001).

John Kurtich and Garrett Eakin, *Interior Architecture* (New York: Van Nostrand Reinhold, 1993).

Peirce A. Lewis, "Common Houses, Cultural Spoor," *Landscape* 19 (1975): 2.

Karal Ann Marling, *As Seen on TV: The Visual Culture of Everyday Life in the 1950s* (Cambridge: Harvard University Press, 1996).

Henry Petroski, *The Evolution of Useful Things* (New York: Knopf, 1992).

Susie McKellar and Penny Sparke, Eds., *Interior Design and Identity* (Manchester: Manchester University Press, 2004).

Brenda Martin and Penny Sparke, Eds., *Women's Places: Architecture and Design, 1860–1960* (London: Routledge, 2003).

Anne Massey, *Interior Design since 1900*, Third edition (London: Thames & Hudson)

Barbara Miller Solomon, *In the Company of Educated Women: A History of Women and Higher Education in America* (New Haven: Yale University Press, 1985).

Lynn Spigel, *Welcome to the Dream House: Popular Media and Postwar Suburbs* (Durham: Duke University Press, 2001).

Sarah Stage and Virginia Bramble Vincenti, *Rethinking Home Economics: Women and the History of a Profession* (Ithaca: University of New York Press, 1997).

George Teyssot, ed., *The American Lawn* (New York: Princeton Architectural Press, 1999).

Eleanor Thompson, *The American Home: Material Culture, Domestic Space, and Family Life* (Hanover: University Press of New England, 1988).

John Turpin, "Omitted, Devalued, Ignored: Reevaluating the Historical Interpretation of Women in the Interior Design Profession," *Journal of Interior Design* 27 (2001): 1–11.

John Turpin, "The History of Women in Interior Design: A Review of Literature," *Journal of Interior Design* 33 (2007): 1–15.

Kate Heinz Watson, *Textiles and Clothing* (Chicago: American School of Economics, 1907), 203.

Gwendolyn Wright, *Building the Dream: A Social History of Housing in America* (New York City, NY: Pantheon Books, 1981).

Gwendolyn Wright. *Moralism and the Model Home* (Chicago: University of Chicago Press, 1980).

Chapter 9: "Principles, not effects"

Edgar Kaufmann, Jr., MoMA and the legitimization of interior design

Lucinda Kaukas Havenhand

As a relatively new field, interior design is still writing its history. In this process, exploring the place where "interior design" emerges as a term, a profession, and a specific body of knowledge is key to understanding the developments that contributed to that. Although those factors and contexts are numerous and complex, one in particularly stands out – the influence of the Museum of Modern Art (MoMA). This essay considers how MoMA, from its position as an arbiter of modern art and design, under the direction of Edgar Kaufmann, jr.[1] their curator of design, created a discourse around the subject of "Good Design" in the 1950s that helped shape interior design's emergent identity. In his 1953 publication written for the museum "What is Modern Interior Design?" Kaufmann identified interior design as based in "principles, not effects" to establish its difference from interior decoration based in "taste."[2] This publication as well as Kaufmann's efforts with the Good Design shows helped the public understand interior design as an occupation distinct from interior decorating and laid the foundations of its development as a profession.

The emergence of interior design as a practice in the United States parallels the development of modern architecture and design in postwar America. The technology and materials of wartime – plastics, fiberglass, synthetic fabrics, and metal welding rods – became the building blocks of a new generation of modern furniture and interior products for American homes. By the late 1940s and early 1950s modern design had become a discernible marker of the United States' step into a new phase of prosperity brought by the war's successful end as advertising, popular journals, industry and museum programs, such as the MoMA's Good Design shows, promoted the modern aesthetic as part of a promise for a better future and as a visual exorcism of America's recent gloomy past.

Interior design as an emerging profession rode the wave of this interest and enthusiasm about modern products. While many Americans were able to build new homes, others chose to renovate and expand their existing ones. At the same time, expanding businesses opened new locations and updated their corporate images. In both scenarios interior design became an important mode of demonstrating the new postwar American way of life. Modern design was also linked to the idea of a return to normalcy as over 16 million military personnel re-entered civilian life. A 1945 *House Beautiful* article written by a war veteran suggested that the returning soldier would have little patience for refinement and pretense because he was a "modern man" whose encounters with "less progressive civilizations" had convinced and made him proud of his own country's progressiveness. "One thing is plain," this soldier wrote, "as far as modern homes and the comforts there of . . . you don't reach the 20th century until you pass the Statue of Liberty or the Golden Gate."[3] Through this lens, modern interior design with its links to technology and its emphasis on functionalism was easily seen as the appropriate mode for creating the new settings of postwar life. Shelter magazines such as *House Beautiful, House&Garden*, and *Better Homes and Gardens* illustrated what the modern interior would look like and employed designers such as Russel and Mary Wright and George Nelson to develop schemes and tips for their readers about how to implement them.

From as early as the late 1920s one can see the initial indicators of this new practice, interior design. By embracing the modern movement's concept of "design," as advanced by the Bauhaus in the 1920s, and using that word instead of "decoration," the field positioned itself as the appropriately modern, systematic, and rational approach to interiors. By the 1930s both a discourse about and practice of interior design had emerged in the United States as its journals, educational programs, and professional organizations developed and more and more Americans reached out to interior designers for professional help in creating contemporary environments.[4] Journals such as *Architectural Review* used the word "design" as well as the phrases "interior design" and "interior architecture" instead of "decoration" to refer to interiors. By the 1940s this language continued to shift and a journal devoted totally to the subject of interior design, called *Interiors*, was initiated. It was followed a decade later by *Interior Design* in 1950. The recognition that MoMA and particularly Edgar Kaufmann, jr. gave to the practice of interior design during the *Good Design* shows from 1950 to 1955 further elevated its legitimacy as a practice and its identification as a distinct profession while simultaneously serving the museum's goal of promoting modern design (Figure 9.1).

By the time the first *Good Design* shows were initiated, MoMA had already played a key role in the advancement of modernism and modern design in the United States. The effort to establish legitimacy for modern art had been long underway from its inception as an institution in 1929. Concentrating on modern painting and sculpture at first, the museum branched out to include exhibitions on modern architecture in the early 1930s and expanded into photography, film, dance, fashion, graphic design and objects by the 1940s. The *Objects: 1900 and today* show in 1933 kicked off a succession of exhibitions about modern home furnishings such as *Useful Objects under $5* (1938), *Useful Objects of American Design under $10.00* (1939, 1942) *Organic Design in Home Furnishings* (1941) and *Design for Use* (1944). Themes of "how to design and plan a modern home" appeared during the war years and continued postwar in exhibitions such as *Planning a Modern House* (1942), *Built in the U.S.A., 1932–44* (1944), *If You Want to Build a House* (1946). The very successful reception of *New Furniture Designed by Charles Eames* (1946), which was hailed by the New York Times as demonstrating the "furniture of the future," propelled Charles and Ray Eames into the spotlight as American modern designers and contributed to the future success of furniture companies such as Herman Miller who manufactured the Eameses' products. This shift from high art to applied art not only created a greater audience for the museum but also a larger market for the modern products and designs endorsed in these shows. As John Elderfield suggests:

> During the war years, this internal reappraisal involved ways to maintain the Museum's fundamental purpose while responding to changed circumstances and needs. In the years after the war, the focus necessarily had to be shifted. The Museums aims had to be reconsidered with the context of a changed world. Increasing

Figure 9.1

Edgar Kaufmann, Jr., and Alexander Girard at the exhibition "Good Design" September 22, 1953 through November 29, 1953. The Museum of Modern Art, New York, Photographic Archive, Musuem of Modern Art Archives, New York. Photo: William Leftwich. Digital Image ©The Museum of Modern Art/Licensed by SCALA/Art Resource, NY.

affluence and, most especially, the emergence of a middleclass consumer society in the United States created a much larger audience for the Museum's program than hitherto.[5]

The museum's dedication of space, exhibition time and the collecting dedicated to design and design products demonstrates its understanding of this.

The museum's promotion of Edgar Kaufmann, Jr. to the role as Curator of Industrial Design in 1946 and to Director of Good Design in 1949 reveals its appreciation for the importance of modern design as a force to promote the ethos of modernism. Kaufmann was an interesting choice for the museum. Unlike his predecessor Eliot Noyes and his colleague and later superior at the museum, Philip Johnson, who were both Harvard-trained and had close associations with European modernists such as Le Corbusier and Marcel Breuer, Kaufmann came from a family of merchants and was educated only briefly with Frank Lloyd Wright, who is credited for awakening his interest in modern design.

Edgar Kaufmann, Jr. was the son of Edgar and Liliane Kaufmann, heirs to the four Kaufmann brothers who emigrated from Germany in the later nineteenth century to found Kaufmann's Department Store in Pittsburgh. Edgar Kaufmann, Sr., through marriage, manipulation, and hard work, ultimately became the controlling owner of the Kaufmann business. Kaufmann, Sr. was a shrewd proprietor who believed that retailing was a skill that needed to be studied and taught. He pushed for educational programs and research about selling and marketing during his lifetime. In 1917 Kaufmann joined with the leaders of six other Pittsburgh department stores to underwrite the Bureau for Retail Training and new programs at the Carnegie Institute of Technology and in the local public schools. Kaufmann's family store was one of the initial users of specific sales techniques developed through the Bureau that began to explore consumer psychology and understood the need for the buyer to create attachments to the products for sale. Kaufmann, Sr. also believed that both his customers and employees needed to be trained in understanding good design. Kaufmann's department store lead the way in creating links between art, design and retailing and the useful exchange between museums and galleries and stores. As early as the 1920s Kaufmann's began to take charge of educating consumer taste after its owner learned that Parisian department stores and art concerns such as Bon Marché, Galeries Lafayette, Printemps, and the Louvre were doing this.[6] Kaufmann's in Pittsburgh may have been the first American department store to convene a design forum and in November of 1926 it hosted a month-long International Exposition of Industrial and Decorative Arts. As part of the event, Stewart Culin, curator of the Brooklyn Museum, gave a talk in which he observed, "The department store stands for the greatest influences for culture and taste that exist today in America. For every one person who goes to a museum to gratify his or her curiosity about new things," he said, "ten thousand visit the department store with the same motive."[7] From his family background and training in his family's business, Edgar Kaufmann, jr. was well aware of the importance of this implication.

When Kaufmann was hired by MoMA he was already well versed in the relationship that retailers and museums and galleries could share. Kaufmann saw clearly that modern design would provide good solutions to the postwar push to set aside old fashion ideas and create the "new American way of Life" for the postwar period. He also understood that he and the museum could provide instruction on how to accomplish this. In the fashion of the many "how-to" books and movements of the postwar period, Edgar Kaufmann, jr. brought to his job as curator at MoMA a specific kind of expertise, different from other curators such as Johnson or Noyes, namely his experience and understanding of home furnishings and retail design, as well as his unabashed acceptance of consumerism as part of American life. Kaufmann moved forward to use the mechanisms of both the museum and retailing to provide training and understanding of modern design in ways both accessible and desirable to the general public.

Kaufmann's expertise and influence began in 1938 when he was hired as a consultant for the museum's first *Useful Objects* exhibit: *Useful Objects under $5*. In this exhibition the objects were arranged in ways that evoked both store and home. Interior design was the medium used for these exhibitions to create the simulated partial domestic interiors that allowed the viewers to experience the objects as if they were being used in their own homes. Historian Mary Ann Staniszewski notes the show,

> was a realization of the Museum's charter to educate the public about all aspects of modern visual culture, but it also directly affected manufacturing and consumption. The show's success was secured by foregrounding the visitor's role as consumer and by presenting modern culture as modest, down-home, democratic housewares.[8]

The demand for the featured objects after the show acknowledged its success, as well as demonstrated to the museum how it could gain access to a broader range of viewers, create a desire for, and an acceptance of, modern products and for daily life.

When Eliot Noyes, Director of the Industrial Design Department of MoMA left for public practice in 1946, the museum named Kaufmann to replace him. Kaufmann continued to build upon the public's interest in modern design with his "International Competition for Low-Cost Furniture" show in 1948. In this show Kaufmann established the philosophy and way of working that would be a hallmark of the *Good Design* shows. First, it was a collaboration between the museum and retailers, in this case The Museum Project, Inc., a group of prominent furniture retailers. Second, the products were limited to designs that were modern and "integrated to the needs of modern living." Third, Kaufmann was actively involved in not only curating but also finding ways to promote, mass produce, and retail the products – even taking on the role of sales agent for designers to be sure they received their share of the profits for their work. The emphasis of the show was clear. It was not just an exhibit that promoted modern design, it was a sales and marketing tool for it.

This is most evident in Kaufmann's work developing the *Good Design* program and exhibitions that ran from 1950 to 1955. Fully titled *Good Design, A Joint Program to Stimulate the Best Modern Design of Home Furnishings*, the program was a combined effort by the Chicago Merchandise Mart and the Museum to "influence their respective audiences: The Museum's members and visitors who may have been disposed toward modern design; and the Mart's wholesale buyers, who were instrumental in determining what goods appeared in retail stores through the country."[9] The shows were organized for two venues, one at the Merchandise Mart in Chicago and the other MoMA in New York (Figure 9.2).

The Chicago Merchandise Mart, originally constructed by the Marshall Field Company, was the largest building in the world at the time it was built in 1930 with 272,000 square feet of space dedicated to the promotion and sales of architectural and interior design trade goods. The Merchandise Mart gave over 5,000 square feet of space to the *Good Design* shows from 1950 to 1955, thus expanding the

Lucinda Kaukas Havenhand ■

Figure 9.2
Cover of "Good Design" An Exhibition of Home Furnishings Selected by the Museum of Modern Art New York, for the Merchandise Mart Chicago" by Edgar Kaufmann, Jr. New York, The Museum of Modern Art, 1950. Offset, Printed in Black, 10"x 71/2". The Museum of Modern Art Library, New York (L1254) The Museum of Modern Art. Digital Image ©The Museum of Modern Art/Licensed by SCALA/Art Resource, NY.

shows' viewership to the over 27,000 design professionals and 80,000 visitors that toured that space annually – effectively contributing to the support for the shows, modern design, and the museum itself. Terence Riley and Edward Eigen point out that "The projected scope of the Good Design program's intervention in the housewares industry – especially its ambition ultimately to influence the buying habits of American consumers and the selling practices of retailers – was without precedent in the United States."[10] Although the format of the shows changed from year to year depending on who designed the exhibition, a consistent feature that Kaufmann oversaw was the ability of the viewers to interact with the products, by touching, sitting on, or interacting with them. Kaufmann understood that for the American public to embrace modern design they must feel comfortable with it and, to a greater extent, understand how they would be able to live with it and benefit from it.

Charles Eames, whose design firm became known for showroom design at Herman Miller and Knoll furniture companies, created the inaugural installation. Using wood-laminate platforms and screen partitions, Eames, with his wife and co-designer Ray, replicated the interior design approach that was used in their own home, Case Study House #8, by creating a harmonious and visually rich arrangement of space, furniture and objects. Designers Alexander Girard, Finn Juhl, and Paul Rudolph continued the strategy of creating interiors to exhibit the work (Figure 9.3). The practice of interior design with its emphasis on intimate scale and rationalist approach was the perfect medium for negotiating this interaction both in the exhibitions spaces and by implication in people's homes. Kaufmann, jr. certainly understood how interior design could be used as both a mediator and a disseminator of modern design. As Alfred Auerbach, design and merchandise consultant, observed in a speech to the Merchants and Manufacturer's Club in 1950, Good Design retailers were "essentially merchants of environments, not just commodities."[11]

Kaufmann's understanding of this is further revealed in his creation of a text about interior design. In 1950 he had produced an explanatory booklet called "What is Modern Design?" the third in the Introductory Series to the Modern Arts published by the museum that had earlier published texts that explained modern art and architecture to the American public. In 1953 he added to the series writing specifically about interior design in "What is Modern Interior Design?" Kaufmann's choice to write an additional booklet to clarify interior design reveals his understanding of the importance of the field.

Kaufmann's outlines in this publication that "modern interior design is planning and making rooms suited to our way of life, our abilities, our ideals. It began a century ago when creative perceptive people reacted to vast problems posed by technological change."[12] Beginning with examples from the Arts and Crafts, Kaufmann carries the reader through an understanding of how his essential characteristics of a good interior – comfort, quality, lightness, and harmony – have been translated through modern technology and materials into comfortable and appropriates spaces for contemporary living. Within its examples and text Kaufmann gives the American public something to aspire to, thus both stimulating and supporting the practice of modern interior design.

Within this context, Kaufmann established two points that specifically supported and helped define the field and its legitimization. The first was to identify interior design as specifically based in "principles, not effects,"[13] which helped the public understand its separation and difference from interior decorating and historical models. Kaufmann notes that nineteenth-century pioneers in the field understood that they "did not want to imitate effects but to follow principles which had produced glorious arts of the past." "This was the decisive change," he states, "principles, not effects. The road was open to a new idiom of design, destined to express the life of its own times."[14] Kaufmann reflects on this to emphasize and explain that modern interior design is not a superfluous bow to taste and style, but reflective of more modern means, in particular the rationalist and technologically-based approach similar to that which had helped the United States win the war and gain recognition as a serious world leader. By making this connection, Kaufmann lends credibility

Figure 9.3

Edgar Kaufmann, Jr., and Alexander Girard at the exhibition "Good Design" September 22, 1953 through November 29, 1953. The Museum of Modern Art, New York, Photographic Archive, Musuem of Modern Art Archives, New York. Photo: William Leftwich. Digital Image ©The Museum of Modern Art/Licensed by SCALA/Art Resource, NY.

not only to the practice of interior design, but also to the modern home furnishing and product industries that were linked to it. As the Good Design shows illustrated, to be modern one must live modernly through modern means and surrounded by modern things – designs that expressed appropriately "the life of its own times." The Good Design shows demonstrated to thousands of Americans how this could be done (Figure 9.4).

Kaufmann also understood that while modern architecture might be attainable to only a few people building new homes, modern interiors were accessible to any existing home that wished to update. Interior design and interior designers could provide the framework and guidance for transforming the old into the new and the modern. Model housing projects with modern interiors were highlighted during this time period in retail concerns, museums and independent programs as instructional guides. In 1941, the Walker Art Center built the first museum display house called *Idea House I* on its grounds, showcasing contemporary approaches to residential architecture and interior design. They followed with *Idea House II* in 1947. MoMA created its own "The House" in the Museum Garden program with a model home designed by Marcel Breuer in 1948, followed by Gregory Ain's Exhibition House in 1950 and the Japanese Exhibition House in 1955. The most extensive of these programs, however, was *Arts and Architecture* magazine's Case Study House program which highlighted the design of over 30 modern houses from 1945 to 1965. The first six houses were built by 1948, mostly in the Los Angeles area and over 368,000 people traveled there

"Principles, not effects" ■

Figure 9.4

Installation view of the exhibition, "Good Design." June 1953. The Merchandise Mart, Chicago, Illinois; organized and shown at the Museum of Modern Art Exhibition Records, 542.13. The Museum of Modern Art Archives, New York. Photographer: Carl Ullrich. The Museum of Modern Art Digital Image ©The Museum of Modern Art/Licensed by SCALA/Art Resource, NY.

to tour them, taking away ideas for their own interiors and promoting the clean, strictly ordered, rational, and precise aesthetic that was being encouraged by interior designers. Programs such as these not only added to the push for Americans to modernize their homes but also the need for interior designers to help accomplish that.

In his 1953 booklet on interior design, "What is Modern Interior Design?" Kaufmann makes it clear that the American public should depend on the expertise and guidance of professional designers and specifically emphasizes that interior design was a professional activity in which one needed to be trained. He states: "The aim of this study is to deepen the appreciation of modern interior design; it cannot begin to teach the practice of it."[15] Kaufmann's implication is that one must rely on the expertise of professionals to gain the benefits of the practice outlined in his text. By further identifying and celebrating various designers who had created examples of what he deemed as "good modern interior design" Kaufmann was purposely showing the public who the experts were.

The publication taken as a whole contributes to many of the necessary goals toward professionalization outlined by design historian Grace Lees-Maffei: recognition of the activity as a profession; providing educational material about the field; establishing standards and criteria; giving a venue for showcasing the work; and contributing to the development of public trust and reputation by giving the approval and support of the well-established and respected museum organization. At the same time, the fact that Kaufmann wrote a separate publication solely about interior design imbues it with importance and sets it up as equal in the museum's eyes to modern art, architecture, and design, which were the other topics of the series.[16]

Kaufmann's support of interior design could only have bolstered and supported the legitimacy of the emerging field. In the 1950s into the 1960s, interior design training programs in New York City at Parsons and Pratt flourished while the design historian's Sherrill Whitton's School of Interior Decoration changed its name to the New York School of Interior Design in 1951, echoing Kaufmann's call for "principles, not effects" in its stated rationale that interior design does not "only concern itself with the details and finishes of a space but the architecture of the interior, everything that is not strictly structural."[17] In 1957 the National Society of Interior Designers (NSID) was founded and in 1961 the older American Institute of Decorators changed its name to American Institute of Interior Designers. Interior design specific groups prospered in companies such as the Knoll Planning Unit and Skidmore Owings and Merrill's interior design department led by Davis Allen, while professional journals devoted totally to the subject such as *Interiors* and *Interior Design* were popularized.[18]

Clearly the recognition of the profession of interior design by MoMA encouraged these trends, but one must ask, what did the museum's support of interior design as a practice do for the museum? It obviously gave full support to Kaufmann's efforts, the Good Design shows, and the publications, and clearly these efforts expanded the range of people who might understand and support modern design and interior design. But I want to speculate here for a moment on some other reasons about how this support might have had political as well as entrepreneurial underpinnings and impact on the museum.

In their essay about the *Good Design* shows, Riley and Eigen mention a "unspoken but obvious antagonism" between Philip Johnson, who headed the Department of Architecture and Design, and Edgar Kaufmann, Jr., who worked for him. Rene d'Harnoncourt, Director of the Museum since 1943 when Alfred Barr was asked to step down, understood clearly how to take advantage of this philosophical set-to to the advantage of the museum. D'Harnoncourt supported Kaufmann's perspective, which was in opposition to Johnson's more elitist stance toward modern design rooted in modern art and architecture and did not share the latter's particular interest or understanding of interior design. By ignoring the implied criticism of commercialism and being "low-brow" inherent in Johnson's elitist viewpoint of the *Good Design* shows and letting Kaufmann have his head with them, d'Harnoncourt allowed the latter to advocate for a "more populist" and "domesticated" modernism that was able to reach and impact thousands more Americans than normally would have been involved.[19] So while Johnson's work and perspective continued to appeal to what critic Rusell Lynes would have labeled as "high brow" taste, Kaufmann's was aimed at a more "middle-brow" audience, and in particular an audience of women as consumers, a market of which he was well aware from his retailing experience and from the response he could directly observe to the MoMA home furnishing and product shows.

In the postwar period women were thrust into a period of flux about their position and identity in society. Women's suffrage and the need for supplemental family income during the early part of the twentieth century had made it acceptable for women to work outside the home and during the 1920s and 1930s women often found jobs as corporate America and the demand for administrative and manufacturing personnel grew. During the Depression years, often it was the woman who was able to find work in a domestic or low-paying capacity while the man of the house could not. During both World War I and World War II, when most of the male working population entered the military, women took places in factories and business in order to keep up wartime production. By the postwar period, women in America had clearly assumed new roles well outside of the domestic sphere and enjoyed new freedoms and possibilities.

But in the late 1940s, after World War II, most women in the United States were encouraged to relinquish their jobs to the nearly seven million male GIs who reentered civilian life and to return to the private sphere to assume more traditional roles as housekeepers and stay-at-home mothers. In the quest for a "return to normalcy" and reinvigorated by the success of the war, American men moved to reestablish their role as the primary breadwinners. As Joanne Meyerowitz points out, women's place in the postwar years was definitively considered to be in the home. "Under cultural pressure and with limited options for work outside the home, women, contained and constrained, 'donned their domestic harnesses.'"[20] Postwar women were asked to return to the home, but, as if in compensation, they were promised they would not have to return to the poorly designed and ill-equipped prewar home. Contemporary literature and advertising make it clear that one of the main concerns of manufacturers during the postwar period was to provide a new modern home appropriate to the "new American way of life" and the role women would play in it.

Books such as Russel and Mary Wright's *Guide to Easier Living*, published in 1950, provided the developing postwar society with instructions for those homes by outlining the processes and products of modern interior design. Shelter magazines such as *Ladies Home Journal*, *Good House-keeping*, *Family Circle* and *Redbook*, along with profession specific journals such as *Interiors* and *Interior Design* also promoted the modern interior and modern design as the indicators of postwar success and contemporariness.

Edgar Kaufmann, Jr. constructed and executed the *Good Design* shows clearly knowing there was a new market and demand for this genre of products by women, who had been designated the primary consumers in the postwar economy. Elaine Tyler May points out that this could be clearly read in popular culture and media. Richard Nixon in his infamous "kitchen debate" with Nikita Khrushchev at the opening ceremony of the American National Exhibition in Moscow in 1959 had argued that "American superiority in the cold war rested not on weapons but on the secure, abundant family life of the modern suburban home."[21] Within this scenario, men occupied the public sphere directly, employed in the businesses of the prospering economy and provided the financial income that would allow women to play their crucial role as the makers, nurturers, and consumers in the modern home.

Women therefore were positioned at the vanguard of this effort and if they did work they considered their jobs secondary to their role as consumers.[22] In this role women appeared to be extremely successful. May reports that "in the five years after WWII consumer spending increased 60 percent, but the amount spent on household furnishing and appliances rose 240 percent . . ." and "in the four years after the war Americans . . . moved into one million new housing units each year."[23] Women's role as consumers and their contribution to the stimulation of the American economy cannot be overstated.

Affluent homes became the marker of the superiority of the American way of life, but these new and renovated homes were not created in the likeness of those of the previous generations, which were seen as symbolic of the historical past. Instead new technologies, labor-saving devices, and modern design became the indicators of a new era of prosperity, success and security. Journals, media and department stores fully understood and took advantage of this and helped to create one of the biggest upturns in spending and consumerism in the country's history.

Edgar Kaufmann Jr. did as well. His long experience and family roots in retailing provided him with clear insights and understandings of the nature of the contemporary market and what an opportunity it was for the museum to link to and take advantage of those trends. Kaufmann understood the potential of women as consumers and purposefully used interior design to target them in two ways: First he established that interior design was the proper modern approach to interiors by explaining its basis in "principles, not effects" in his 1950 publication, making it an acceptable practice in modern terms and the proper alternative to interior decorating which was rooted in historicism and taste. In doing this he also demonstrated how the interior, which is historically associated with women and their self-expression, could also be modern and an indicator of being a modern and progressive woman. He made a direct appeal to women as consumers by promoting interior design, which is still mostly regarded and characterized as a feminine profession and interest despite its efforts to escape this characterization. MoMA and Edgar Kaufmann, jr. therefore celebrated a women's field as applied to a women's place and by doing so made modern interior design the vehicle for transformation for the thousands of women who returned to the role of homemaker in the postwar period and were acting as the major consumers of home furnishings.

An advertisement for *Better Design* magazine pointed out in 1951 that: "Design is potentially the single most important selling factor in modern retailing."[24] Edgar Kaufmann, Jr. fully understood this, and d'Harnoncourt knew that he did. By supporting Kaufmann's efforts, the museum opened the door to allow women buyers in and a kind of acceptable consumerism to insert itself in the museum's operation. This consumerism still today buoys the museum, financially as well as popularly, through its museum shops, retail, and online outlets for selling products. Allowing Kaufman to define and foreground interior design so that it was not identified as elitist or based in class or taste like interior decorating (i.e. in principles that were democratic and rational) made it an accessible means for American women to bring modern design into their homes and accept it. As a result of his efforts, Kaufmann and the museum were strong advocates for the newly professionalized practice of interior design by helping the American public, particularly women, understand its purpose and its potential – an effort that mutually benefited both interior design as a profession and MoMA as a promoter and arbiter of modern design.

NOTES

1 Edgar Kaufmann, Jr., always preferred the lower-case version of the abbreviation for junior.
2 Edgar Kaufmann, Jr., *What Is Modern Interior Design, Introductory Series to the Modern Arts, No. 4* (New York: Museum of Modern Art, 1950), 7.
3 Major Arthur Gordon, "The House I Left Behind Me," *House Beautiful* (January 1945), 44.

"Principles, not effects" ■

4 Design historian Grace Lees-Maffei outlined in in her article the process of developing an activity into a generally recognized profession. This is accomplished by "the setting up of professional organizations, the articulation and monitoring of standards and codes of conduct, the institution of clear educational routes and means of assessment, networking and gate keeping." She also noted that interior design in order to professionalize "needed to shift its emphasis from taste to skill" in order to move away from the taint of amateurism and personal preference embedded in interior decoration (p. 1). This new focus on skill required that interior design establish courses of training, modes of evaluation, regulation, and acknowledgment to define and maintain that expertise. Further, Lees-Maffei stated that professionalization "represents the institutionalization of trust and reputation for the benefit of practitioners, their colleagues and clients." Trust and reputation require both recognition and understanding of the scope, purpose and accomplishments of the field or its individual practitioners. The creation of professional organizations, journals and training for interior designers helped identify, professionalize, and legitimize the field. Grace Lees-Maffei, "Introduction: Professionalization as a Focus in Interior Design History," *Journal of Design History* 21, no. 1 (2008).

5 John Elderfield, "Preface" in the *Museum of Modern Art at Mid-Century: At Home and Abroad* (New York: Museum of Modern Art; Harry Abrams, 1994), 6.

6 Jan Whitaker, *Service and Style: How the American Department Store Fashioned the Middle Class* (New York: St. Martin's Press, 2006), 144.

7 Ibid, 145.

8 Mary Ann Staniszewski, *The Power of Display A History of Exhibition Installations at the Museum of Modern Art* (Cambridge, MA: The MIT Press, 1998), 160.

9 Terrance Riley and Edward Eigen, "Between the Museum and the Marketplace: Selling Good Design," in the *Museum of Modern Art at Mid-Century: At Home and Abroad* (New York: Museum of Modern Art; Harry Abrams, 1994), 155.

10 Ibid, 151.

11 Auerbach in speech given at the Merchants & Manufacturers Club, Chicago, 16 January 1950; typescript, n.d. Architecture and Design archive.

12 Edgar Kaufmann, Jr., *What Is Modern Interior Design, Introductory Series to the Modern Arts, No. 4* (New York: Museum of Modern Art, 1950), 3.

13 Ibid, 7.

14 Ibid.

15 Ibid, 3.

16 The other books in the series were: Edgar Kaufmann, Jr. *What Is Modern Design?* (1950); Alfred Barr, *What Is Modern Painting* (1946); Margaret Miller, *What Is Modern Architecture* (1942).

17 "About NYSID: History of NYSID," NYSID-New York School of Design, accessed March 19, 2018, https://www.nysid.edu/about/history.

18 See also in this volume, Penelope Dean "Imaging Interior Design: Beneath, Beside and Within Architecture for more information on interior design journals and Mark Hinchman "The Skyscraper had a Glass Ceiling: Modernism, the Free Plan, and Women Designers After WWII," for more information on interior design firms.

19 Terrance Riley and Edward Eigen, "Between the Museum and the Marketplace: Selling Good Design," in the *Museum of Modern Art at Mid-Century: At Home and Abroad* (New York: Museum of Modern Art; Harry Abrams, 1994), 155.

20 Joanne Meyerwitz, ed. *Not June Cleaver: Women and Gender in Postwar America, 1945–1960* (Philadelphia: Temple University Press, 1994), 3, quoting Betty Friedan in *The Feminine Mystique* (New York: Norton, 1963).

21 Elaine Tyler May, *Homeward Bound: American Families in the Cold War Era* (New York: Basic Books, Inc., 1988), 17.

22 Ibid, 167.

23 Ibid, 165.

24 Riley and Eigen, 169.

Chapter 10: "Apology areas"

Interior decorating and the marketplace in the 1950s

Kristina Wilson

Readers of a 1950 product catalogue published by the Associated American Artists were greeted on page one with a striking graphic: photographs of domestic living spaces, silhouetted in irregular, quasi-biomorphic shapes, branded with insistent black "x"s – three in the living room, two in the stairway, one in the dining room (Figure 10.1). What were these troubling "x" marks? The legend in the corner indicated that the X equaled "Apology Areas," and then explained: "When your guests enter a room, are there certain blank spots (like those shown above) which you always really feel like apologizing for – wall areas that seem to 'cry' for pictures? This catalogue shows you how inexpensively you can win compliments for tasteful use of these areas."[1]

Associated American Artists (AAA) is best known as the mail-order business that sold prints by American artists to consumers for five dollars during the Great Depression.[2] By the late 1940s, AAA had considerably expanded its product line in pursuit of affordable art, and was selling color reproductions of paintings, as well as artist-designed ceramics, fabrics, and small sculptures. AAA was not an interior decorating business; it was in the business of selling art. However, as the page from the 1950 catalogue demonstrates, the company understood that interior decorating could be an effective strategy for selling its products.

This chapter will examine the use of interior design as a sales strategy in the American marketplace of the 1940s and 1950s through a comparative case study of AAA and the Herman Miller Furniture Company (now Herman Miller, Inc.). Although the National Society of Interior Designers was not established until 1957, businesses catering to the housewares market had a well-developed understanding of the effectiveness of interior design and decorating as a sales tool in the years immediately following World War II. Indeed, furniture manufacturers had been exploring the power of commercial displays – and advocating for well-designed installations – since at least the 1920s.[3] In the context of this anthology, the current essay sheds light on the multifaceted ways that interior design and decorating were practiced in the first half of the twentieth century. The study of interior design in the marketplace provides information that helps us to further understand both the structure of the interior design profession and the public reception of design. For example, through the marketing materials generated by AAA and Herman Miller, members of the public were exposed to numerous interior design strategies, and were encouraged to emulate them. While the marketplace educated the public, the interior designs generated by AAA and Herman Miller were not apparently the product of a single professional designer or decorator. Instead, based on archival

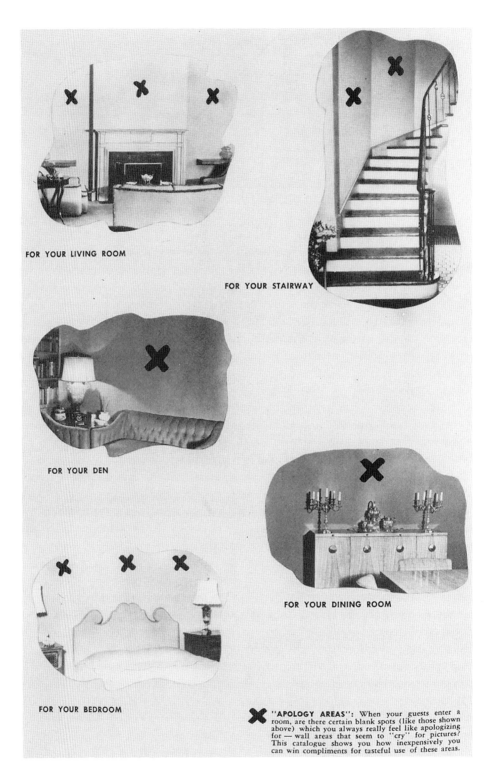

Figure 10.1

"Apology Areas," *Full Color Masterpieces* (New York: Associated American Artists, 1950), p. 2.

"Apology areas" ∎

evidence, it seems that the practice of interior design in these two companies was a fluid, often collaborative process shared by designers, artists, journalists, and salespeople. Thus, the case study of interior design in the American marketplace of the 1940s and 1950s reveals an ad hoc, not yet fully professionalized, understanding of design work. At the same time, this study demonstrates the full-bore embrace of interior design's capacity for rhetorical persuasion. While these companies may not have hired interior designers per se, they knew interior design and decoration were essential for selling their products.

From our current vantage point in the second decade of the twenty-first century, Herman Miller is a better known corporate name than Associated American Artists. Notably, Herman Miller is the company that manufactured and sold many of the iconic objects of mid-century modernist design, including works by George Nelson, Isamu Noguchi, and Charles and Ray Eames. Although AAA and Herman Miller might initially seem to be a surprising pairing for a case study, they share several key features. First, both companies firmly situated their products in the so-called élite world of the fine arts. AAA actively advertised its products as works of art; a typical advertisement touted the "exquisite, signed originals" for sale, and claimed that many of them had been "already purchased by leading museums."[4] Herman Miller promoted the individual designers of its products as artists and art-world celebrities, turning their signatures into logos and even using expensive advertising to promote not products but its famed, world-weary designers (a well-known 1954 advertisement from the company depicts no objects, only Nelson, Eames, and Alexander Girard as "Traveling Men").[5]

Yet even as both companies conspicuously allied themselves with the élite fine arts, they also attempted to reach a much broader, non-élite consumer audience, and this is their second point of similarity. AAA's entire business model was predicated on the idea of making fine art affordable to "every American home."[6] Herman Miller, especially in the designs of the Eameses, claimed it wanted to create "improved performance at reduced cost."[7] In the 15 years following World War II, the landscape to which both Herman Miller and AAA looked in pursuit of customers was the booming world of suburbia: the single-family home, oriented around a nuclear family with several children, and filled with material goods that functioned to identify and define the family for its circle of peers. AAA's product catalogues regularly addressed the reader's home, with catalogue copy such as this: "There are so many ways these Signed Originals can beautify your home."[8] Herman Miller strategically targeted suburban living in a low-cost educational pamphlet from the early 1950s, in which photographs of furnishings, arranged in domestic vignettes, were capped by graphic renderings of a roof gable; the cluster of four photographs capped by four gabled roofs echoed popular aerial views of suburban developments.[9] Both companies sought out the young families in new homes outside of city centers who understood intuitively, through reading an endless parade of women's and shelter magazines, that possessions could function as status-signifiers.[10]

Neither Herman Miller nor AAA were interior design firms, but both of them used interior design to sell their products. Why did they do so? What did they hope to convey through the lens of interior design? I propose that both companies understood how interior design could be a tool to help consumers imagine the lifestyle their products would enable. They understood that customers would see interior design as a way to establish an identity for themselves. How the commercial marketplace taught consumers interior design, and how it insinuated that interior design could construct identity, are the questions this essay will examine in further depth. I will discuss, first, how Herman Miller used interior design to sell its products, and then turn, in the latter half of the essay, to the Associated American Artists.

HERMAN MILLER

Interior design pervaded several levels of the Herman Miller postwar marketing plan. In keeping with established industry practice, the company sold its products through department stores, where it shared floor space with a cacophony of other brands. However, its major sales innovation – and its most impressive use of interior design – came in the development of the company showroom, a space it controlled entirely, where the complete furniture line could be presented. Access to these showrooms was through the trade – the member of the general public had to be accompanied by a designer or architect – in contrast to the more democratic, open access of the department store. In addition to its showrooms, Herman Miller used interior design in its numerous product catalogues and pamphlets. In those publications, photographs of fully staged interiors offered compelling, seductive images of the furniture in use. Some photographs were taken on the showroom floor, while others were staged specifically for the promotional publication. In both cases, the photographs served as a surrogate for the experience on the showroom floor: if the consumer could not physically walk into a thoughtfully designed interior created by Herman Miller products, she could imagine her way into one through a photograph.[11]

Herman Miller opened its first showroom in 1939, when Gilbert Rohde was its design director, and by 1956 a corporate report noted:

> The chain of showrooms that has been established since then [1939] is in many ways the backbone of this business. Again the reason is obvious. This new way of life not only involved furniture which had to be shown in its entirety but its use and arrangement and its backgrounds had to be visualized for the people who were interested. Trained sales personnel also had to be ready to give counsel and service to the dealers and their clients.[12]

Rohde exercised artistic control over the early showrooms in New York and Grand Rapids, a practice that his successor, George Nelson, continued in the late 1940s and early 1950s. (The notable exception in these years was the Los Angeles showroom, which was designed by the studio of Charles and Ray Eames.) Nelson hired Irving Harper and Ernest Farmer from Rohde's office, and the design of the Nelson-era showrooms was a product of collaborative work by these men.[13] As is clear from internal correspondence, the company's sales strategy was built around the distinctive experience created by its showrooms; Nelson's office provided drawings that not only placed each item of furniture in the showroom space, but also specified types of plants and their location, as well as other decorative accessories, and Nelson insisted that these plans be followed in every detail.[14] Nelson exercised further control over the presentation of his furniture designs by spending considerable energy on product photography. As early as 1945, he suggested that the showrooms be designed with their photography in mind, and he repeatedly called for careful attention to arrangement, accessories, and lighting for all catalogue photographs in the late 1940s and early 1950s.[15]

While Nelson's office took the lead on interior design, the showrooms were staffed entirely by sales professionals. Jim Eppinger, the company's director of sales, described the ideal showroom representative as someone who was aesthetically oriented, but ultimately stronger as a salesman; in his words: "51% gregarious-sales minded and 49% design-aware, that was the thing, and an architectural student who made it as an architect, but didn't practice architecture, or didn't graduate, he worked out best. . . . You had to have just slightly more ability to sell."[16] In addition to sales, the company provided interior design services through its showrooms. This began as early as the Rohde years, with the work of Elizabeth Kaufer: an early history of the company noted that "Eppinger and Rohde worked together closely to train a girl (Elizabeth Kaufer) from Rohde's office to act as a home planner, or interior design consultant, advising customers in the choice of furniture for their home needs."[17] These services apparently continued, no longer led by Kaufer, through the mid-1950s, when advertisements announced that the company's showrooms provided "planning facilities . . . for you and your decorator."[18]

Interior design was clearly integral to the Herman Miller sales program, but how did it function to promote sales? It is important to think of the fantasy interiors created in the showrooms and the product catalogues as having two audiences: client-hired decorators and the general public. While decorators might read more logistics into Herman Miller's model interiors than the general public, the emotional effect generated by the photographs and furniture groupings was something both professionals and the public would have responded to. Two photographs (one of a showroom, and one from a catalogue) show imaginary living rooms made possible by products from the Herman Miller furniture company, and what kind of life do they portray (Figures 10.2, 10.3)?[19] Despite the severity of the furniture lines – crisp, finely pointed edges in the cabinetry as well as the upholstered sectional sofas – the props tell a story of casual, informal living: books piled in various different directions, leaning against one another as if they have just been consulted and shoved back on the shelf; magazines left open by the bored reader. In each of these rooms, the arrangement of furniture fosters an undeniable sense of community. In Figure 10.3, the focus is the fireplace. In Figure 10.2, the chair pulled toward the sofa makes it seem as if the communication between the two is the focal point. And, indeed a shared conversation might be the focus of both of these scenes: the furniture is gathered so that people can gather. The sense of a tight community is heightened by the interplay of photography and architecture: as photographed (by the highly accomplished Ezra Stoller) neither of these "rooms" appear to give onto another space; there is never any obvious way out; the direction of one's attention is always inward toward the center of the group.

But even as these rooms conjure up an imagined sense of community through the dramatis personae of the seating furniture and props, at a visual, formal level, the spaces as a whole are structured around prominent pairings of binary opposites. We see circles versus squares, curved lines versus right angles, textured fabrics versus planar wood. Perhaps the larger metaphysical duality is nature versus the industrial. The crisp geometries and machine-milled forms are contrasted against the plants, which spill over edges or cast dramatic shadows, making the industrial modernism hard to read in places. Nature further appears in Figure 10.3 in the woven reeds that encase a large jug, alluding to pre-industrial patterns of living where indoors and outdoors are fluid.[20] If, for a minute,

Figure 10.2
Showroom display, Herman Miller Furniture Company, 1950. Courtesy Herman Miller, Inc.

we consider expanding the metaphysical binary, then on the side of rustic, craft, and nature (in opposition to industrial, machine-made, and modern) we would have to put "female." Where are the women in these rooms? In Figure 10.2, she is a selected prop, like the plants or the basket in Figure 10.3: contained within the pages of a magazine left idly on the ottoman.

In drawing attention to these binary pairings, my larger point is that these are rooms of constant contrast: something is always standing out, whether it is the circular side table or the piled wood for the fire. The consumer who pauses in a daydream contemplating these interior design vignettes is being shown how to create a community with these objects, and she is being told she can create a community with these objects. More subtly, she is being given a lesson in forging contrasts, in standing out. She might stand out, or stand in contrast, if she purchases these products.

ASSOCIATED AMERICAN ARTISTS

This essay's own binary "other" is the role of interior design in the sales materials of the Associated American Artists. Unlike Herman Miller, which relied on the visual communication of its interior design models (in photographs and showroom floors), AAA used textual communication alongside

"Apology areas"

Figure 10.3
Display of Herman Miller furniture, Kresge Department Store, Newark, New Jersey, 1947. Photograph by Ezra Stoller.
© Esto. All rights reserved.

small images to convey its interior design directives.[21] Reeves Lewenthal, the impresario behind AAA, clearly had connections to the shelter magazine industry, based on his product placement success; examples of AAA ceramics appeared in issues of *Better Homes & Gardens* and *House Beautiful* in the early 1950s.[22] However, to date, scholars have been unable to identify the author/s of AAA's decorating texts, many of which are recycled, rephrased, and repackaged repeatedly through the 1940s and 1950s. They may have been drafted by journalists in the magazine arena, but were undoubtedly polished by Reeves's own team of sales copywriters.

One prominent message, conveyed through both text and image, was that the artwork offered through AAA would be appropriate in homes of any stylistic disposition. For example, a 1948 catalogue assured buyers with these words: "Remember, whether your décor be modern or classical; French, English, or Early American; you are assured that these works cannot clash with the color scheme of any room."[23] Sketches that were published in the 1954 product catalogue make the same point (Figure 10.4).[24] Despite the small size, each image gives us an impressively detailed room: in the upper right sketch, tall windows are capped with triangular pediments as they frame

Kristina Wilson

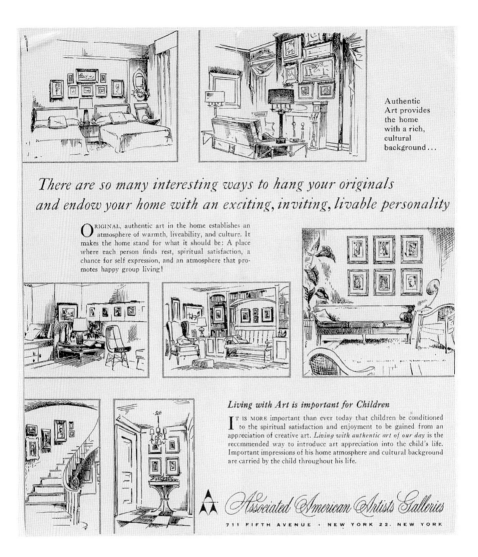

Figure 10.4
"There are so many interesting ways to hang your originals," *Annual Catalogue* (New York: Associated American Artists, 1954), p. 2.

a neoclassical mantelpiece; the center of the page features a room decorated in the popular "early American" style, complete with a spindle-back settee and a wing chair; to the left of the early American room is a modernist bedroom, indicated by the built-in sofa, horizontal arrangement of art, and a stilted rendering of an Eames chair with an Eiffel Tower base.

The catalogue texts also repeatedly argued that AAA's art would "unify" the consumer's home; this term is significant, in particular, as a point of contrast to the binaries that structured the Herman Miller interiors. Throughout the 1940s and 1950s, AAA taught its customers that " 'orphan' wall

"Apology areas" ■

spaces" were a problem to be avoided in interior decoration, and explained that its products could eliminate the orphans and help one achieve decorative unity in a room. For example, the 1950 print catalogue introduced the problem as follows: "That difficult wall over a chair in the living room – those 'orphan' wall spaces in the bedrooms – that staircase landing . . . all have perhaps been begging for the ideal pictures." Then, just as quickly, it provided a solution: "Notice the room shown at the bottom of this page. Here the pictures have been used to *unify* the sofa and book-case arrangement, composing the whole into one *unified* pattern."[25] What might have been the significance of these words? In an era of burgeoning birth rates, when the nuclear family assumed its indisputably dominant position as social role model, an orphan was associated with not just loss, but also failure to achieve a socially acceptable family model. Likewise, "unity" could have evoked the model family unit living together under one roof, part of a larger, unified suburban community. Indeed, "unity" is the premise of the style-based interiors featured in Figure 10.4 and referred to above: AAA presumed that its customers' rooms were decorated in a unified style such as "neoclassical," "early American," or "modern."

Coursing beneath this rhetoric of "orphans," "unity," and "apology areas" is an undeniable tone of judgment. These catalogues encourage the reader to look at her house through the unforgiving gaze of a competitive neighbor and to imagine taking steps to defend against that gaze: under the headline "How to Dress up Awkward Spots," the consumer is urged to:

> Look around your home, study those corners and furniture arrangements that don't seem to be "just *right.*" That chair-table-lamp unit near the window or that open and perhaps unattractive space between the hall door and corner. Visualize originals on those empty walls. Not only as lovely things in themselves, but as integral parts of a balanced, inviting arrangement.[26]

The small sketches that accompanied such catalogue text contribute to the air of defensiveness: they tend to depict walls, not rooms; something to look at, not something to live in. They show decor that would pass the test, not "inviting" rooms where people could really relax or have intimate gatherings. Admittedly, AAA was selling art to hang on empty walls, and thus had an obvious reason to show sketches that focused on the walls of rooms. The attention to walls, however, may have been multiply determined: walls are where a homeowner hangs her art, what she shows off to visitors, how she demonstrates that she fits in. The consumer who follows the interior design advice of AAA will find herself in an impeccable house, defensible against the most critical guests.

CONCLUSION

If the Associated American Artists used interior design examples to condone a wide variety of furnishing styles, the Herman Miller Furniture Company was, of course, purely modernist. AAA preached an idea of the unified interior design, wherein art and furnishings created a seamless fortress of propriety; Herman Miller offered interior designs structured around bold contrasts. On the whole, between its stylistic catholicism and emphasis on unity, AAA seemed to be striving for consensus, and it used interior design to demonstrate a cautious, even conservative, taste. Herman Miller used interior design to embrace the idea of standing out, whether through the austere, machine-like sofa or the out-of-control plant; it was not conservative, but rather the taste of the avant-garde. Both companies anchored their products in the élite world of fine art, but AAA used its interior design advice to allude to a mythical ideal of "old money," a world where showing one's ownership of history and tradition had high value. Herman Miller, in contrast, used interior design to evoke an attitude of "new money," a culture that marked itself by breaking from past traditions and that did not need to fit in.

Ultimately, we might surmise that the differences between AAA and Herman Miller in the post-war years can be understood primarily as a question of class. AAA more successfully reached a broad middle-class consumer, and its conservatism and old-money allusions were better suited to a public that had less experience with actual histories of wealth. Herman Miller was ultimately more successful in cultivating an upper-middle-class consumer whose greater financial freedom embold-ened them.[27] We might even be tempted to say that these two companies addressed two different sides of the binary ideology of the postwar suburbs: the ideology of conformity versus individuality, or the ideology of fitting in versus standing out. AAA used interior design to show customers how they could fit in to the conforming culture of the postwar suburbs. Herman Miller used its interior design to convey how a consumer might resist conformity, embrace her individuality, and enjoy standing out.

However, rather than close with the suggestion that perhaps Herman Miller has "won" the con-test posed by this chapter's comparative structure, I suggest that scholars consider the landscape of 1950s suburbia through Slavoj Žižek's analysis of ideology. Žižek argues that whenever we think we have stepped outside the boundaries of a dominant ideology, we must remember that the place beyond is also defined by ideology.[28] If resistance to suburban conformity in the postwar decades was to be found in the expression of individuality – if, in other words, individuality was the place beyond the ideology of conformity – then we must appreciate that individuality itself was a part of the larger dominant suburban ideology. Both AAA and Herman Miller used interior design to give their suburban consumers an anchor in the ideological world in which they lived. Whether by helping them to fit in or to stand out, their fantasy interiors simply gave their consumers different locations to occupy within the same ideological map.

NOTES

1 *Full Color Masterpieces* (New York: Associated American Artists, ca. 1950), 2.

2 For a comprehensive account of AAA, see Elizabeth Seaton and Jane McNamara Myers, eds., *Art for Every Home: Associated American Artists* (Marianna Kistler Beach Museum of Art, Kansas State University, and Yale University Press, 2015).

3 Kristina Wilson, introduction to *Livable Modernism: Interior Decorating and Design During the Great Depression* (New Haven: Yale University Art Gallery), 17–19.

4 Advertisement for AAA, *New Yorker*, 15 November 1952, 112.

5 The ad is reproduced in Jochen Eisenbrand, ed., *George Nelson: Architect, Writer, Designer, Teacher* (Weil am Rhein: Vitra Design Museum, 2008), 96.

6 Associated American Artists records, c. 1934–1981, Archives of American Art, Smithsonian Institution (hereafter cited as Associated American Artists Papers, AAA-SI), reel D256, frame 296.

7 *The Herman Miller Collection 1952* (Zeeland, Michigan; reprint: New York, Acanthus Press, 1995), 88.

8 *Annual Catalogue* (New York: Associated American Artists, ca. 1950), 6.

"Apology areas" ■

9 *ABCs of Modern Furniture* (Zeeland, Michigan: Herman Miller Furniture Company, c. 1951), 30–31.

10 The literature on postwar suburbia is extensive. Examples of contemporaneous accounts are: William H. Whyte, *The Organization Man* (1956; repr. Philadelphia: University of Pennsylvania Press, 2002); and Jack Keats, *The Crack in the Picture Window* (New York: Ballantine Books, 1956). For more recent scholarship, see: Elaine Tyler May, *Homeward Bound: American Families in the Cold War Era*, Revised edition (New York: Basic Books, 2008); Kenneth T. Jackson, *Crabgrass Frontier: The Suburbanization of the United States* (Oxford: Oxford University Press, 1985); and Dianne Harris, *Little White Houses: How the Postwar Home Constructed Race in America* (Minneapolis: University of Minnesota Press, 2013).

11 Herman Miller charged a reasonably hefty fee for its product catalogues ($3 for the 1948 catalogue; $5 for the 1955 edition). Advertisements from the mid-1950s encouraged individuals to buy the catalogue, but it is clear from the language inside the publication that it was written for an audience of professional interior designers as well as the general public. (See, for example, Herman Miller Advertisement, *New Yorker*, 9 June 1956, 46.) In addition, Herman Miller published booklets for the general public, such as the "ABC of Modern Furniture." This publication was promotional, disguised as educational and informational, was about 35 pages long, and sold for 25 cents; it was illustrated with full-room decorating views as well as isolated product images.

12 Herman Miller Furniture Company, pamphlet, Zeeland, Michigan, April 1956, in folder: Corporate Histories 1956–78, Gray Box Series #80, Corporate Archives, Herman Miller International (hereafter HMIA).

13 A typed memo lists a "Design Staff" "responsible for this furniture and showroom on exhibition" from 1953: George Nelson, Charles Eames, Isamu Noguchi, Paul Laszlo, Ernest Farmer, and Irving Harper. Typed ms. entitled "These are the men and women who are responsible. . .," c. 1953, in folder: Corporate Histories 1956–78, HMIA. See also Stanley Abercrombie, *George Nelson: The Design of Modern Design* (Cambridge: MIT Press, 1995), chapter 5.

14 See, for example, correspondence between Nelson and Herman Miller president D.J. DePree: Nelson to DePree, 14 August 1946; DePree to Nelson, 23 December 1946. In folder: Correspondence with George Nelson, 1945–47, HMIA.

15 Nelson's original report to DePree about his vision for Herman Miller included this statement: "Showrooms should be so set up that we can get all necessary photographs of complete rooms for use in the catalogues." "Report from George Nelson, 1945," in folder: Corporate Office Box 6, Folder 8, George Nelson File, HMIA. See also Nelson to DePree, 27 January 1947; Nelson to DePree, 17 March 1947, in folder: Correspondence with George Nelson, 1945–47, HMIA.

16 Marilyn Neuhart and John Neuhart, *The Story of Eames Furniture*, 2 vols. (Berlin: Gestalten, 2010), 487.

17 Typed ms., "Evolution of Furniture By William S. Gamble 1958 or 1959," p. 5, in folder: "D J DePree's Papers on HM History, Jones, Candill, Burleigh. Folder 9, Box 81," HMIA.

18 Advertisement for Herman Miller Furniture Company, *New Yorker*, 9 June 1956, 46. I have been unable to find any further information about the planning services offered in the showrooms, although it is likely that sales people provided this service at least on occasion. In 1956 Herman Miller also established a "Planning Service Division," which it described as a "service to our dealers and their clients." This division was led by an architect, William Smull, "who has specialized in space analysis." See "The President's Report to the Stockholders at the Annual Meeting of the Herman Miller Furniture Company, Zeeland, Michigan, on August 14, 1956," p. 8, PUBS 296, HMIA. In addition to providing direct services, the division was tasked with training "sales people in planning and layout work" in Herman Miller franchise dealerships. See "Sales Department Handbook, Herman Miller Furniture Company, January 1956," 25–26, HMIA.

19 Figure 10.3 was published in the 1952 Herman Miller catalogue, but was actually taken around 1947. It was first published in Better Homes and Gardens (August 1947): 49, as a display in Kresge Department Store, Newark New Jersey. Correspondence indicates that Nelson may have been responsible for the staging, and hired Ezra Stoller to photograph it. See Nelson to DePree, 16 December 1946; and Nelson to DePree, 26 February 1947, in folder: Correspondence with George Nelson, 1945–47, HMIA.

20 This particular item was apparently used again in the New York showroom in the early 1950s, as evidenced by photographs in the Herman Miller Archives. See folder: New York Showrooms, 1951–1954, HMIA.

21 For a slightly different version of this discussion, framed within the context of AAA's larger business plan, see my "How to Decorate with Pictures," in *Art for Every Home*, 186–88.

22 See, for example, "The American Marriage of Elegance and Easy Upkeep," *House Beautiful* 92, no. 12 (December 1950): 142–145; and Florence Byerly, "Make the Most of Fabrics," *Better Homes and Gardens* (February 1954): 60–63.

23 *Catalogue of Miniature Prints* (New York: Associated American Artists, 1948), AAA D255, frame 470.

24 *Annual Catalogue* (New York: Associated American Artists, 1954), 2.

25 Emphasis added. *An Invitation From America's Greatest Artists* (New York: Associated American Artists, 1950), 6–7. This same language appeared as early as the 1943 catalogue.

26 Emphasis original. Ibid.

27 For a more extensive discussion of the class implications in Herman Miller's postwar marketing strategy, see Kristina Wilson, "Like a 'Girl in a Bikini Suit' and Other Stories: The Herman Miller Company, Gender, and Race at Mid-Century," *Journal of Design History* 28, no. 2 (May 2015): 161–181.

28 Slavoj Žižek, "The Spectre of Ideology," in *Mapping Ideology*, ed. Žižek (London: Verso, 2012), 16–17.

Chapter 11: Imaging interior design: beneath, beside, and within architecture

Penelope Dean

In November 1960, *Interiors* magazine released an anniversary issue celebrating "Two Decades of Interiors." Reflecting on the achievement of interior designers finally becoming independent professionals, the editors attributed the accomplishment to the resolution of a very simple bookkeeping problem: how, and for what, was the interior designer being paid.[1] Whereas interior designers had historically been remunerated on commission for reselling merchandise, by 1960 they were being recognized as the sellers of a high caliber *service* – which *Interiors* defined as "the training, knowledge, skills, talent and experience to design and produce an interior" – compensated in its own right.[2] The editors further argued that it was not until interior design work was given a price tag, measured and analyzed by contracts and billing systems, that the activity could be elevated in standing from a business into a profession, from a retail operation into a service as late as 1960. Yet financial independence would only arrive after interior designers had defined their services, and specifically in relation those of architects.

Interiors' celebration of interior design *as service* would coincide, roughly, with architectural critic Reyner Banham's inverse advice to architects in his essay "Design by Choice," published in *The Architectural Review* in July 1961. There, Banham recommended that British architects redirect their professional activities toward specifying interior furnishings and merchandise for purchase, rather than providing a traditional architectural service.[3] In Banham's opinion, architects held superior experience over the consumer when it came to fitting out interiors, and urged them to exert their influence by working with the furnishing industry directly. His call was not only a testament to the strength and independence of the interior design profession at the time, but also signaled the competitive threat it posed, as well as the opportunities it presented for architects.

The question *how* to define qualifying standards in North America for interior design practice had dogged designers during the first half of the twentieth century, since the formation of the American Institute of Decorators (AID) in 1931, the National Society of Interior Designers (NSID) in 1957, and up until the establishment of the American Society of Interior Designers (ASID) in 1974. The same question would beleaguer architects offering the design of interiors as part of their architectural services in parallel. For even though architecture had been long established as an organized profession – the American Institute of Architects (AIA) was founded in 1857; the first licensing law established in the State of Illinois in 1897[4] – the more recent rise of an autonomous interior design profession alongside the long-established architecture profession

169

was regarded by many architects as an encroachment into a design territory they had ostensibly laid claim to in theory, but not often in organized practice. The professional and ideological *distinctions* between the nature and scope of services offered by an emerging profession and an already established one would prove to be long lived, and only resolved through the question of how each profession's interior activities resembled and differed from one another over an extended period of time.

Nowhere does the process of delineating the distinctions between interior design and architecture appear more vividly than in the feature stories, stocktaking reports, opinion pieces, and news items published in professional architecture and interior design magazines between the early 1940s and late 1960s. In the period's key journals – *Interiors, Architectural Record, The Architectural Forum, Progressive Architecture*, and *Arts & Architecture* – interior design activity is reported on in two general ways. The first might be understood in terms of service *principles* and reaches for what actually constituted interior design ideologically and in scope – i.e., the rules for selecting furnishings, material finishes, space planning – undertaken by architects, interior designers, and industrial designers, and relayed through specific projects, technical data, practitioner profiles, historic examples, and design criticism. The second might be characterized as service *logistics*, and evidences the stages of interior design's professionalization in relation to the growing number of specialist societies and showroom news, market reports, career information, education accounts, trade associations, and economic data that accompany it. If the first offers a *qualitative* portrait of interior design activity, the second presents a *quantitative* picture of its *contexts* through increasing numbers: new institutions, new events, and new societies.

Together – principles and logistics both – they reveal the professionalization of interior design playing out at the intersection of evolving design values – which with few exceptions during the period, were indebted to architects – and furnishing markets that not only sustained the professionalization of interior design but also stimulated architectural practitioners toward new kinds of specialized, interior activities. Indeed, the magazine layouts, images, and essays show the professionalization of interior design largely forming, developing, and separating, along the lines of an architectural culture under constant revision.

It is not surprising that in this fluctuating context the journals also provide conflicting perceptions and definitions of what actually constitutes an interior design service. Indeed, they present alternating portraits of interior design in relation to architecture through three overlapping and staggered acts of exchange that correlate with contemporaneous socio-economic developments. First, between 1940 and 1951, as both fields respond to rising consumer confidence and a growing domestic interior market, the journals publish project reviews that inconsistently position interior design simultaneously *beneath* and *beside* architecture. The discrepancies largely revolve around the *status* of the interior designer in relation to the architect.

Second, between 1948 and 1959, against the background of a burgeoning service economy, the journal's critical essays and special segment features expose interior designers and architects revising their professional identities but in opposing directions: interior design from the *outside in* (by emulating architectural design *values*); and architecture from the *inside out* (by entering the interiors *industry*). In this period, marked by a postwar office building boom and new demands for office interiors, the magazines focus on the *identities* of interior design – understood as a form of

Imaging interior design: beneath, beside, and within architecture ∎

furniture arranging – and the new specialization "interior architecture" – understood as a form of space planning.

Third, between 1960 and 1968, as interior markets continue to segment into niche markets, and as architects and designers continue to specialize their interior services, anniversary and themed issues shift attention away from the qualitative distinctions of status or identity toward legal title and the logistics of remuneration. This focus emphasizes the professional *organization* of interior design and interior architectural practices.

In their recordings of the shifting priorities of architects and interior designers, the journals fabricate the ground intelligence for interior designers and architects to define and redefine their professional activities in relation to one other. They also demonstrate that it was not simply that interior design became professionalized, but that the process of professionalization collaterally impacted the architecture profession, instigating architects to re-invent their service, which in turn provoked interior designers to re-invent theirs. A closer comparison of the journals' content through these three stages shows how these reciprocations factored into interior design's professionalization process.

1940–1951: BENEATH OR BESIDE ARCHITECTURE?

In September 1940, *Architectural Record* published a review by designer Virginia Conner entitled "Making Maximum Use of Minimum Space." In her article, Conner criticizes the "common faults" of architectural design in small apartment interior: "the greatest architectural handicap that the interior designer faces is the indiscriminate location of openings."[5] She suggests collaboration between architects and interiors and a more holistic approach to design by, for example, "mapping out a room for living, sleeping and dining," as a way to solve the problem.[6] Interior designer Walter P. Margulies, in a more derisively titled essay "Interiors vs. Architecture" published in *Interiors* in August 1945, also reiterates the need for professional cooperation, this time in relation to hotel rooms. He too proposes "interiors with architecture" as a way to rectify the unfortunate situation where "the harassed interior designer" is bequeathed "rooms of random sizes and shapes – and the thankless task of fitting them to do their jobs."[7] And in May 1951, *Architectural Forum*, the leading "Magazine of Building," takes a passive-aggressive swipe at architects when it credits architect-trained designer, Florence Knoll, then director of interior design services at Knoll for providing an "outstanding example of interior camouflage" for Knoll Furniture's New York showroom.[8] The interior cover-up, achieved though applications of air, color, light and water – techniques incidentally employed by Mrs. Knoll's architect mentor Mies van der Rohe – is praised for "effectively kill[ing] most of the existing architecture."[9] Collectively, the journals articulate, from a designer's perspective, the frustrating predicament of interior design being *beneath* (or inferior to) architecture while striving to be recognized *beside* it.

Conversely, features published by architect-editors in the same magazines at exactly the same time construct an entirely different portrait of the relationship between the two professions. Instead, they emphasize the *equivalence* between the two sets of activities graphically and editorially. This is clearly communicated in a built-in lounge feature published in *Architectural Record* in April 1940, for example. Here designs for built-in domestic furniture by interior designers and architects are graphically depicted side-by-side, in identically sized photographs, drawings, and with captions

171 ▢

describing forms, colors, and materials.[10] Without image captions, it would be very difficult to figure out who authored what. Similarly, equivalence is directly stated by Jan Reiner in his "Notes on the New Interiors" published in *Arts & Architecture* in May 1944 and, despite mistaking the word "decorator" for "designer" when he writes "[a] modern interior should be a happy fusion of the work of an architect and decorator," and exhibit "principles of harmony," which cannot be achieved "by concentrating upon interior design alone."[11] And it is demonstrated graphically in a mosaic-spread of images and captions published in *Architectural Record*'s "Coordinated Interior Design" of November 1947, where designers – the Saarinen-Swanson Group – equivalently permeate the "spirit of architecture" through rooms, furniture, decor, and textiles, to achieve "harmony in spirit, form, scale and color."[12] In each article, the journals situate interior design work *alongside* that of architecture, neither beneath nor in opposition to it.

How does one account for such different perceptions of the architecture-interior design relationship at this moment? Both fields are responding to a growing domestic market for consumer items – including housewares, appliances, and new furniture – and both are expanding their interior services in response to this expansion of goods. The answer lies in how each field *views* the interior. On the one hand, interior designer-author's articles place their emphasis on the design of the whole – spaces and rooms – rather than the design parts – traditional furnishings. Their focus is at an *architectural* scale. On the other, the architect-author's pieces place emphasis on the coordination of parts – furniture, décor, and textiles – rather than rooms or spaces. Their focus is at an *interior design* scale. As interior designers scale up their activities toward the scale of architecture, architects scale down their activity toward the details of the interior. The orientations are different attempts to gain control of the interior.

These approaches reflect real-time shifts taking place in the furnishings industry as well as in architectural offices. For example, during the 1940s, leading furniture companies like Knoll quickly grew and shifted their focus away from importing and manufacturing furniture and objects, to designing entire interiors, particularly office interiors.[13] In this shift, architects were hired to design furniture pieces. Herman Miller, for example, hired architect-trained designer George Nelson as the company's first design director in 1945.[14] Similarly, in corporate architectural offices like Skidmore, Owings and Merrill (SOM), architects began purchasing and specifying furniture as part of their architectural service, a move that led to separate interior design sections being formed within offices in the 1950s.[15] Against the background of industry and office shifts, it is perhaps not surprising that interior designers would focus on pragmatic issues of territory and expertise. Significantly, however, both perspectives paradoxically represent interior design in architecture's image: an ideological image projected before the professional "fact" of interior design.

1948–1959: FROM WITHOUT AND FROM WITHIN

Interiors magazine would be a central venue in proposing a version of interior design conceived in architecture's image. In a series of articles published between 1948 and 1959, George Nelson and Edgar Kaufmann jr. called upon designers to precisely distinguish themselves from decorators by adopting design "principles," which invariably were established by modern architects ranging from Le Corbusier, to Mies van der Rohe and Frank Lloyd Wright. The magazine communicates these

Imaging interior design: beneath, beside, and within architecture ■

ideas in text and/or image. In his imageless essay, "Problems of Design: Ends and Means" published in May 1948, Nelson calls for more design "integrity" in reference to the example of architecture.[16] In his better-known essay "Problems of design: modern decoration," published in November 1949, he makes a visual argument for design "principles not formulas" through text, cartoons, and three very large photographs of interiors designed by Le Corbusier, Mies, and Wright.[17] And in a particularly architectural point of view, *Interiors* presents a domestic interior from the waist down through a series of worm's-eye photographs in Nelson's "Problem's of Design: Notes on the New Subscape" published in November 1950. Here, voyeuristic photographs magnify the lower halves of interior spaces like an architectural section drawing, to show furniture legs designed by Charles Eames, among others.[18] The essay's emphasis on comfort and lightness parallels Edgar Kaufmann jr.'s ideas for good design – later reformulated as "principles, not effects" – in his 1953 catalogue essay "What is Modern Interior Design?"[19]

It would not be until 1960, however, that the *Interiors* editors would retroactively admit that the subject matter of "Interiors to Come" – a futures feature published every January between 1941 and 1956 – was, by 1956, no longer about interiors per se, but rather "architectural works comprising at least a building [whose] décor was wholly incidental."[20] In imaging interior design in architecture's appearance, *Interiors* had shifted the emphasis of interior design away from the pragmatics of furniture arranging, toward the articulation of design *values* that were derived from modern architecture. This campaign, which paralleled the lead up to the formation of the NISD, recast the interior designer's relationship to the architect in a new way: architects were no longer perceived to be inhibitors of practice as they had during the 1940s, but rather role models for it. The intellectual guidance of architects was now recognized as a means to the interior designer's professional elevation.

Meanwhile, as *Interiors* dispensed advice and show interior designers redefining their game from the *outside* in, architects are redefining interior design from the *inside* out in their journals. Under the auspices of the new specialization "interior architecture," the journals insert new monthly features. For example, in June 1953, *Progressive Architecture* introduces an "Interior Design data" segment that reviews a broader range of interiors designed by architects, including those of banks and offices. It also initiates an "interior design products" section to specify furnishings, cabinetwork, lighting, wall, ceilings and flooring finishes for offices.[21] In October of the same year, *Architectural Record* begins a recurring "Architectural Interiors" segment profiling different designs, details, materials and equipment for corporate interiors.[22] And *The Architectural Review*, in the British context, introduces a regular monthly "interior design" supplement in April 1958, accompanied by one of the clearest pleas by an architectural editor "for a more open-minded approach to the problem of interior design in general, seeing it neither as something absolutely within the architect's control, nor as something entirely outside his responsibility, but rather as a field of expert, integrated, sympathetic consultancy, like structural engineering."[23] As if in anticipation of Edgar Kauffman's 1962 speculation in *Progressive Architecture* that interior designers might just be influencing architects rather than the other way around, the American journals present architects recalibrating their interior design activity at a moment in the interior industry's fortification.[24] New journal segments like "Interior architecture" not only correspond with emerging interior niches in a segmenting market culture – indeed, the term "market segmentation" first appeared in 1956[25] – but also parallel

173 □

interior design's formation into a national society in 1957. In this regard entry into the interior designer's contract industry is a means for architects to redefine interior design as a specialized activity *within* their traditional practice.

This outward shift was a function of two related developments in the 1950s: an economic building boom and the rise of a service economy. The building boom produced more construction – office buildings in particular – and more undecorated space in need of fitting out. In turn, specialists were needed to perform the new work. In a report published in February 1957, *Architectural Forum* succinctly identified the need for specialists experienced "in the science of making interior office space work out logically, i.e. profitably."[26] This new science was a "science of coordination," as Dutch architect Rem Koolhaas retroactively put it; not just about choosing furniture, but coordinating ceiling tiles, lighting fixtures, partitions, air-conditioning grills, electrical outlets, and floor finishes as well.[27] In many ways, the journal's new architectural interiors segments reflected market demand in the same way that the introduction of "interiors" divisions into American corporate architecture firms met the demand for new kinds of commissions. Both evidence the extent to which a burgeoning furnishings industry had become as lucrative for architects to engage with, as the traditional construction industry.

This expansion reflects an important turn in orientation regarding the architects' interior activities, away from what might be called proficiency in interior design "theory" toward a competence for interior design in organized "practice." *Progressive Architecture* and *Architectural Record* illustrate this shift well in their newly inserted interior segments, making visible architecture's newly specialized professional services, the scope of commissions being undertaken, and the emergence of new kinds of residential and corporate clients. The public relations turn seems to inspire the *Interiors* editors in turn, who insert new segments into their issues a couple of years later like the aptly titled "Race to Design Series" in February 1955, and "Design Firm Case Studies" in January 1959. Both offer in-depth features on architect-designed interiors but with different focuses: on public and institutional interiors in 1955 – offices, banks, hotels, restaurants, shops, showrooms, religious buildings, hospitals, schools – and on architectural firms in 1959.[28] As architects colonize the contract furnishing industry as a way to redefine interior design territory, their published successes provide an editorial model for interior designers to emulate, this time not in terms of principles, but of practice.

1960–1974: FEE SIMPLE; FEE SEPARATE

It was not until 1960 that a focus on these professional permutations would subside in the magazines, as editors and writers turned toward articulating the specifics of architecture and interior design as independent practices, and the organizational logistics of interior design service, in whatever forms it might be offered. On the interiors side, this most vividly came into focus in an anniversary issues and two profile reports, which consecutively presented interior design as an autonomous profession. In Interiors' 1960 anniversary, "Two Decades of Interiors," the editorial emphatically states that "interior design [is] no longer a by-product of other professional services like architecture."[29] This liberation is attributed to numerous factors including the rise of the furnishing industry,

Imaging interior design: beneath, beside, and within architecture ∎

trade associations, markets, clients, and fee structures. It is made visible, through an accumulation of small images, statistical data, graphic timelines, and short text columns: graphic density gives weight to interior design's growing professional independence. The visual emphasis on logistical quantity marks a divisive moment in the profiling of the interior design profession. In Interiors' subsequent "Profile of the Profession" published in February 1968, the editors carefully distinguish the "profession" of interior design from the "art" of interior design, which as they point out, can be practiced by any number of people including architects, interior designers, and artists.[30] Quantity, therefore, not only announces the emergence of a particular kind of practitioner, but also implies a shift away from defining *what* professional interior design is, to *who* has the right to claim its professional (as opposed to artistic) title. This question of entitlement would not be resolved until well after the merging of the AID and NSID into the American Association of Interior Designers (ASID) in 1974 when the legal title of interior designer became partially effective.[31]

In contrast, as *Interiors* were chronicling the logistics of independence, *Progressive Architecture* and *Architectural Record* were articulating how architects were addressing the professional minutiae of "interior architecture" in terms of contract specification, fee arrangements, staffing, and client relations. At the basis of this logistical focus was an attempt by architects to regain control of the design of interiors through highly organized business operations. *Progressive Architecture's* presumptuously themed issue "The Architecture of Interiors" published in October 1962 pushes for this effort, publishing several exchanges between interior designers and architects under another grandiose title: "Architectural Control of Interiors."[32] *Architectural Record* also unpacks the question of why and how architects are providing services in interior design in its two-part series "How Architects Practice Interior Design" (1964–1965) authored by architect W. B. Foxhall. In part one Foxhall provides three reasons for *why*: one, to control the palette of materials and colors of a whole building (inside and out) so as to maintain unity and depth of concept; two, to perform a total professional service by coordinating all aspects, technical and aesthetic of buildings; and three, to get paid for that service on a professional basis.[33] In part two, he suggests two reasons for *how*: one, set up interior design operations as a separate business from the architectural firm; and two, separate the interiors contracts and billing systems from the building contracts.[34] The office of "Interior Space Design" (ISD) – another semantic spin on interior architecture – incorporated in 1961 as a subsidiary of the corporate architectural firm Perkins & Willis, exemplifies this business model.[35]

By duplicating the scales and scopes of their services, architects could contract interior design services separately from building services. As Robert Gutman explained in his book *Architectural Practice*, the willingness of architectural firms to offer interior architecture made good sense economically:

> The design of interior space, especially office space for high-level personnel and floor space in department stores and other shops marketing consumer items, produces high fees for the practitioner. Interior space is also replaced much more frequently than the building shell and facades. It therefore offers the possibility of repeat work, which generally results in bigger profits.[36]

But the motive behind this level of control was ostensibly more than profit and professional competition between fields. It also meant "substantially a return to the 'mother art' of architecture," as

Architectural Record put it in a profile of emerging trends in practice in June 1969.[37] In other words, the expanding scope of architectural services was a means to reassert the theoretical ideal of interior activities taking place under the umbrella of architectural practice, even if economically. As *Interiors* places the legal authorization of interior design beyond decorating, but beside architecture, both *P/A* and *Record* reposition interior design back *within* the scope of architecture.

By the end of the 1960s, the journals anticipate Gutman's analysis of interior work being split at least three ways: between interior design consultants responsible to architects; interior designers and architects working directly with clients; and in-house interior departments as subsidiaries in architectural offices.[38] This segmentation was a direct product of the back and forth between interior designers and architects, as well as of a growing service economy and inflationary furnishing industry. As the independent profession of interior design evolved between 1940 and 1960, it did so in very close proximity to the architectural profession. While serving as forums for the professionalization of interior design and the specialization of a facet of architecture into interior architecture, the journals and magazines redefine the professional responsibilities of both fields, whether by redirecting interior design's status and identity, or by defining the logistical terrain of both architectural and interior design practice. In its quest for greater control in the design of interiors, the architect needed to enter the consumer market and occupy the territory interior designers had just left. This was the inverse case in interior design's quest for professionalization, where the interior designer needed to leave the consumer market of furnishings in order to become a billable service.

NOTES

1 "Two Decades of Interiors: The Profession," *Interiors* 120 (November 1960): 161.
2 Ibid.
3 See Reyner Banham, "Design by Choice," *The Architectural Review* 130 (July 1961): 46.
4 Robert Gutman, *Architectural Practice: A Critical View* (Princeton: Princeton Architectural Press, 1988), 61.
5 Virginia Conner, "Making Maximum Use of Minimal Space," *Architectural Record* 88 (September 1940): 61.
6 Conner, 62.
7 Walter P. Margulies, "Interior vs. Architecture," *Interiors* 105 (August 1945): 88.
8 Knoll had been working full time for Knoll Associates since 1943. See "Knoll Timeline, The 1940s." www.knoll.com/discover-knoll/timeline#y_1941. Accessed 9 June 2016.
9 "Walls of Air, Color, Light and Water," *Architectural Forum* 94 (May 1951): 141, 143.
10 See "Units Lounging," *Architectural Record* 87 (April 1940): 70–71.
11 Jan Reimer, "NOTES on the New Interiors," *Arts & Architecture* 61 (May 1944): 25.
12 "Coordinated Interior Design: The Saarinen-Swanson Group," *Architectural Record* 102 (November 1947): 78–79.
13 For example, in 1946 Florence Knoll launched the "planning unit at Knoll" aimed at controlling the design of an entire space. See "Knoll Timeline, The 1940s." www.knoll.com/discover-knoll/timeline. Accessed 9 June 2016. For an historical account of Knoll and the Knoll Planning Unit, see Bobbeye Tigerman, "'I am Not A Decorator': Florence Knoll, the Knoll Planning Unit and the Making of the Modern Office," *Journal of Design History*, 20, no. 1 (2007): 61–74.
14 See "Company History 1950 – Herman Miller," www.hermanmiller.com/about-us/who-is-herman-miller/company-timeline/1950.html. Accessed 9 June 2016.
15 SOM attributes this shift in scope of service to when "the firm's wealthier corporate clients began to provide funds for items such as plants, sculptures, paintings, and various other decorative objects to

Imaging interior design: beneath, beside, and within architecture ∎

provide an attractive atmosphere in their workplaces" in the 1940s. The company was commissioned "to purchase or design furniture that was particularly comfortable, so that employee morale would remain high and performance during long hours remain effective. Adequate lighting and suitable coloring also became concerns." As more clients requested such services, SOM "became one of the first architectural firms to include interior design in its contracts, attending to space, lighting, color, furniture, and the overall effect of the enclosed environment." See "History of Skidmore, Owings & Merrill LLP," www.fundinguniverse.com/company-histories/skidmore-owings-merrill-llp-history/. Accessed 9 June 2016. Following SOM, Perkins and Wills would introduce an in-house interior design staff in 1949. This department eventually became a separate division within the company and was incorporated in October 1961 as Interior Space Design. See "Perkins and Will and Its satellite, Interior Space Design," *Contract Interiors* 120 (July 1961): 59.

16 George Nelson, "Problems of Design: Ends and Means," *Interiors* 107 (May 1948): 84–87.

17 George Nelson, "Problems of Design: Modern Decoration," *Interiors* 109 (November 1949): 68–75. With its focus on design principles, this essay shares a similar argument to Albert Auerbach's essay "What is modern?" published a year earlier. See Alfred Auerbach, "What Is modern?" *Arts & Architecture* (March 1948).

18 George Nelson, "Problems of Design: Notes on the New Subscape," *Interiors* 110 (November 1950): 140–143.

19 See Edgar Kaufmann, *What Is Modern Interior Design?* (New York: Museum of Modern Art, 1953), 3–30.

20 See "Guesses on Interiors to Come: Hindsight and Foresight," *Interiors* 120 (November 1960), 181.

21 See, for example, "p/a Interior Design Data," *Progressive Architecture* 34 (June 1953): 125–131.

22 See for example, "Color Enlivens Offices" in the Architectural Interiors section published in *Architectural Record* 114 (October 1953): 173–177 and "Space Definition Within the House," *Architectural Record* (May 1954): 164–169.

23 Contents page description, *The Architectural Review*, 123, no. 735 (April 1958): 228.

24 In his 1953 essay (see footnote 19) Kauffman attributes principles of interior design to the work of architects. In his 1962 essay, he disputes the architect's sense of entitlement over the interior design practice, stating that historically this superiority was more an exception than a rule. See Edgar Kauffmann, Jr. "Interior Design: Architecture or Decoration?" *Progressive Architecture* (October 1962): 141–144, 260.

25 See Wendell R. Smith, "Product Differentiation and Market Segmentation as Alternative Marketing Strategies," *Journal of Marketing* 21, no.1 (July 1956): 3–8.

26 See "Who Gets What Office?" *Architectural Forum* 106, no. 2 (February 1957): 118–121.

27 Rem Koolhaas, "Typical Plan," in *SMLXL* (New York: The Monacelli Press, 1995): 338.

28 See "Race to Design: Offices, An Untypical Collection," *Interiors* 114, no. 7 (February 1955): 70–81; "Race to Design: Retail Shops and Stores," *Interiors* 114, no. 8 (March 1955): 64–85; "Race to Design: Showrooms," *Interiors* 114, no. 9 (April 1955): 92–107; "Race to Design: Hotels," *Interiors* 114, no. 10 (May 1955): 87–99; "Race to Design: Hospitals," *Interiors* 114, no. 11 (June 1955): 78–91; "Race to Design: Restaurants and Bars," *Interiors* 114, no. 12 (July 1955): 75–81; and "Design Firm Case Studies: SOM," *Interiors* 118, no. 6 (January 1959): 90–109.

29 Olga Gueft, "20 Years and 240 Issues Ago," *Interiors* 120 (November 1960): 128.

30 See "Profile of the Profession," *Interiors* 127 (February 1968): 69–73.

31 For a history of this transition, see "A Salute to the ASID," *Interiors* 134 (January 1975): 76–87, 178. As late as 1988 legal title was still not resolved. In his book, *Architectural Practice: A Critical View*, Robert Gutman notes that interior design was "still engaged in a battle to become a licensed profession" and that chapters of the American Institute of Architects were still lobbying against the registration of interior designers. He notes that in 1986, "the title of interior designer was protected in only three states" and that the competition between architects and interior designers was "probably more intense now than ever before in the history of architecture." He attributes this rivalry to the growing domination of service industries. See Robert Gutman, *Architectural Practice: A Critical View* (Princeton: Princeton Architectural

177 ☐

Press, 1988), 65. Stephen MacDonald, "Building Battle: Interior Designers Pitted Against Architects in Licensing Dispute," *Wall Street Journal*, 6 May 1987, 33.

32 See entire issue of *Progressive Architecture* 43 no. 10 (October 1962), and in particular "Architectural Control of Interiors," 43, no. 10 (October 1962): 156–157.

33 William B. Foxhall, "How Architects Practice Interior Design: The Architect in Practice – Part 1," *Architectural Record* (November 1964): 89.

34 William B. Foxhall, "How Architects Practice Interior Design: The Architect in Practice – Part 2," *Architectural Record* (April 1965): 108.

35 See "Perkins+Will History," http://history.perkinswill.com accessed 9 June 2016 and "Space Illusions in ISD's New Chicago Office," *Interiors* 125 (January 1966): 104.

36 Gutman, 13.

37 "The Design of Interiors: A Profile of Emerging Trends in Practice," *Architectural Record* 145, no.7 (June 1969): 130.

38 Gutman identifies four ways, but I am only referencing three here. See Gutman, 66.

Chapter 12: Modernism's glass ceiling

Women in commercial design after WWII

Mark Hinchman

The early years of the interior decoration business is often told with a set of stock characters: Elsie de Wolfe, Nancy Lancaster, Syrie Maugham, Dorothy Draper, and others.[1] Providing professional services involving interiors proved a welcoming environment for working women. The dynamics of the interiors business changed dramatically after World War II, when some women, as either interior designers or architects, started working on large commercial projects for firms that were themselves big corporate entities.

SOM was the firm that became the economic and design model of corporatism, in developing an administrative structure that could handle client's large projects, and whose own administrative model it emulated. They were so successful that they spawned legions of imitators around the world, including Harry Seidler, Hugh Stubbins, and HDR. SOM took the teachings of Mies van der Rohe to heart.[2] Part of the design mantra of modernists, from Mies to Alvar Aalto, was a variant on *Gesamtkunstwerk*, or total work of art, that all parts of a project should relate. SOM architects, including Gordon Bunshaft, Bruce Graham, and Walter Netsch, interpreted this by encouraging their clients to hire them also for the interiors of their office buildings. According to this view of project development, a building's interiors were an extension of the architecture.

Looking at the careers of four women who worked at SOM on interiors projects, two as architects, two as interior designers, is a means to trace a range of experiences of those who specialized in non-residential interiors. Gertrude Kerbis, Margaret McCurry, Nathalie de Blois, and Margo Grant Walsh worked for a time at SOM in the postwar period, and their careers reveal how many women initially fared in the world of corporate interior design. Their own words tell the stories of how women both prospered and encountered difficulties in the commercial design workforce.[3] Additionally, a number of aesthetic issues arose, from the relationship of interior designers to Miesian modernism, the creation of SOM's interiors department, the conceptual connection between a building and its interiors, and the circumstances that led to the creation of the world's largest interiors firm, Gensler.

GERTRUDE KERBIS, MIES VAN DER ROHE, AND WALTER NETSCH

The career of Gertrude Kerbis (1926–2016) demonstrates that there is an approach to interior design that is not concerned with furnishings and finishes, but with crafting interior space by focusing on

179

structure, especially long-span structures, considering modularity as an initial approach to space planning, and developing custom-manufactured elements such as concrete panels.[4]

Once Kerbis started her education, her degrees came in a non-linear fashion. After studying at Wright Junior College, and the University of Wisconsin, she received a Bachelor of Science in architectural engineering from the University of Illinois in 1948. She spent a semester at Harvard, and finished her Master's degree in architecture at the Illinois Institute of Technology (IIT) in 1954; as a student, her instructors included no less than Walter Gropius and Mies van der Rohe. She worked for the foremost modernists of her day, including Carl Koch, Bertrand Goldberg, Gordon Bunshaft, Walter Netsch, and Bruce Graham. What is evident in her oral history is that for much of her early career, her bosses did not treat her as an equal to the men on the design teams on which she worked.[5] She emphasized that she was an architect, and that the list of projects that came her way, a restaurant, a dining hall and notably, no high rises, is because she was a woman. Yet, by any measure, she was an accomplished architect with several of the most prominent interior projects of the twentieth century to her credit: before SOM she worked on the Lustron House, and furniture for a MoMA Low-Cost Furniture exhibition; at SOM, she did the USAFA dining room, and their own offices; at C.F. Murphy, she created the Seven Continents Restaurant, and C.F. Murphy's offices. In these projects, she focused on creating a structure which allowed for a broad expanse of uninterrupted space, delineated by non-structural partitions, and furnishings.

After her graduation from IIT, Netsch hired Kerbis to work at SOM. She started working on Mitchell Hall, the dining hall that was one part of the campus of the USAFA, in 1954.[6] From the start, her interest was in creating a column-free interior, an idea her IIT mentor, Mies van der Rohe, was exploring. Her solution involved a giant space in which all 3,000 cadets could eat at the same time, a client requirement (Figure 12.1). The finished structure is a 308 x 308 foot square, made of steel, aluminum, and pre-cast concrete, with an interior clear span of 266 feet. It is one story at its entry level, and, because of a sloping site, the interior dramatically drops away to a three-story high southern elevation of glass. Mies' team was investigating a similar structural system for Chicago's Convention Hall, an unrealized project. Thus, Kerbis put into reality ideas about long-span structures that Mies and his engineers only had theorized. On the completion of Mitchell Hall, Kerbis joined the select group of experts in long-span construction with real-life experience. Another innovation of Mitchell Hall was the construction method, in which the roof was built in its entirety on the ground, on site, and then hydraulically lifted into place. Construction took place in 1958; raising the roof took six hours, an event which the press referred to as "instant construction."[7]

The dining area lay underneath the two-way truss system, initially held aloft by eight columns on the perimeter, which was changed to 16 as the project developed. Despite being the principle designer on the project, Kerbis was not allowed to interact with the client, nor to be present for the lifting of the roof, the first time a project of this scope had been attempted. Kerbis attributed these and other slights to her being a woman: "I always felt that the reason I never designed a high-rise building was that the commercial world was not ready to accept a woman designing an office building."[8] She had a contentious relationship with Bruce Graham, one of the SOM executives overseeing the design of USAFA, and he fired her in 1959. It was a conflation of two situations: Graham

Figure 12.1
SOM, Walter Netsch and Gertrude Kerbis. Mitchell Hall, USAFA dining facility, 1954.

was having marital difficulties and, Kerbis said, "Bruce sort of came onto me."[9] He was the partner in charge of a hotel project, and he developed one design direction, Kerbis another. Before a client meeting that he could not attend because of a broken leg, he instructed Kerbis to present his idea. She presented her idea, and not his.[10] He was furious.

In her oral history, Kerbis repeatedly declines to attribute the vicissitudes of her career exclusively to sexism. She straightforwardly mentioned that she was attracted to Graham, and that the impediment to a potential romance was that he was married. By then, in 1959, she was in discussion with C.F. Murphy, a firm known for its collaboration with Mies on many projects. They were doing preliminary work on a huge project: Chicago's O'Hare International Airport. Kerbis was to work at C.F. Murphy until 1963. Because of her experience with Mitchell Hall, she was given the highly visible Seven Continents Restaurant at the airport. The master plan, done by others, called for a round building that served as a knuckle between the two terminals. Its geometry thusly called for a different structural system than Mitchell Hall.

Kerbis remained attracted to the possibilities of a giant column-free space. She developed a concrete circular beam at the building's perimeter. At the center of the circle was a smaller steel ring, and steel tension rods connected the interior ring to the exterior circle. This resulted in a slightly inverted dome with a clear span of 200 feet. The open space allowed for a circulation path that connected the terminals and the restaurant. The roof was only five inches thick. Again, her innovation created considerable buzz. The opening of Terminals 2 and 3 and the Seven Continents Restaurant, in 1962, was a grand affair with Mayor Daley and President Kennedy present. Kerbis was not initially invited and, in response, she, in her term, created a "ruckus" that included writing to the

President.[11] She attended the opening, but later complained "I felt again that I was powerless, that I was not given a partnership, that I was not brought into the inner circle."[12]

At multiple points in her career, and later when reflecting on it, Kerbis distanced herself from the aspects of her projects that were interior design. At SOM she did the firm's offices when they relocated to the Inland Steel building. Similarly charged with designing C.F. Murphy's offices, she did the space planning, but left the furnishings and finishes to others. In the case of the Seven Continents Restaurants, George Larson did the interior design work, which included draperies, table clothes, and table ware. Kerbis was offered a position at Holabird and Root, as an architect but, told that she would be sitting in the interior design studio, she declined. With no expressed interest in interiors, as a woman architect, her superiors nonetheless gave her multiple interiors projects.

Kerbis's work on Mitchell Hall and the Seven Continents Restaurant influenced Mies' work on the National Gallery in Berlin, C.F. Murphy's work on McCormick Place, and Buckminster Fuller's geodesic domes. She monetized the concept of the open plan, in that she took what had been an idea and made it real, and functional for clients. A staunch modernist, her story also indicates that even highly accomplished women at the world's largest architectural firm trod a difficult path.

NATHALIE DE BLOIS, FLORENCE KNOLL, MARGARET MCCURRY, AND DAVIS ALLEN

Nathalie de Blois' career explains the genesis of SOM's interiors department. The firm did a new headquarters for Connecticut Life Insurance Company, in Hartford, 1954–1957. An eight-story low-rise building set in a suburban campus, it was one of the early office examples to exploit the possibilities of a metal and glass curtain-wall and open office planning. Because it was one of the first suburban office headquarters, and its uncompromising modernism, the project garnered a lot of attention. Gordon Bunshaft was the architect.

An article in 1958 extolled the virtues of "The Team Approach" that resulted in the Connecticut Life headquarters, which included the client, the architect, an interior designer, a graphic designer, and a sculptor.[13] Yet, as is often case with SOM projects, design was credited to the partners in charge, and the dynamics of how the rest of the team contributed remain unclear.

De Blois related that in 1953–1954, 15–20 people at SOM worked on the design of the project, while another SOM studio handled the production of working drawings.[14] The client had a women's committee, with whom de Blois met multiple times. She worked on details as specific as the layout and location of the women's toilets, recreation area, and a library. She was acutely aware of how designing the interiors unfolded, with Bunschaft creating the layouts and general design direction, and the office furniture being developed later.

Florence Knoll, of the Knoll Planning Unit, designed the furniture and office layouts.[15] Knoll, like Bunshaft, was a modernist who believed in total design, or that the interiors should be an extension of the architecture.[16] In multiple records of the project's development, Bunshaft had no major disagreements with Knoll about her design direction. What rankled Bunshaft was her on-going relationship with the client, and her prominence in the press. For Bunshaft's conception of how the project should run, Knoll "got too much attention."[17] Committed modernists, Bunshaft, de Blois,

Modernism's glass ceiling ■

Figure 12.2
SOM, Gordon Bunshaft, Florence Knoll, and Nathalie de Blois. Connecticut Life, 1954. (Ezra Stoller photographer)

and Knoll got their way with the design direction of most aspects of the projects, including the building and work areas (Figure 12.2). Yet designing the executive area was a different story. Speaking about Connecticut Life's board members, de Blois said that "those who wanted their Georgian furniture got what they wanted."[18]

Because of his success in supervising the creation of interiors with his in-house team of architects, and his dissatisfaction with the attention the Knoll Planning Union garnered, Bunshaft supported the creation of SOM's interiors department, largely so that he could control them.

Another of Bunshaft's famous works was the Chase Manhattan Building of 1961. The 60-story building was lower Manhattan's first international style building. The work for the vice-presidents' offices initially was outsourced to the designer Ward Bennett. Bennett came to interior design after a start in fashion and window display. He clashed with Bunshaft over the design of the offices as he encouraged their individuality and worked with executives' desire to use antiques. Bunshaft preferred to work with SOM's own Davis Allen.

This was the environment Margaret McCurry encountered when she started at SOM in 1966; her time there overlapped with that of de Blois. McCurry had a different academic and professional background than Kerbis and de Blois, with degrees in Art History and English.[19] Her father was an architect and she grew up in an international style house he designed. After college, she started out as a secretary at Quaker Oats in Chicago, and was promoted to package-design coordinator, her first design position.

She interviewed at SOM, and took a position in interiors, as they had an opening. SOM in the 1960s, was, in her words, "firmly entrenched in reinterpretations of Mies."[20] De Blois, who worked with McCurry, concurred: "Everything was Mies."[21] Richard McKenna led Chicago's interiors

183 □

department, while Davis Allen, in New York, was SOM's head interior designer. His longevity suggests that he was a survivor of the company's demanding corporate culture, and he got along with some famously big egos, including Graham, Netsch, and Bunshaft. Allen's body of work for SOM indicates that he was a talent in his own right, and that given the opportunity to veer away from – but not oppose – the company's Miesian modernism, he did so with considerable agility.[22] Two of the many projects on which he worked represent different aspects of his commercial interior design work, the interiors of the Mauna Kea Beach Hotel, Hawaii, 1965, and the interiors of the National Life and Accident Insurance Company in Nashville, 1970.

After working in a subsidiary capacity on a number of projects, McCurry took on more responsibility with a prominent SOM project for both the building and interiors of an office building in Nashville. Graham designed the National Life and Accident Building in 1970 and Allen did the interiors.[23] The building had a crisp curtain-wall, but the interiors were less modern than Connecticut Life. In a more subtle direction, Allen and McCurry softened their approach to the interiors, particularly in the cases of the executive offices (Figure 12.3). Some executives expressed an interest in certain art forms outside of modernism, from antiques to art. Evidently Graham was slightly more accepting, or uninvolved in the interiors. Allen selected Berber rugs and folk arts. With McCurry, he designed a guest chair, the Andover chair, which took as its point of departure the eighteenth-century Windsor chair, a paean to hand-crafted turning. Allen and McCurry modernized the look, using rods instead of turned spindles, and the chair appeared throughout the National Life offices.[24] It was such a success that it became a mainstay of SOM corporate interiors.

During McCurry's time at SOM, she had two mentors, McKenna and Allen. In contrast to Kerbis' experience with Bunshaft, Graham, and Netsch, McCurry writes fondly of her direct supervisors, both interior designers. De Blois and McCurry worked together on multiple projects, which the former described as "a lot of fun."[25]

Davis Allen worked at SOM for 40 years, beginning in 1950, and SOM's leadership named him associate partner in 1965. Despite the length of his SOM tenure, most of it as head of its interiors, he was never made full partner. Unlike Kerbis, de Blois designed high rises, although she reports at one point Bunshaft told her "You'll never be made partner." De Blois relocated to SOM's Chicago office, and eventually, after 30 years at SOM, she left.

McCurry worked at SOM for 11 years, and there were two reasons for her leaving: one regarding the potential for promotion, the other her growing dissatisfaction with the firm's allegiance to modernism. She noted that after a decade in interiors, she had progressed as far as she likely would. She was never made partner. Additionally, she was becoming increasingly disillusioned with modernism. Along with her husband, the architect Stanley Tigerman whom she met in 1975, she became one of the foremost figures in postmodernism.[26] She opened her own office in 1977; in 1979, she married Tigerman, and they merged their independent practices to form Tigerman/McCurry.[27]

McCurry described her career thusly: "My work has gradually evolved into a synthesis of modern classicism and the eccentric romanticism often found in the naïve architecture of the American vernacular."[28] Vernacular architecture and folk art became major influences of her work in the twenty-first century, but for over ten years at SOM, they subtly inflected the modern office designs she and Allen created.

Figure 12.3
SOM, Davis Allen and Margaret McCurry. Nashville Life And Accident Insurance Company, Nashville, 1970. (Ezra Stoller photographer).

MARGO GRANT WALSH, DAVIS ALLEN, AND ARTHUR GENSLER

Of Chippewa and Scottish lineage, Margo Grant Walsh was born on a Blackfoot Indian Reservation in Fort Peck, Montana, in 1936.[29] The family moved to Portland, Oregon where she attended Portland State, then the University of Oregon, graduating in interior architecture in 1960. Her professional introduction to corporate modernism started with working as a receptionist for Herman Miller in San Francisco.[30] Shortly thereafter, Alexis Yermakov lured her away to work for SOM. She started out as an all-round worker, whose duties included typing letters. While at SOM, Grant Walsh worked on multiple large projects. This experience led to a decades-long career during which she was at the highest level of design in two of the largest architecture and interior design firms: SOM and then Gensler. Looking at her career is also to visit the trajectory of a successful designer who started out doing clerical work, and ended up as a vice-president.

At SOM, her many projects included Tenneco, and the Mauna Kea Beach Hotel. Grant Walsh also considered Davis Allen to be her mentor, and recalls working with him with fondness. Despite considerable success, as a designer and a manager, she was one of the women who could not break the firm's glass ceiling; the position of partner eluded her. One of her first projects was the Mauna Kea Beach Hotel, a sprawling three-story building set in 23 verdant acres on Hawaii's big island. Edward Charles Bassett was the architect in charge.[31] That Miesian modernism proved adept as a model for corporate office buildings was becoming abundantly clear. How it would apply to the élite hotel sector was less certain. Additionally, how modernism was to adapt to different – read non-Western – cultural environments remained an unanswered question. The work of Allen and Grant Walsh on Mauna Kea Beach Hotel provided an answer to both questions.

Allen brought Grant Walsh in to serve as his "lieutenant."[32] As the first step in understanding Hawaii's cultural context, the duo took a trip around Hawaii, examining hotels, houses, gardens, restaurants, clubs, museums and hospitals. The client was Laurance S. Rockefeller, a relative of David Rockefeller for whom SOM had designed the Chase Manhattan Building. Grant Walsh's responsibilities came to include a dizzying number of responsibilities, large and small. She had Allen's trust, and he relied on her to execute his ideas.

After the extended Hawaiian tour that the two of them took, Allen convinced Rockefeller to fund a trip he took to Hong Kong, Thailand, India, and Japan, with a budget of $100,000 to purchase Asian artworks, handicrafts, and textiles.[33] Grant Walsh lived in San Francisco, but Allen ran the project out of New York, and asked that she relocate. She rented a maid's room in the Plaza Hotel and, for the next two years, was commuting between San Francisco, New York, Hawaii, and Sydney, where she started work on a subsequent hotel, the Wentworth. She was involved with the Mauna Kea from beginning to end. While Allen toured Asia, Grant Walsh managed the telexes, payments, and shipments; she wrote, "He did some ridiculous things, just assuming 'Margo will get it done.' "[34] In Hawaii, she stayed through construction and move-in, living in a shack on the construction site, and coordinating the arrival and installation of the artworks that Allen sent her way.

The hotel opened to generally wide acclaim, and received an AIA National Honors Award in 1967.[35] Much of the building's favorable press was due to its interiors, in which Allen and his team did not proceed from Bassett's reinforced concrete structure as their starting point, but provided a lively contrast to it (Figure 12.3). An essay in *The Source Book of American Architecture* explained that: "Mauna Kea's greatest impact comes from the unfolding and interweaving of its inner spaces, both vertical and lateral; these are almost staggering in their three dimensional sensuousness."[36] In contrast to Connecticut Life, the interiors of the Mauna Kea Beach Hotel were not an extension of the architecture, but a counterpoint to it.

An SOM report documented that "Rockefeller assembled an exceptional collection of Asian and Pacific arts, and working with SOM . . . saw to it that these objects were incorporated into the structures and on the grounds with greater sensitivity than had been brought to virtually any hotel project elsewhere." A sense of place for Rockefeller, Allen, McCurry and Grant Walsh was not limited to Hawaii's culture, but the broader backdrop of Asia. The work of the interiors team created a new direction for the modern luxury resort.[37]

One of Grant Walsh's managerial strengths was her ability to retain clients for repeat business. She was one of the people who established how the interiors business handled turning modernist principles into a method of dealing with large corporate interiors projects that included both offices and workstations. In his insightful dissertation on SOM, Hyun-Tae Jung relates that SOM architects initially focused on the technical challenges of high-rise construction, and that a consistent approach to modern interiors was developed later.[38] Looking at her overall body of work as it unfolded, it is clear that her methods and the results varied; for law offices, a specialty of hers, the business culture required partner offices. She developed a model which she relied on repeatedly, in which a race-track shaped circulation path opened up in strategic places to bring natural daylight to areas of workstations. Over the course of her career, she increasingly was less beholden to modernism.

At SOM, Grant Walsh did multiple projects for the Marine Midland Grace Trust Company, and the firm did both the base buildings and the interiors (Figure 12.4). For the Marine Midland Building

Modernism's glass ceiling ■

Figure 12.4
SOM, Edward Charles Bassett, Davis Allen and Margo Grant Walsh. Mauna Kea Beach Hotel, 1967.

in Manhattan, 1968, Bunshaft did the architecture, and Allen and Grant Walsh the interiors. This was one of the projects on which Grant Walsh learned the intricacies of large-scale projects. She stated multiple times in print that if one could handle a large project, one could handle a small project, but that the reverse was not necessarily true.[39] The Marine Midland buildings in Manhattan, Rochester, and Buffalo demonstrated the ultimate expression of SOM's approach to modern interiors. As the architect of the Manhattan building, the prickly Bunshaft no longer had to deal with outside consultants, like Florence Knoll and Ward Bennett, but administered SOM's in-house interiors department.

Marine Midland Manhattan was 52 stories tall, and the bank occupied the first 12 stories. SOM Interiors created the interiors, including offices, open work areas, and the lobby and banking floors. Floors 1, 2, and 3 are the banking floors. About the interiors, an article opined: "The solution was executed with SOM's customary precision and authority."[40] Bunshaft, Allen and the team convinced Midland Bank that their business was commensurate with modernism. Although Allen was capable of multiple design approaches, the Marine Midland designs suggest that when working for Bunshaft, design-wise he toed the party line. The furniture and seating selections were simple modern

Mark Hinchman ■

Figure 12.5
SOM, Davis Allen and Margo Grant Walsh. Marine Midland Bank Rochester, 1970. (Ezra Stoller photographer).

pieces; the color palette relied on bold, flat colors. The project's opulence derived from its use of rich, natural materials, including travertine, marble, burl wood, glass, and leather. These were applied in a fashion credited to Mies van der Rohe, of luxurious materials, used with painstakingly developed simple detailing.

The lobby, second and third floors of Marine Midland were true to the concept of the open plan. Other than for the base building's core, the fire stairs, the elevators, and the toilets, there were no rooms and no doors. On the second and third floors, carpets, plants, and non-structural partitions delineated the spaces. All the vestiges of a historic bank, a visible vault, tellers behind glass and metal grills, and bank officers in rooms reached through ante rooms, were gone.

Visitors arrived at the second-floor banking area from the lobby via open escalators. Antique green marble wrapped the building core, which also acted as a locational device. On the second floor, the banking floor, on the long sides of the building (in the space between the core and Bunshaft's curtain wall), there were two sides: the tellers' side, and the bank officers' side.

On the teller's side, a check counter (for writing checks, and deposit and withdrawal slips), cantilevered out from the green marble core. Running parallel to the check counter, but separated from it, a continuous travertine tellers' counter ran parallel to the perimeter.

The opposite side contained bank officers who met individually with clients. The officers' area was broken up into sub-areas, with each officers' area delineated by a custom red carpet, and a massive U-shaped low-height secretarial station. Behind this configuration, bank officers worked not in offices, but at free-standing desks.

It is striking how the Marine Midland design was beholden to the idea of open planning, with furniture and no walls. The ceiling was a continuous plane of drywall with a sea of evenly spaced incandescent downlights (which decades later would be criticized as an energy hog). The ceiling did not respond to departmental areas, but provided a uniform wash of light.

Modernism's glass ceiling ■

While the Marine Midland banking floor was one of the modern projects that set a new direction for banking, the design of the third floor was even more striking because the same design principles were at play in the executive areas. The top three men in the firm were not in offices but open "workstations," the qualifier being that they were huge and made of expensive materials. Each of the three executives had a lavishly sized work area of 20' x 30'. Their "workstations" had no doors. Non-intersecting partitions, covered in either ash or burl oak, delineated the individual executive spaces. Bright green emerald rugs on the travertine floors further demarcated the opulent work stations.

For an executive to be in what was essentially a workstation, albeit gargantuan in size, and with a private toilet and expensive finishes, Marine Midland was a game-changer. It is noteworthy that Robert Probst's Action Office, for Herman Miller, had been available since 1964. Yet there was no attempt in SOM's projects of the period to create semi-enclosed spaces with a panel system. De Blois in her oral history discussed SOM's dissatisfaction with the existing panel systems, and declined to use Action Office at Connecticut Life, Nashville Life, and the Marine Midland Banks.[41]

Yet, as with Connecticut Life, traditional gestures to hierarchy reigned in the executive areas. Marine Midland's top management enjoyed tufted leather sofas and club chairs, although still with crisp rectilinear profiles, in what became known as "transitional," neither modern nor historically based. The atmosphere of the executive areas was described as "clubby."

Grant Walsh worked at SOM for 13 years. She worked increasingly on larger projects, and SOM partners considered her an expert at handling complicated projects, both in terms of the client's demands, and managing the team of SOM designers. At one point after Marine Midland, Grant Walsh asked to speak to one of SOM's partners. She had a design issue on her mind, but he thought she wanted to discuss a promotion. He countered her by saying "You're f – ing never going to be made partner."[42]

Grant Walsh had had an auspicious meeting with Arthur Gensler in 1965; his firm at the time had three employees. By 1973, she was ready to move. Gensler offered her a job, and she accepted.[43] Once at Gensler, one of her early large projects was the massive Pennzoil Place, Houston. She was promoted multiple times at Gensler, and ended her career as one of its vice-presidents. Asked why Gensler's corporate culture differed from SOM, she responded "That's who Art was. Who you were didn't matter to him as long as you could do the work."

At Gensler, Grant Walsh was known for her management techniques as much as her design skills: she drew on her SOM experience, and specialized in large projects, multiple projects with the same client, and opening new offices. Grant Walsh opened Gensler's New York Office, 1979, whose prominence she considers part of her legacy. The office pursued clients in the legal and financial sectors, including Covington Burling in New York and Washington, Bank of America Headquarters, and the Goldman Sachs Headquarters. She was head of the New York Office for six years. She was instrumental to opening several Gensler offices: Washington DC, 1982; London, 1988; and Boston, 1993.[44]

An example of her realizing the importance of repeat clients came with Credit Suisse Boston, which was followed by projects in Moscow, London, and Singapore. As Grant Walsh moved up the management hierarchy, she was increasingly interested in the design process, how projects were managed. She emphasized communication, so that clients were aware of all design decisions

189 ❑

and agreed with them, or in her words "bought into them." With many clients to her name over decades, it is not surprising that her portfolio of projects does not have the same design consistency, for example, of her one-time mentors, Bunshaft or Allen.

A 1994 article published several projects that Gensler had done in London, two of them law firms.[45] Nearly 30 years after Marine Midland's uncompromising modernism, Gensler's work on law offices showed that the open plan, with spaces formed by free-standing furniture, remained a tough sell stylistically in many quarters of the commercial interiors market. Both conceptually and with details, law offices remained beholden to a design strategy of having individual offices, with full height walls, and doors. What was changing in the second half of the twentieth century was the number of support staff who supported the lawyers. Because of the number of lawyers, law firms were expanding and moving into high-rises. The culture of law firms in skyscrapers led to plans with a perimeter lined with offices, with secretarial and other support staff in workstations in the inner areas. Law firms were nonetheless experiencing the changes that affected all workplaces, because of technology: electric typewriters, dictaphones, word-processing systems, and then computers. Lawyers, senior and junior partners, no longer each needed their own secretary.

One of Gensler's 1994 projects was Luce, Forward, Hamilton, and Scripps. A 115,000 SF law office, it spread out on seven floors in London. Gensler designers under Grant Walsh employed strategies to achieving openness in parts of the project: they used clerestories, glass conference rooms, and an interconnecting stair.

For Sherman and Sterling, an 11,000 SF law office also published in 1994, again a perimeter of lawyer's offices left an expanded circulation space between perimeter and core. Gensler's work, and Margo Grant Walsh's designs in particular, demonstrated the designers' willingness to forego one of modernism's central tenets, the open plan, and to embellish seating areas, and partners' offices, with historical furniture, from Georgian to Queen Anne, and Chinese antiques, oriental carpets, and a variety of accessories and art works.

Grant Walsh's lack of an ideological position about the furnishing of offices proved sympathetic to executives, some of whom approached an upcoming interior design project from the perspective of their individual collecting. A serious collector herself, she looked at the beginnings of modernism. Her interests included wooden foot stools, and she focused on Arts and Crafts pieces, especially American and British early twentieth century silver. She had over a thousand pieces that she donated to the Portland Art Museum, where they constitute the Margo Grant Walsh collection that includes pieces by Gio Ponti, Josef Hoffman, C.F.A. Voysey, and Charles Rennie Mackintosh.

CONCLUSION

Stylistically, it is tempting to draw a line from early twentieth-century historicism to modernism, as though this happened in a linear fashion. In some quarters it did, as with Chase Manhattan and Connecticut Life. But this was not always the case. Depending on the designer, the client, and the function, some projects were rife for a modernist expression in their interiors, others less so. Several women's experiences with SOM, in regard to their not being made partner, including Kerbis, de Blois, McCurry, and Grant Walsh, do not paint the firm in a positive light. In the era before feminism and diversity, SOM architects such as Bunshaft, Graham and Netsch, were in competition with each

Modernism's glass ceiling ■

other, and focusing on building a firm. They were all committed modernists. It took strong-minded personalities to convince clients of purely modern projects, such as Marine Midland and Connecticut Life. While the women mentioned in this chapter suffered from a corporate culture at SOM that hindered their promotion, they are all careful to not tell the story exclusively in terms of their gender. SOM partners supported the nominations of Kerbis, de Blois, and McCurry to FAIA. De Blois said that she was happy with the projects she worked on, and never expected to be made partner. It is unlikely that McCurry could have sustained her position as one of the principal questioners of modernism had she remained at one of the firms at its center. SOM named its first woman partner, Diane Legge Lohan, in 1982. Not coincidentally, she was married at the time to Mies van der Rohe's grandson, Dirk Lohan.[46] Yet it is telling that of these women, with their varying experiences with modern interiors, the one who achieved the greatest position within corporate interiors was Grant Walsh, when she decamped to an interior design firm, Gensler.

If larger implications can be made from McCurry and Grant Walsh's work, as interior designers within modernism, it is that interior designers were less beholden to strict formal definitions of modernism, and were more open to historical and ethnic influences, from Queen Anne chairs to Berber rugs. In the projects looked at here, there were two competing paradigms for the relationship of a building's interiors to its exterior. Bunshaft, Netsch and Graham espoused one: that an interior was integral to the overall architectural concept. Allen, McCurry, and Grant Walsh, when working in high rises, put forth a different paradigm. It is a theory of interiors in which the inside of the building is not exactly the same conceptually as its outside. And, among the three, their motivations for blending historicism and modernism differed: Allen's was instinctual, McCurry's theoretical, and Grant Walsh's was practical.

The usual periodizations for the post-World War II period are modernism, postmodernism, and deconstruction. Architectural historian Sylvia Lavin steps outside stylistic names, and addresses multiple issues of twenty-first-century art, architecture, and design. About the relationship between a building and its interiors, she offers a paradigm that differs considerably from the total work of art. She uses the metaphor of kissing, indicating that a building's interiors and its exteriors are in a relationship similar to two bodies who embrace, for there is a "centrifugal force of attraction between two exquisitely similar but yet distinct things."[47] This conceptualizes a relationship between inside and out, one based on resonance, and some similarity, but more than slight differences. The works looked at here suggested that modernism's trajectory into corporate offices took many directions, and that commercial interiors after WWII took modernism in its own distinct direction.

NOTES

1 Buie Harwood, Bridget May, and Curt Sherman, cover this material in their chapter, "Modern Historicism", from *Architecture and Interior Design From the 19th Century*, Vol. 2 (Upper Saddle River: Prentice Hall, 2009), 760–783. While it seems self-evident that women figure significantly in this narrative, John Turpin points out that it is often nonetheless presented as a masculine narrative: "The History of Women in Interior Design," *Journal of Interior Design* 33 (2007): 1–15.

2 Sigfried Giedion, "Das Experiment S.O.M.," *Bauen + Wohnen* 12 (April 1957): 109–114.

3 For Kerbis and de Blois, I used the oral histories that the Art Institute of Chicago conducted. For Margaret McCurry, I relied on the chapter "Inside Out: Becoming an Architect" from her book *Constructing*

Twenty-Five Short Stories (New York, Monacelli Press: 2000), 6–21. I spoke to Margo Grant Walsh by telephone in February 2016, and we have had numerous e-mail exchanges since then. Knowledge of all four women's careers was furthered with the coverage of their projects in the contemporary design and architectural press.

4 Blair Kamin, "Gertrude Kerbis, groundbreaking architect, dies at 89", *Chicago Tribune*, 15 June 2016. Business section and www.chicagotribune.com/news/obituaries/ct-gertrude-kerbis-obituary-kamin-met-0616-20160615-story.html.

5 Gertrude Kerbis. Oral History of Gertrude Kerbis, Interviewed by Betty Blum (Chicago: The Art Institute of Chicago, 1997), 78-79.

6 Robert Allen Nauman, *On the Wings of Modernism: The United States Air Force Academy* (Urbana: University of Illinois Press, 2004), 95–98.

7 Sheri Olson, "Raising the Roof: The Dramatic Construction of Mitchell Hall," in Robert Bruegmann's *Modernism at Mid-Century: The Architecture of the United States Air Force Academy* (Chicago: University of Chicago Press, 1994), 74–75.

8 Kerbis, 79

9 Kerbis, 88.

10 Kerbis, 89.

11 Kerbis, 104.

12 Ibid.

13 Frazer Wilde, Gordon Bunshaft, Florence Knoll, and Lester Beall, "The Team Approach: a Round-Table Discussion Reveals How Connecticut General Got Just What It Wanted," *Industrial Design* 5 (1958): 48–57.

14 De Blois, Oral History of Natalie de Blois, Interviewed by Betty Blum (Art Institute of Chicago, 2004), 57.

15 "Insurance Company Headquarters, Hartford, Conn," *Architectural Design* 28 (1958): 281.

16 "Die Räume sollten so gestaltet warden, daß sie in Harmonie mit der Architektur ein Teil des Ganzen bilden." Fred Ruf and Ernst Zietzschmann, "Connecticut General Life Insurance, Bloomfield, Conn," *Bauen + Wohnen* 12 (1958): 179.

17 De Blois, 106.

18 De Blois, 61.

19 Her two degrees were from Vassar. She studied neither architecture or design, but eventually passed the architecture AIA and interior design NCIDQ exams. McCurry, 12.

20 McCurry, 7.

21 De Blois, 85.

22 Maeve Slavin, *Davis Allen: Forty Years of Interior Design at Skidmore, Owings, and Merrill* (New York: Rizzoli, 1990).

23 McCurry, 13; and Slavin, 64.

24 Allen redesigned the chair and Stendig produced it in 1983.

25 De Blois, Oral History of Natalie de Blois, 102.

26 Eds. John and Pirrie Aves, *Best: From the Interior Design Magazine Hall of Fame* (Grand Rapids: Vitae Publishing, 1992), 212–215.

27 McCurry, 16.

28 McCurry, 7.

29 "Hall of Fame '87," *Interior Design* 58 (1987): 152.

30 Kim Mandel, "An Interview With Margo Grant," *Avenu* 19 (1989): 7.

31 Nicholas Adams. "Chuck Bassett and Mauna Kea" *SOM Journal* 6 (2010): 168.

32 Slavin, 50.

33 Slavin, 54.

34 E-mail from Grant Walsh, January 2017.

35 James Hunter, R. Max Brooks, Vladimir Ossipoff, Joseph Smith, and Philip Will, "1967 Honor Awards," *American Institute of Architects Journal* 47 (1967): 60.

Modernism's glass ceiling ■

36 G.E. Kidder Smith. *The Source Book of American Architecture*. (New York: Princeton Architectural Press), 1996, 508.

37 Douglas Haskell, "Ten Buildings That Climax an Era," *Fortune* 7 (1966): 162.

38 Hyun-Tae Jung.

39 Kim Mandel, "An Interview With Margo Grant," *Avenu* 19 (1989): 7.

40 "New Star on Broadway . . . the Marine Midland Building" *Contract Interiors* 127 (1968): 92.

41 De Blois, 60.

42 Phone conversation with Grant Walsh, February 2016.

43 Mandel.

44 Eds. John and Pirrie Aves, *Best: From the Interior Design Magazine Hall of Fame* (Grand Rapids: Vitae Publishing, 1992), 86.

45 Beverly Russell. "Gensler Goes International" *Interiors* 153 (1994): 36-53.

46 Cynthia Davidson-Powers. "The Next Generation: Work By Young Architects" *Inland Architect* 29 (1985): 38.

47 Sylvia Lavin. *Kissing Architecture* (Princeton: Princeton University Press, 2011).

Chapter 13: The future of cross-disciplinary practice

Joel Sanders

The design professions are in transition. The era of Starchitecture is drawing to a close as a new generation of designers recognize that they need to address urgent environmental, technological and social justice issues that have spatial consequences. These include climate change, war and migrations, making accessible and safe public spaces for diverse communities and considering the transformative impact of digital technologies on the spaces of our everyday lives.

But the nature of professional practice driven by the demands of consumer capitalism frustrates this goal. Star-architecture rewards eye-catching form over social responsibility, encouraging name-brand architects and interior designers to craft signature photogenic trophy buildings and interiors that can be disseminated in the mass media. This mentality represents the last gasp of the now discredited image of the heroic Modern architect, exemplified by Howard Roark as depicted in Ayn Rand's *Fountainhead*, an invincible white male who single-handedly can save humanity through design. Modernism, for all of its arrogance and heroic delusions, at least rooted itself in utopian social ideals.

The challenges posed by contemporary global culture are far too complex, wide-ranging and interconnected to be solved by a single author representing one design field alone. Instead they require cross-disciplinary problem solvers from allied disciplines – architects, interior designers, and landscape architects – to work together to craft a new way of thinking and working, an integrated conception of environmental design that regards interiors, buildings, and landscapes as linked inter-active systems.

Interdisciplinary collaboration is easier to achieve in theory than in practice. The first hurdle is to dismantle the silos that divide these three overlapping fields into separate professions each governed by their own systems of education, training, licensing and codes of professional conduct. But to do that we first must acknowledge the deep-rooted and often problematic cultural and ideo-logical values and prejudices that led to this disciplinary segregation in the first place. In the same way that individuals work with therapists to outgrow engrained patterns of behavior received from the past, the design professions are in need of counselors who can help them see and ultimately transcend the inherited cultural baggage that inhibits cross-disciplinary alliances.

Hence the value of design history books like *Shaping the American Interior: Structures, Contexts, and Practices*. Rather than recount the usual story of lone male geniuses who craft signature mas-terworks, this book departs from convention and shifts its emphasis from practitioners to practices, looking at how the designed environment is shaped by networks of individuals whose ways of working are dictated and shaped by the structure of professional practice.

While I am not a design historian, as an architect and a professor I have grappled with some of these questions, teaching history seminars and writing articles like this one that look at the way history can shed light on issues confronting contemporary practice. These forays into history and theory came from my own experiences as a designer wanting at different times in my career to bridge three fields – architecture, interiors, and landscape – that have been professionally segregated since the late nineteenth century. Why was I never taught to think about how the layout of furniture and the choice of fabrics and upholstery influenced the way people occupy and interact with each other in a room? Why did my education leave me unequipped to expand my materials palette to include living materials – trees and vegetation – as space-defining elements? Why was I trained to conceive of the building envelope as the limit where architecture ends rather than as a porous membrane that facilitates the transition between interiors and landscape, both precincts understood as inter-communicating designed spaces that foster social interaction?

Considering these questions from a historical and social perspective, has led me to conclude that the seemingly straightforward differences in design approach and professional conduct between architecture, interiors and landscape stem from deep-seated cultural values often rooted in class and gender. Over the past 20 years, I have written papers that treated the relationship between architecture and interiors and architecture and landscape as independent subjects. In this essay I will attempt a synthetic overview that explores the affinities and differences between them. After examining the issue of professional segregation from a historical context, I will conclude with proposals about how we might go about overcoming the obstacles that divided the professions in the past with the goal of forging productive associations in the future.

STUD

My longstanding interest in uncovering the foundations of disciplinary segregation began in 1996 when I edited *Stud: Architectures of Masculinity*, a book that invited a group of architects, critics, and artists to explore the role architecture plays in the *performance* of male identity.[1] *Stud* borrowed the notion of gender as "performance" from queer theorists who argue that human identity in general, and gender identity in particular, are not inborn biological traits but rather culturally constructed, learned modes of behavior. Theorists like Judith Butler and Jack Halberstam, then known as Judith, frequently referred to drag queens and drag kings whose exaggerated gestures, make-up, and costumes expose how gender is not innate but performed.[2] But the performance of gender identity depends, at least in part, on space: impersonation relies not only on the materials that clothe the body but also upon the designed environment that frames it.

Two insights derived from queer studies inspired me to think about architecture in a new way. First, if architects tend to consider buildings as photogenic objects, the notion of "performance" encouraged me to shift my attention to the interplay between human bodies and space and to embrace a conception of the built environment as a "stage" that enables people, like actors, to perform various roles. Second, Butler's analysis of the way drag performers rely on costume to construct identity led me discover the affinities between clothing and cladding – the ephemeral elements like wallpaper, paint, fabrics, curtains upholstery, and furniture – that interior designers use to dress the interiors designed by architects: both are culturally coded applied surfaces that we use to fashion identity.

CURTAIN WARS

Discovering the crucial yet overlooked relationship between clothing, cladding, and human identity while editing *Stud* sparked my interest in architecture's devalued sister discipline – interior design. In 2002, I wrote an essay, "Curtain Wars: Architects, Decorators and the 20th Century Interior," that explored how the conflicts that pit architects against decorators, "wars" that are waged over something as seemingly innocuous as curtains, are bolstered and sustained by broad cultural stereotypes and anxieties about the nature of gender transmitted through a variety of "high" and "low" cultural discourses from architectural theory to Hollywood films.[3]

"Curtain Wars" explored how problematic assumptions about gender and class shaped both design approaches and professional identities. Ever since the emergence of the interior decorator as a design professional in the mid-nineteenth century, interior decoration has been dismissed as a superficial pastime associated with economically privileged upper and later middle classes. By the twentieth century, interiors, a field practiced by women and gay men, became tainted by its association with femininity and homosexuality. It was thought that architects, typically men, worked conceptually, organizing space by manipulating durable materials and elements (structure and walls), while decorators, typically women and gay men, worked intuitively, adorning rooms with ephemeral materials (fabrics and upholstery) linked with fashion and domesticity. In contrast to architects who think in abstract terms to solve practical programmatic and technical problems, interior designers create spaces that cater to corporeal needs, the material body considered a female principle, as opposed to immaterial male intellect.

GROUNDWORK

Ten years after completing "Curtain Wars," my academic interests converged with my professional practice, leading me to consider the obstacles that kept another one of architecture's allied disciplines at a distance – landscape. The emergence of Green design at the turn of the millennium put pressure on architects to think in a new way. My studio, JSA, received commissions to design residential and institutional projects that encouraged and sometimes required architects to incorporate what at that time was a new set of LEED certified green building standards that, while focused on buildings, also included ecological landscape techniques as well.

At the same time, I became interested in the work of progressive ecologists who underscored how climate change required us to recognize that nature and civilization, although not the same, have always been intertwined and are becoming more so. There is not a square inch of the planet that does not in some way bear the imprint of humans. Landscape and culture intermix in various combinations; while constructed elements are more common in urban areas and natural elements predominate in rural zones, organic and synthetic operate as a gradient of differing intensities that forms a continuum across the surface of the earth.

Joel Sanders ■

If the design disciples were to pursue the design consequences of this interconnected conception of humans and nature, then they needed to integrate their efforts. However, sustainable design, although driven by commendable goals, stymied this goal. Taking for granted the long-standing professional division of labor between architects and landscape architects, it was largely driven by a product-oriented mentality that evaluated materials and techniques on the basis of their performance and efficiency while rarely taking into consideration issues of form and human use. How could the two fields join forces to forge an innovative landscape/architecture design vocabulary that could tap into the formal and programmatic potential of sustainable design principles?

Professional frustrations again let me to design history. I soon realized that sustainable design recapitulated the professional segregation of landscape and architecture that dates back to the nineteenth century. In the introductory essay to Groundwork "Human/Nature: Wilderness and the Landscape/Architecture Divide," I argued that this problematic division of architecture and landscape into independent disciplines in the United States has ideological underpinnings that can be traced to a deep-rooted Western polarity that opposes humans and nature and as a consequence buildings and landscapes.[4]

I soon discovered many parallels between the troubled relationship between architecture and interiors and architecture and landscape. Architects again enlisted problematic assumptions about the nature of class and gender to marginalize landscape and to justify the notion that buildings and nature were inherently and qualitatively different from one another. Like interiors, landscape was a discipline discredited for its association with women and the domestic realm. In the mid-nineteenth century, gardening had become a pastime reserved for upper class women and by the mid-twentieth century a hobby for middle class housewives, publicized in popular magazines like *House and Garden*, whose title and content made explicit the affinities between interiors and landscape. And while landscape, like interiors was embraced by the mainstream media, it too was largely overlooked by the academy. Up until recently there has been a conspicuous absence of serious scholarly books and exhibitions devoted to landscape as compared to architecture, a phenomena that both reflects and reinforces landscape's secondary status.

Moreover, landscape design methodologies, like interiors, are shaped by problematic assumptions about the gendered body. The landscape/architecture divide, mirrors the long-standing split between the spirit and the flesh, the Western binary that opposes immaterial intellect, considered a male prerogative, with the material corporeal body, deemed a female principle that since antiquity has been linked with Mother Earth. In addition, the design disciplines have accepted a Western bias espoused by philosophers and art critics including Aristotle, St. Augustine, Goethe, and Clement Greenberg, who all categorize the human senses in a hierarchy, differentiating between the immaterial higher senses – sight and sound – and lower senses – touch, taste, and smell. Modern architects like Le Corbusier famously validated this ocular-centric perspective. They privileged the visual rather than the multi-sensory dimension of architecture in contrast to interiors and landscape, two professions that work with soft ephemeral elements – fabrics and vegetation – to create indoor and outdoor spaces that engage not only sight but the lower senses, touch and smell.

The long-standing personification of nature as woman has also perpetuated the human/nature, landscape/architecture divide. Until the nineteenth century, the design disciplines mirrored a conception of nature inherited from the Old Testament that conceived of nature as a wily and temperamental

The future of cross-disciplinary practice ■

female that needed to be tamed by men. But the rise of industrialization in the nineteenth century ushered in a new conception of nature as women. A first generation of environmentalist thinkers and activists like Henry David Thoreau, Charles Muir, and Theodore Roosevelt active during the second half of the nineteenth century were confronted with an intimidating prospect not unlike that which we face today – the disappearance of Wilderness. The vanishing wilderness paralleled imperiled white male masculinity now threatened by a range of emerging forces like technology, immigration, and women' rights. But for men like Theodore Roosevelt, Wilderness, the home of the frontiersmen and the cowboy, represented a haven that sustained "vigorous manliness," a refuge where robust individuals could resist the emasculating and domesticating forces of urban culture. If Nature was traditionally conceived of as an unruly woman that needed to be subdued and cultivated through the labor of men, Wilderness thinking now cast Nature as a virgin in desperate need of male stewardship that needed to be conserved and protected from the ravages of industrial civilization.[5]

Not only did Wilderness thinking give birth to the American environmentalist movement, but it also shaped the evolution of landscape and architecture in America from the nineteenth century until today: its dualistic conception of people and nature, bolstered by problematic gendered stereotypes, only reinforced the age-old Western conception of the building as a man-made artifact qualitatively different from its ostensibly natural surroundings. In turn, this way of thinking impacted professional conduct, reflected in the professional segregation of architects and landscape architects into parallel professional organizations: in 1899, at the height of the Wilderness movement, a new professional academy, the American Society of Landscape Architects (ASLA) was established.

Wilderness core values not only resulted in dual design professions but it also shaped design approaches: by positing that the human is entirely outside the natural, Wilderness presents a fundamental paradox: how to reconcile the ideal of untouched nature with the imprint of human design? The result is a deep and persistent suspicion of designed nature that still endures today.

BREAKING NEW GROUND

Since I wrote "Curtains Wars," the status of interior design has risen. No longer relegated to periodicals like *House and Garden* and *House Beautiful* geared to a largely female and gay readership, home improvement has expanded its reach. Internet and cable TV channels cover home design and appeal to a broader, although still principally white, demographic.

Interior design's reputation within the architectural community has improved as well. Fifteen years ago, most self-respecting architects still subscribed to Modern Architecture's disdain for interior design, seemingly oblivious to the contradiction that some of the great designers of furniture and interiors were men like Le Corbusier, Mies van de Rohe, Alvaar Aalto and Eero Saarinen. In contrast, today Stararchitects of both sexes, like Rem Koolhaas and the late Zaha Hadid, have no qualms designing interiors, furniture, and even clothing, often for fashion brands like Prada and Chanel. And unlike their Modernist predecessors who repudiated ornamented buildings in favor of stripped-down structures that employed materials associated with male authenticity like stone, wood, steel and glass, today celebrated Pritzker Prize winning architects like Peter Zumthor and Jean Nouvel create diaphanous veil-like facades of patterned glass and perforated metal that recall seductive female garments.

Clearly these significant professional inroads stem from recent changes in cultural attitudes about sex and gender. Thanks to the efforts of feminist, gay, and, more recently, transgender activists, mainstream society is gradually adopting more expansive models of human identity that has impacted design over the past 15 years. At the turn of the millennium, innovative magazines like *Wallpaper** emerged that combined fashion, design, and architecture to a mixed audience that included a new breed of self-proclaimed "Metrosexuals." Today mainstream newspapers, like the New York Times *T Magazine* publish an eclectic mix of fashion, design, and architecture that represents the pervasive influence of a young generation of hipsters and genderqueers who freely cross design genres and gender codes in their quest to express fluid multiple identities.

Likewise, the status of landscape has risen in recent years. Sustainable design has impacted the work of an international roster of progressive architects and landscape architects like Snohetta, Weiss Manfredi, and West who all blur the lines between buildings and sites. Progressive city agencies across the country are investing in public infrastructural projects for sustainable urban parks like the Highline, NYC and Millennium Park, Chicago. The visibility and acclaim given to these projects and to their authors like James Corner and Adriaan Geuze, are attracting a new generation of students who are enrolling in landscape programs. Meanwhile, old-school gendered stereotypes that shaped the image of landscape are shifting as well. The success of large-scale infrastructural projects designed by male practitioners convincingly demonstrates that landscape need no longer be regarded as an exclusively feminine domain confined to the domestic realm.

THE FUTURE: CROSS-DISCIPLINARY COLLABORATION

But despite significant improvements in the status of interiors and landscape over the past 15 years, made possible by changing attitudes in the culture at large, we still have a long way to go. Here are a few recommendations that might instigate a new way of thinking and working.

Design scholars and historians can help us overcome the constraining cultural ideologies that hold us back. Understanding the history of practice from a cultural perspective will allow us to overcome engrained cultural conceptions, often rooted in suspect notions about the gendered body that continue to shape design approaches and professional conduct.

With the help of design history, we can repudiate the problematic ideologies that brought into being binary thinking and establish an alternative design methodology based on interdisciplinary cooperation. No longer will architects prioritize buildings, relegating the design of interior and exterior as an afterthought that will be addressed, if at all, later in the design process. Instead, as soon as we put pen to paper or keyboard to monitor, we need to assemble teams of like-minded architects, interior designers and landscape architects to collaborate on projects that from their very inception employ sustainable design principles to generate designs that weave together people, interiors, buildings, and landscapes. Ultimately, teams will need to expand to include not only design professionals, but also engineers, ecologists, and computation experts. The challenge is to train confident practitioners who welcome the prospect of dissolving the already unstable boundaries between inside and outside, organic and synthetic, humans and nature, while at the same time respecting the kind of in-depth knowledge and expertise that can only be acquired from specialization. We

The future of cross-disciplinary practice ■

need to cultivate a new frame of mind that merges integrated thinking with expert knowledge based on the recognition that the world's problems are too complicated and interconnected for one kind of professional to solve alone.

Training open-minded designers that value both interdisciplinary exchange and specialization inevitably requires revamping the existing structure of design education that, mirroring the structure of the design professions, educates students in separate programs, that inevitably shape the thinking, values, design approaches, and skill sets of the students they educate. Design education and professional licensing are inter-connected, linked by accreditation boards that approve schools that can demonstrate that they adequately prepare students with the required skills necessary to become licensed professionals when they graduate. For example, only graduates of architectural programs accredited by the National Architecture Accrediting Board (NAAB) are qualified to apply for a license that will allow them to practice architecture in 37 states.

Curriculums are the bridge that links the academy and practice. For example, to obtain NAAB accreditation, programs must demonstrate that they offer curriculums that cover a range of required subjects in design, history/theory, technology and professional practice. Consequently, curriculums tend to be relatively uniform, leaving little room for substantial variation. We can begin reforming design education by formulating a revised NAAB-compliant prototypical design curriculum that will expose architecture students to the principles, values, and skills of two allied fields – interior design and landscape – that intersects with their own. For example, now architecture curriculums require students to take courses that acquaint them with the rudiments of technical subjects like mechanical systems, structures, and acoustics, subjects that will prepare them to work with licensed consultants representing these fields when they enter the profession. In a similar vein, why not expand architecture curriculums to include courses that treat the basics of furniture, fabric, and plant specification?

While revising architecture curriculums is a modest first step, the best way forward would be to imagine the consolidation of separate design departments into a single degree-granting program with areas of specialization. For example, in the first three years of a five-year program, students could follow a core curriculum that acquaints them with the fundamental principles needed to think across a range of indoor and outdoor sites and scales. Then, in the final two years, they could elect to pursue majors in inclusive subjects that span disciplines like hardscape, softscape, building envelopes, sustainability, and ergonomics that would allow them to graduate with specialized degrees.

In both short-term and long-term scenarios, pedagogy will not only equip students with a broader set of skills not taught in most architectural schools but will encourage synthetic interdisciplinary thinking that will make them aware of the value of introducing interiors and landscape issues from the very inception of a project.

The existing structure of practice in which each field is organized under independent professional organizations – American Institute of Architects (AIA), American Society Interior Designers (ASID), and the American Society of Landscape Architects (ASLA) – each governed by different standards of professional protocols, needs to change as well. A modest first step would be for each organization to rewrite and to coordinate the boiler-plate legal documents that define the scope of services that each offers to clients. While we tend to take these purportedly objective descriptive documents for granted, these texts prescribe professional working relationships between client,

201 □

architect, and consultants, including interiors and landscape, based on unchallenged assumptions about the nature of the design disciplines and the people who practice them.

In complex architectural projects that involve the participation of representatives from interiors and architecture, the respective division of labor that governs how the three parties will work together is outlined in three separate contracts that are written in a way that prescribes a hierarchical relationship between them. Consultants are typically retained either by the client or in many cases directly by the architect who then becomes legally and financially responsible for overseeing their work. In a typical project, the architect is the project leader, overseeing the course of the design process. During the first phase of the project, Schematic Design, the architect generally establishes the design direction. Only later in the process, typically in the second and third phases, Design Development and Construction Documents, are the interiors and landscape consultants brought in to elaborate or embellish the design concept already generated by the architect.

In the spirit of efficiency, contracts parse the work between architect and consultants into discrete tasks to avoid redundancy and ultimately save the client time and money. In the end, contracts dictate a rigid linear design process that ignores the inherently blurred boundaries between disciplines. For example, at first glance the line between building shell, freestanding furniture, and vegetation is clear. But who, architect or decorator, should be responsible for picking wall colors, tiles, and finishes? Who, architect or landscape architect, should design the outdoor hardscape elements like terraces and paths that define the perimeter of buildings and articulate the threshold between inside and outside? Moving forward we need to draft more flexible and inclusive contracts that promote collaboration. They should allow for all three parties at the beginning of a project to brainstorm design concepts. And as the project unfolds, contracts need to differentiate roles and responsibilities in a way that acknowledges that there is inevitably a certain measure of productive redundancy between the overlapping tasks that need to be shared between disciplines.

Contracts are not the only professional documents that need revamping. Tenders and RFQs (Request for Qualifications) and RFPs (Requests for Proposals) issued by clients looking to hire qualified designers also presume a hierarchical division of labor between design professionals. They are typically addressed to the architect, who is responsible for submitting the proposal that must include an assembled team of consultants that may or may not include, interiors and landscape. Even design awards programs and project credits in design publications presume disciplinary segregation: awards submissions are typically divided into rigid disciplinary categories and publications – both analog and on-line – typically credit the lead designer, generally the architect, listing the supporting consultants if at all, in the fine print.

EMBODIMENT

Cross-disciplinary alliances ultimately depend on reworking the intricate procedures and protocols, from curriculums to contracts, which underpin the interconnected relationship between design education and the design professions. However, this ambitious project depends on a form of consciousness-raising that requires us to look at how the past informs the present. The contribution of design history is essential. A new generation of scholars needs to think across design fields to map

The future of cross-disciplinary practice ■

the interwoven histories of professionalization that have come to dictate the design approaches and working relationships that have yielded the arbitrary division of labor between architects, interior designers, and landscape that we have inherited to this day. These engrained habits have prevented us from seeing that, in the end, all three fields are but a single enterprise dedicated to a common goal, the design of spaces where embodied humans can perform a variety of roles as they interact with one another in public and private space.

We rarely address this shared imperative. The names assigned to the design disciplines – architecture, interiors, landscape – are telling: they attest to the way we define them and differentiate them from one another in terms of the sites upon which they operate, be it a building, a room, or a park. More often than not, the representations that designers make and that scholars and curators reference are evidence of our indifference to the body. Human beings are either conspicuously absent from or mindlessly photoshopped into drawings, photographs, and renderings. Another even more telling symptom of this problem is that we continue to ignore what critiques of representation have been telling us for years, that images tend to see the world from the narrow perspective of a privileged few. We must not take for granted the structure of Western spectatorship that, by default, presumes the default point of view of a Western heterosexual white male, the implied but invisible occupant of the space being depicted whose body lies outside the picture frame.

Design handbooks, like the popular *Time-Saver Standard* series are among the rare exceptions when designers directly address the requirements of human bodies. These three manuals, *Time-Saver Standards for Architecture*, *Time-Saver Standards for Interior Design* and *Time-Saver Standards for Landscape*, although aimed at different audiences, nevertheless all depict men, and sometimes women, as eviscerated diagrams. These two-dimensional line drawings reduce the corporeal body in all of its diversity into a universal abstraction that illustrates the "normal" body, whose standardized dimensions determine the ergonomic measurements established in building codes that designers incorporate into their projects. Scholars from Disabilities Studies like Douglas Baynton have persuasively demonstrated that this conception of the "standard" body is historically contingent, a problematic product of nineteenth century science and medicine, whose supposedly objective findings were and continue to be used to uphold the oppression of those considered deviant.[6] Rejecting the convention of the "normal" body as ideologically bankrupt will allow designers to turn their attention to addressing the needs of a wide range of non-conforming bodies marked by race, gender, and disability.

In the end, design histories like this one will allow us to recognize that the triad architecture, interiors and landscape are in fact continuous practices whose common denominator is the corporeal experience of differently embodied people in the world. This recognition will allow us to refocus our energies. No longer will we create projects differentiated by scale and location (building, interior, exterior) treated as isolated commodities that can be consumed in two-dimensional images. Instead, adopting a new mentality will free us to conceive of environmental design as a single practice spearheaded by teams of individuals with different levels of expertise but all dedicated to a common goal, the creation of a gradient of indoor–outdoor spaces that combine living and non-living materials where a diverse range of differently embodied humans of different ages, races, classes, and genders can productively interact.

NOTES

1 Joel Sanders, *STUD: Architectures of Masculinity* (Princeton: Princeton Architectural Press, 1996).
2 Judith Halberstam, *Female Masculinity* (Durham: Duke University Press, 1998); Judith Butler, *Gender Trouble: Feminism and the Subversion of Identity* (New York: Routledge, 2010).
3 Joel Sanders, "Curtain Wars," *Harvard Design Magazine No. 16* (2002).
4 Joel Sanders, *Groundwork: Between Landscape and Architecture* (New York: The Monacelli Press, 2011).
5 William Cronon, "The Trouble With Wilderness; or Getting Back to the Wrong Nature," in *Uncommon Ground: Toward Reinventing Nature* (New York: W. W. Norton, 1965).
6 Douglas Baynton, "Disability and the Justification of Inequality in American History," in *The Disability Studies Reader* (New York: Routledge, 2013).

Index

Note: Page numbers in italics indicate figures or photographs.

Aalto, Alvar 179, 199
Ackerman, Frederick Lee 108
Aesthetic Movement 72–73
aesthetic style 14,15
Ain, Gregory 150
Allen, Albert M. 80
Allen, Davis 152, 183–8, *185*, *187–8*
Altman, Benjamin 37
American Institute of Architects (AIA) 169, 201
American Institute of Decorators (AID) 152, 169, 175
American Institute of Interior Decorators 56
American Institute of Interior Designers 152
American National Exhibition 153
American Society Interior Designers (ASID) 56, 169, 175, 201
American Society of Landscape Architects (ASLA) 199, 201
America Redecorates (TV show) 110–3
Annual Conference of the Society of Architectural Historians, 2014 1
apology areas, in 1950s 3, 157–66, *164*
Architect and the Industrial Arts (exhibit) 101
Architectural Forum, The (magazine) 170–1, 174
Architectural Practice (Gutman) 175
Architectural Record (magazine) 171–6
Architectural Review (magazine) 144, 169–70, 173
architecture: in 1940–1951, beneath or beside 171–2; in 1948–1959, from without and from within 172–4; in 1950s, apology areas in 161; in 1960–1974, fee simple/fee separate 174–6; branding of oneself 51; coeds and t-squares 134, 137; commencement houses 131–6, *132–3*, *135*; in cross-disciplinary practice, future of 195–203; designing professionals 5–6, 15; expanding, in United States 53; gender and 69–70; history 1–4; Hoggson Brothers 77–80, *78*; home economics differentiated from 126; imaging interior design 169–76; interior, from domestic economy to 126–9; MacAlister 107–8; McMillan 77, 80–81; modernism's glass ceiling 179–80, 182, 184–7, 191; multi-step process to coordinate decoration with 82; Museum of Modern Art 143–4, 150, 152; New York salon (drawing room), Mrs. Rice's 37–38, 41, 47–48; in postwar America 143; professionalism, modeling 77; project development and 179; specialist firms 74; Starchitecture 195
Armour, J. Ogden 48
art and antiques dealers: business practices 33–34; business records 29, 31, 33; project management 34, 43
Art Institute of Chicago 3
Art-in-Trades Club 89–101
Arts and Crafts interiors 73, 83–84, 149, 190
Arts and Crafts Movement 92
Arts & Architecture (magazine) 150–1, 172
Arts & Decoration (magazine) 94
Associated American Artists (AAA) 3, 157–9, 162–6
Association Men 72, *76*
Auerbach, Alfred 149

Bach, Oscar 96
Bach, Richard F. 90–91, 101
Baldwin, Billy 59, 64
B. Altman 99
Banham, Reyner 169
Barr, Alfred 152
Barron, Leonard 90
Bartlett, Apple 47
Bassett, Edward Charles 185
Baynton, Douglas 203
Belmont, E. A. 92, 97, *97*
Bennett, Ward 187
Better Design (magazine) 154

205 □

Better Homes and Gardens (magazine) 144, 162
Bigelow and Wadsworth 54
Billings, Frederick 2, 5–18
Billings, Julia 5–9, 11–18
Billings residence in Woodstock, Vermont 5–18,
       8–10, 16–7
Boucher, François 38
Breuer, Marcel 146, 150
Brides Magazine 132–3
British collectors 42
Brotherhood of Painters and Decorators of America 62
Brothers, Ernest L. 31, 32, 40–41
Bunshaft, Gordon 179–80, 182–3, *183*, 184, 187

Carlhian (Firm) 32–34; business practices 33–34;
       critique 40–41; departments 32; design
       process 34; Duveen partnership 29–30;
       history 32; interior design 37–38;
       maquettes 34, *35–6*, 38; Mrs. Rice
       and 29–30, 37, 39–41, 43; project
       management 34, 43
Carlhian, André 32, 34, 40
carpet: Billings house 5, 9–11, 15–16, 18; de Wolfe
       51; interior decorating instruction on early
       television 110; New York salon (drawing
       room), Mrs. Rice's 34, 39–40; women in
       commercial design after WWII 188, 190;
       YMCA 80, 82
Carrère and Hastings 54
Cary, Elisabeth L. 98
Case Study House (exhibit) 150–1
Cawthra, Thomas A. 90
ceramics 93–94, 157, 162
C.F. Murphy 181–2
Charlap, Danielle 2–3
Charmois, Victor 11
Chase Manhattan Building 183, 186
Cheney Brothers 99
Chicago Merchandise Mart 147
Clark, William Andrews 31
Clifford, Chandler Robbins 91
Clifford & Lawton 62
Codman, Ogden 54
coeds and t-squares 125–38; *see also* home
       economics
Coffin, William Sloan 1–3, *71*, 71–72, 81–82,
       89–91, 101
Cole, Henry 92
collectors and collections 29, 32, 42; Billings 15;
       British 42; Duveen Brothers 30–32; French
       42; Frick 42; Gardner 42; Huntington
       42; Kahn brothers 31; Margo Grant
       Walsh collection 190; Marie-Antoinette
       42; Metropolitan Museum of Art 81–82,
       90–91, 95; Mrs. Rice 29, 38, 40, 42
College of Architecture, Art, and Planning 128
College of Architecture and Design 128

College of Engineering 128
College of Home Economics 128
College of Human Ecology 128–9
commencement houses 131–6, *132–3, 135*
Company of Master Craftsmen 89
Connecticut Life Insurance Company 182–3, 189
Conner, Virginia 171
Conran, Terence 48
consumption 1, 5, 53, 147
contract interior design services 3, 175
Cooley, Anna B. 130–1
"Coordinated Interior Design" (Saarinen-Swanson
       Group) 172
Copeland, Robert Morris 7–9
Cornell University 128
Corner, James 200
Council of Interior Design Accreditation (CIDA) 128
*Country Life: A Handbook of Agriculture, Horticulture
       and Landscape Gardening* (Copeland) 8
Crater, Susan 47
Credit Suisse Boston 189
Crocker, William H. 48
cross-disciplinary practice, future of 195–205;
       breaking new ground 199–200;
       collaboration 200–2; "Curtain Wars" 197;
       embodiment 202–3; *Groundwork* 197–9;
       Stud: Architectures of Masculinity 196–7
Culin, Stewart 146
Cumming, Rose 47
"Curtain Wars: Architects, Decorators and the 20th
       Century Interior" (Sanders) 197

dealing in interiors 29–43, *35–6, 40; see also* New
       York salon (drawing room), Mrs. Rice's;
       Rice, Mrs. Alexander Hamilton (née
       Eleanor Elkins); Carlhian 30–34; client
       34–37; Duveen Brothers 30–32; style and
       meaning 41–42
Dean, Penelope 3
de Blois, Nathalie 179, 182–4, *183*, 189
Decorating is Fun! How to Be Your Own Decorator
       (Draper) 108
decorative arts, in Mrs. Rice's New York salon
       (drawing room) 29, 31, 37–38, 42
Decorative Furnisher (magazine) 90, 92, 95, 98
decorative painting 9–10, 11, 15
Decorative Textiles (Hunter) 91–92
Decorators' Club 56, 62–63
Delineator, The (magazine) 50
Department of Interior Architecture and Product
       Design 128
"Design by Choice" (Banham) 169
Design in Line Notan Color (Warner) 81
de Wolfe, Elsie 1–2, 47–56, 61–62, 64, 108, 179
d'Harnoncourt, Rene 152
Disabilities Studies 203
Doe, Hunnewell & Co. 12, 14–16

Index ■

Doe, Joseph Merrill 11
Doe & Charmois *10*, 10–11
Doe & Hazelton 15
do-it-yourself (DIY) decorators 110, 117
domestic economy 126–9
Domestic Science and Domestic Art
school 127
Donnis, Erica 2
Doucet, Jacques 50
Draper, Dorothy 47, 64, 108, 179
drapery: Billings house 12, 16–18; coeds and
t-squares 135; gay decorators 61, 63;
interior decorating instruction on early
television 116; New York salon (drawing
room), Mrs. Rice's 33–34, 38, 40–41;
women in commercial design after WWII
182; YMCA 72
drawing room *See* New York salon (drawing room),
Mrs. Rice's
dream house context 129–31
Du Fais, John L. 15–18
Durgan, Jack C. 128
Duveen, Joseph 1–2, 31–32
Duveen Brothers (Firm) 31–32; Carlhian partnership
29–30; favors for clients 32; history 31;
maquettes 31; marketing 32; Mrs. Rice
and 29–30, 37, 39, 43; New York gallery
30–32, 37, 39; spying 32

Eames, Charles 144, 149, 152, 159, 173
Eames, Ray 144, 149, 159–60
Eastern Association of Indian Affairs (EAIA) 93
Edgewater Tapestry Looms 92
Edmonson, Patricia 2–3
Eero Saarinen, 199
Ehrlichman, John D. 59
Eigen, Edward 147
Elderfield, John 144–5
Eleanor Elkins *See* Rice, Mrs. Alexander Hamilton (née
Eleanore Elkins)
Elias, Megan 126
"Elizabethan Motif" 83
Ellis, John A. 15
"Elsie de Wolfe" brand 51
"Elsie de Wolfe Studio" 52
embroidery 92
Emerson, William Ralph 8, *17*
Eminent Actors in the Their Homes (Hamm) 48
Entertaining is Fun! How to Be a Popular Hostess
(Draper) 108
Eppinger, Jim 160–1

fabrics: apology areas, in 1950s 157, 161; Art-in-
Trades Club 96, 98; Billings house 5, 10,
14–16; coeds and t-squares 130; cross-
disciplinary practice, future of 196–8,
201; gay decorators 60; Kaufmann, Jr.

and MoMA 143; New York salon (drawing
room), Mrs. Rice's 33–34; YMCA 71
Family Circle (magazine) 153
fashion houses 54
Fehmer, Carl 8
feminine achievement in interior decoration 47–56
feminine drift 64
Foundation of Interior Design Education and
Research 128
Fountainhead (Rand) 195
Foxhall, W. B. 175
France, eighteenth-century 29, 31–32, 37–38, 41–43
Frankl, Paul 99
Frick, Henry Clay 54–55
F. Schumacher & Co. 91
Furnishings Service 2, 69–70, *82*, 81–85
furniture: Art-in-Trades Club 89–92, 94, 96, 98–99,
101; Billings house 6–7, 9–10, *10*, 11–12,
14–17, *17*, 18; coeds and t-squares 126–7,
129–31, 133–7; future of cross-disciplinary
practice 196–7, 199, 201–2; gay decorators
62–63; imaging interior design 169–76;
interior decorating instruction on early
television 107, 110, 112–7, *114*; Kaufmann,
Jr. and MoMA 144, 146–7, 149–50, 152–4;
manufacturers 2, 5, 17, 71–73, 81, 83, 157;
manufacturing 10–11, 12, 14–15 New York
salon (drawing room), Mrs. Rice's 29–34,
37–41, *40*, 42; 1950s 157, 159–61, *162–3*,
165–6; Plan-a-Room in 112–6, *114–6*;
Wolfe 48, 51, 54–55; women in commercial
design after WWII 179–80, *183*, 187–8, 190
182–3; YMCA 69–96, *73–6*, *83–5*
"Furniture of the Fourth Dimension" (Frankl) 99

Gabriel, Jacques-Ange 38
Garden Magazine 90
gay decorators 59–67; gender "drift" 60–64;
"Interior Desecration" 64–67
gender "drift" 60–64
gendering 70
genderqueers 200
genres and gender codes, cross designing 200
Gensler, Arthur 185, *187*, 189–90
George IV 42
Geuze, Adriaan 200
Gilded Age 2, 29, 34, 41
Girard, Alexander *145*, 149, *150*, 159
Goldberg, Bertrand 180
Goodbye Mr Chippendale (Robsjohn-Gibbings) 48
Good Design program 143–4, *145*, 147, *148*, *150*
Good Furniture (magazine) 90–91, 98
Good Housekeeping (magazine) 108, 153
Goodnow, Ruby Ross 48, 55
Graham, Bruce 179–81
Grand Tour 41
Green design 197

207 ☐

Gregory, John 127
Gregory Ain's Exhibition House 150
Groundwork (Sanders) 197–9
Guide to Easier Living (Wright and Wright) 153
Gulledge, Eugene 133–4
Gutman, Robert 175

Hadid, Zaha 199
Hadley, Albert 47
Haldeman, H. R. 59
Halperin, David 64
Hamm, Margherita Arlina 48
hangings 34, 73, 78, 82, 97
Harris, William Laurel 89, 93, *93*
Hay, David Ramsay 9
Hazelton, Jonathan Eastman 14–15
Hazelton, Joseph T. 14–17
Hazelton & Goddard 16
Herman Miller Furniture Company (Herman Miller, Inc.) 157–8, 160–2, *162*, 165
Heun, Arthur 54
Hinsdale, Kenneth 134–5
"Historic Ornament in Textiles" (Hunter) 90
"Historic Styles, The" (Walker) 90
Hoggson, Noble 77
Hoggson Brothers 77–80, *78*
Holly, Henry Hudson 12–14, *13*
HOME (TV show) 111–2, 117
home economics 3, 108–9, 125–38; commencement houses 131–6, *132*; disciplinarity 137–8; from domestic economy to interior architecture 126–9; dream house context 129–31; home management houses 136
home management houses 136
House Beautiful (magazine) 143–4, 162, 199
House & Garden (magazine) 99, 144, 198–9
House in Good Taste, The (de Wolfe) 48–49
"How Architects Practice Interior Design" (Foxhall) 175
"Human/Nature: Wilderness and the Landscape/Architecture Divide" (Sanders) 198
Hunnewell, Elias R. 12, 14
Hunter, George Leland 91
Huntington, Henry E. 31, 37, 39, 42

Idea House exhibits 150
imaging interior design 169–76; in 1940–1951, beneath or beside 171–2; in 1948–1959, from without and from within 172–4; in 1960–1974, fee simple/fee separate 174–6
instruction on early television 107–18
interior decoration: apology areas, in 1950s 157–66; Art-in-Trades Club 89–101; Billings house 5–18; coeds and t-squares 125–38; Coffin *71*, 71–72; credibility in 59, 91, 94, 149–150; critique 40–41; cross-disciplinary

practice, future of 195–205; de Wolfe 47–56; feminine achievement in 47–56; gay decorators 59–67; gendering 70; history 1–4; Hoggson Brothers 77–80, *78*; imaging interior design 169–76; instruction on early television 107–18; Kaufmann, Jr. and MoMA 143–54; legitimacy in 59, 63, 144, 152; by men for men, YMCA 69–86; New York salon (drawing room), Mrs. Rice's 29–43; professionalism, modeling 77; women in, after WWII 179–91
Interior Decoration (TV show) 111
Interior Decoration: Its Principles and Practice (Parsons) 48, 62
"Interior Desecration" (Rothschild) 64–67
Interior Design (magazine) 144, 153
Interior design education 125–38
Interiors (magazine) 144, 153, 169–76
"Interior Space Design" (ISD) 175
"Interiors *vs.* Architecture" (Margulies) 171
"International Competition for Low-Cost Furniture" (show) 147
Ivy, Gregory 134–5

Japanese Exhibition House 150
John A. Ellis & Co. 15
Johnson, Philip 146, 152
JSA 197
Juhl, Finn 149
J. Walter Thompson 53

Kansas State Agricultural College 127
Kansas State College 128
Kansas State University 128
Kantack, Walter 99
Kaufer, Elizabeth 161
Kaufmann, Edgar, Jr. 3, 143–54, *145*, *150*
Kaufmann, Edgar, Sr. 146
Kaufmann, Liliane 146
Kerbis, Gertrude 179–82, *181*, 183–4
Khrushchev, Nikita 153
Kimball, Fiske 29, 42
Kinne, Helen 130–1
Kirkham, Pat 64
"kitchen debate" 153
Kleiser, Lorentz 98
Knoll, Florence 171–2, 180, 182–3, *183*, 187
Knoll Planning Unit 152, 182–3
Koch, Carl 180
Koolhaas, Rem 174, 199

Ladies Home Journal 50, 153
La Farge, John 15
Lake Placid Conferences 125–6
Lancaster, Nancy 47, 179
land-grant institutions 3, 125–8, 136
landscape architects 195, 199–200

Index ■

landscapes 195–203
Larson, George 182
Lavery, John 39–40
Le Corbusier 146, 172–3, 198–9
LEED certified green building standards 197
Lees-Maffei, Grace 152
legitimization of interior decoration 143–54
L'Exposition Internationale des Arts Décoratifs et Industriels Modernes 98
Little and Browne 54
Living for Young Homemakers Magazine 132
Loewenstein, Edward 131–5
Loewy, Raymond 51
Louis XVI style 29, 37–38, 41–42, 54, 94
Louis XV style 41, 98
Lucas, Patrick Lee 3
Luce, Forward, Hamilton, and Scripps 190
Lucky Strike tobacco 51, *52*
Lupkin, Paula 2

MacAlister, Paul 2–3, 107–18
Macy's 90, 99
Macy's Exposition of Art and Trade 99
"Making Maximum Use of Minimum Space" (Conner) 171
mantels 8–10
maquettes 31, 34, *35–6*, 38
Marbury, Elizabeth 50
Margo Grant Walsh collection 190
Margulies, Walter P. 171
Marie-Antoinette 42
Marine Midland Grace Trust Company 186–9, *188*, 190
market segmentation 173–4
Marsh mansion 7–8
Martinez, Maria 93
mass production 1, 51, 53, 55, 70, 83
Maugham, Syrie 47, 179
Mauna Kea Beach Hotel, Hawaii 184–6, *187*
May, Elaine Tyler 153
McBurney, Robert 73, *74*
McCall's Magazine 132
McClelland, Nancy 47, 56, 81, 108–9
McCurry, Margaret 179, 183–4, *185*
McKenna, Richard 183–4
McMillan, Neil 77–78, 80–82
McMillen, Eleanor 47, 108
McPherson, William J. 9–12, 15, 17
Mellody Hall 48
merchandising 1, 3
Merchants and Manufacturer's Club 149
Metropolitan Museum of Art (MMA) 81–82, 89–90, 95, 101, 108
Metropolitan Museum of Art Bulletin 90
Metrosexuals 200
Meyerowitz, Joanne 153
Miller, Herman 3, 144, 159–62

Mitchell Hall 180–1, *181*, 182
modernistic interiors 2, 93, 96, 98
Morales, Teresa 2
Moran, Walter J. 134
Morgan, J. P. 37, 39
Morrill Act 125
Muir, Charles 199
Muscular Christianity 72, 74
Museum of Modern Art (MoMA) 3, 143–54
Museum Project, Inc., The 147

Nancy Smith, Herbert and 135
Nast, Condé 50
National Architecture Accrediting Board (NAAB) 201
National Life and Accident Insurance Company, Nashville 184, *185*, 189
National Society of Interior Designers (NSID) 56, 59, 152, 157, 169, 173, 175
National Television Systems Committee 117
natural drift 64
nature as woman 198–9
Nelson, George 144, 159, 172–3
Netsch, Walter 179–80, *181*
New Furniture Designed by Charles Eames (Eames and Eames) 144
New Place 48
New York City townhouse *see* New York salon (drawing room), Mrs. Rice's
New York salon (drawing room), Mrs. Rice's 29–43, *35–6, 40*; *see also* Rice, Mrs. Alexander Hamilton (née Eleanore Elkins); Carlhian 30–34; Duveen Brothers 30–32, 39; furnishings 38–41; salon design 37–38; style and meaning 41–42
New York School of Art 90
New York State College of Agriculture 128
New York State College of Home Economics 128
New York Times 62–63, 90, 94
Nixon, Richard 59–60, 153
Noguchi, Isamu 159
North Carolina College for Woman in Greensboro 127
North Carolina State University 127
"Notes on the New Interiors" (Reiner) 172
Nouvel, Jean 199
Noyes, Eliot 146–7

Objects: 1900 and today (TV show) 144
objets d'art 39, 51, 54
O'Connor, Justin 53
O'Hare International Airport 181
Origins of Graphic Design in America (Thomson) 47
orphan wall space 163, 165

paintings: Art-in-Trades Club 96; Billings house 6, 9, *10*, 15; coeds and t-squares 133; de Wolfe 53; Kaufmann, Jr. and MoMA 144; New

209 □

York salon (drawing room), Mrs. Rice's 31, 38–39; 1950s 157; YMCA 70, 82–83

paneling: Billings house 8; New York salon (drawing room), Mrs. Rice's 29–30, 32–34, *36*, 38, 40, *41*

Paquin, Jeanne 50

Parish, Sister 47, 49

Parmly, Julia *see* Billings, Julia

Parsons, Frank Alvah 1–2, 48, 62, 71, 89–90, 101, 152

Parsons School of Design 90

pedagogy 201

Pennzoil Place, Houston 189

Period Furnishings: An Encyclopedia of Ornament (Clifford) 91

Perkins & Willis 175

Permanent Exhibition of Decorative Arts and Crafts (PEDAC) 107

Philadelphia Museum of Art 29, 42–43

Plan-a-Room (TV show) 111

Plan-a-Room kit 2, 107, *109*, 109–16, *113–4*, *116*, 118

porcelain 29, 31, 37, 39, 41–42

Porter, Susan 2

Pottier, Auguste 12

Pottier & Stymus Manufacturing Company 12

Potvin, John 2

Pratt Institute 70, 81, 90

Preston, Jonathan 8

"Problems of Design: Ends and Means" (Nelson) 173

"Problems of Design: Modern Decoration" (Nelson) 172–3

"Problems of Design: Notes on the New Subscape" (Nelson) 173

professionalism, modeling 77

Progressive Architecture (magazine) 170, 173–5

project management 34, 43

Pueblo ceramics 93–94

Queen Anne style 12–13, 92

Radio Corporation of America (RCA) 107

Rand, Ayn 195

Ranken, William Bruce Ellis 39–40

Redbook (magazine) 153

Reiner, Jan 172

Renaissance Revival style 8, 11

Rensselaer, Martha Van 127

reproductions: Art-in-Trades Club 91–92, 96; New York salon (drawing room), Mrs. Rice's 29, 32–34, 41; 1950s 157; YMCA 82–83, 85

RFPs (Requests for Proposals) 202

RFQs (Request for Qualifications) 202

Rice, Alexander Hamilton 37

Rice, Mrs. Alexander Hamilton (née Eleanore Elkins); *see also* New York salon (drawing room), Mrs. Rice's: collecting 29; life story 34, 37; Newport, Rhode Island residence 8, 34

Riley, Terence 147, 152

R. J. Haddock Inc. 96

Robinson, Gertrude Gheen 56

Robsjohn-Gibbings, T. H. 48

Rockefeller, David 186

Rohde, Gilbert 160–1

Rome, James P. 90

Rooms for Improvement (TV show) 111

Roosevelt, Theodore 73–74, 199

Rose, Flora 127

Rossiter, Ehrick Kensett 14

Rothschild, Dorothy 64–67, *65*

Rothschilds 41–42

Rudolph, Paul 149

Ruhlmann, Jacques Emile 99

Saarinen-Swanson Group 172

Sanders, Joel 3, 196–7

San Ildefenso 93

Schaaf, Anne-Marie 2

School of Family Resources and Consumer Sciences 127–8

School of Home Economics 127–8

School of Human Ecology 128

sculptures 29, 31, 38–39, 157

Seidler, Harry 179

Seven Continents Restaurant 181–2

Seventh Regiment Armory 15

shelter magazines 144, 153

Sherman and Sterling 190

Simple Life, The (Wagner) 73

"Single Contract Method" 77

Sixteenth Century Ships (Wearne) 94, *95*

Skidmore, Owings and Merrill (SOM) 172, 179–91, *185*, *187–8*

Snohetta 200

Society of Decorators 62–63

Source Book of American Architecture, The (Kidder) 186

"Spanish Motif, the" 83, *83*

Sparke, Penny 2, 64

Staniszewski, Mary Ann 147

Stararchitects 195, 199

Starck, Philippe 51

State University of New York (SUNY) 128

Stephenson, John W. 62

Stewart, Marjorie 128

Stickley, Gustav 1, 81, 83

Stoller, Ezra 161

Stonewall Riots 59

Storey, Walter Rendell 94, 98

Strenuous Life, The (Roosevelt) 73

Stubbins, Hugh 179

Stud: Architectures of Masculinity (Sanders) 196–7

"Study-Hours on Practical Subjects Conducted by Grace Cornell" (Ackerman and McClelland) 108

Stymus, William Pierre, Sr. 12

tapestries: Art-in-Trades Club 92–93, *93*, 98; New York salon (drawing room), Mrs. Rice's 29, 31, 37–41; YMCA 84
tastemakers 2, 18, 43
Taylor, Frederick Winslow 74
Taylor, John 134
television, interior decorating instruction on 107–18; *America Redecorates* 110–3; debut 109–11; expanding 112–7; *HOME* 111–2, 117; *Interior Decoration* 111; on-air professional 111–2; *Plan-a-Room* (TV show) 111; Plan-a-Room kit 2, 107, *109*, 109–16, *113–4*, 118; popular 108–9; *Rooms for Improvement* (TV show) 111; technology needs 117
Tenders 202
textiles: Art-in-Trades Club 91–94, *95*, 96, 98; coeds and t-squares 125, 127–8, 135; gay decorators 61; imaging interior design 172; New York salon (drawing room), Mrs. Rice's 32–34, 40
Thomson, Ellen Mazur 47
Thoreau, Henry David 199
Tiffany, Louis Comfort 1, 15–17
Tiffany Glass Company 15–17
Tiffany Studios 90
Tigerman, Stanley 184
Time magazine 51
Time-Saver Standard series 203
T Magazine 200
toile de Jouy 94, 97–98
Town Topics (magazine) 48
Trumbauer, Horace 31, 34, 37, 38

Union League Club, New York City 15
US Department of Housing and Urban Development 126
unity areas 165
University of Kentucky (UK) College of Design 128
Upholsterer and Interior Decorator, The (magazine) 62–64
upholstery: Art-in-Trades Club 97; Billings house 5, 10, 16–18; coeds and t-squares 133; future of cross-disciplinary practice 196–7; gay decorators 64; New York salon (drawing room), Mrs. Rice's 32–34, 38–40; YMCA 71, 80, 82, 84
USAFA 180, *181*
Useful Objects under $5 (exhibit) 144, 147

Valentiner, Wilhelm Rudolph 90
van der Rohe, Mies 171–2, 179–80, 188, 191, 199
Victoria and Albert Museum 42
Vider, Stephen 61
Villard, Henry 7
Vogue magazine 50, 65, 96, 98–99

Wagner, Charles 73
Walker Art Center 150

Wallace Collection 42
wallpaper: Art-in-Trades Club 94, 96; Billings house 8–11, 15, 18; coeds and t-squares 131; cross-disciplinary practice, future of 197; feminine achievement 54; gay decorators 66; instruction on early television 108; MMA's historic collection 108; New York salon (drawing room), Mrs. Rice's 32–34
Wallpaper (magazine) 200
Walsh, Margo Grant 179, 185–90, *187–8*
Warner, Lamont A. 81–85, *82*
Wearne, Harry 94, *95*, 101
weaving 92–93
Weiss Manfredi 200
"What is Modern Interior Design?" (Kaufmann) 149, 151–2, 173
Wheeler, Candace 1, 61, 69–71, 80–81, 108
Wheeler, Gervase 12
Wheeler, Laura 13
White, Stanford 50, 54
W. H. S. Lloyd Company 94, 96
Why Study Home Economics? (film) 130
Widener, George 34
Widener, Mrs. George D. *See* Rice, Mrs. Alexander Hamilton (née Eleanore Elkins)
Widener, P. A. B. 37
Wilderness thinking 199
Willson, Winifred 94
Wilson, Kristina 3
W. & J. Sloane 81, 83, *83*, 89, 91–92, 98
Woman's College of North Carolina 131–2, *132*, 136
women: in commercial design, after WWII 179–91; feminine achievement in interior decoration 47–56; feminine drift 64; nature as 198–9
Wood, Ruby Ross 48
woodcarving 92
Worth, Charles Frederick 50
Wright, Frank Lloyd 146, 172–3
Wright, Russel and Mary 144, 153

YMCA 69–86; *see also* Furnishings Service; Coffin and *71*, 71–72; gendering interior decoration 70; Hoggson Brothers and 77–80, *78*; manly interior decoration and 72–76, *73–5*; McBurney's room 73, *74*; Milwaukee parlor 72, *73*, 75; New York West Side 84, *85*; professionalism, modeling 77; steps in achieving 78, *79*
YMCA Building Bureau 69, 76–83, *79*
Young Men's Christian Association *see* YMCA

Zimmerman, Paul 98–99, *99*
Zizek, Slavoj 166
Zumthor, Peter 199